OSINT Investigations
We know what you did that summer

By Information Warfare Center

OSINT Investigations
We know what you did that summer
Cyber Secrets 8
First Edition First Published: January 1, 2022
Copyright © 2022 Information Warfare Center

Authors: Jeremy Martin, Carolina Christofoletti, Diana Prusova, Mirjana Ivanic, Luna Winchester, Bonnie Betz, Khadija Naz, Prabhu Rajasekar, Zack Jones, LaShanda Edwards, Syed Shayan Abbas, Justin Casey, Jerry Hartsell, Khadija Naz, Kevin John O. Hermosa, Muhammad Abubakar, Maria Segarra, Umar Farooq, Frederico Ferreira, Ed Cabrera, Andrea Martinez, Abel Mateo, Nicole Consuegra

Editors: Jeremy Martin, Daniel Traci, Joshua Martin, Diana Prusova, Steve Bartimote
Illustrator: Daniel Traci

The writer and publisher of this article do not condone the misuse of Tor for illegal activity. This is purely instructional for the purposes of anonymous surfing on the internet for legal usage and for testing Tor traffic monitoring in a subsequent article. **To access .onion sites, you must have access to the Tor network. To access i2p sites, you must have access to the I2P network. To access any Surface Web site, you must have access to the Internet. Be careful when accessing unknown sites.**

Cataloging-in-Publication Data:
ISBN: 9798786923194

Disclaimer: Do NOT break the law!

About the Team

Jeremy Martin, CISSP-ISSAP/ISSMP, LPT
CSI Linux Developer
linkedin.com/in/infosecwriter

A Security Researcher that has focused his work on Red Team penetration testing, Computer Forensics, and Cyber Warfare. He is also a qualified expert witness with cyber/digital forensics. He has been teaching classes such as OSINT, Advanced Ethical Hacking, Computer Forensics, Data Recovery, AND SCADA/ICS security since 2003.

Daniel Traci
CSI Linux Contributor
linkedin.com/in/edanieltraci

MERN full stack developer, Certified Professional Scrum Master, and experienced project manager. Master of Science in Diplomatic Studies. Permanently in love with international relations, security, and the creative part of marketing. Previously held roles such as Program Coordinator at the Information and Documentation Center on NATO and served as Parliamentary Advisor to the Office of the President of the European People's Parliamentary Group in Moldova.

Carolina Christofoletti
linkedin.com/in/carolina-christofoletti-26b0a01b1

Attorney-at-Law (OAB/SP), Brazil, Criminal Law, Cybercrime and Digital Law. University of São Paulo | Advogada, (OAB/SP), Brasil. Direito Penal,Direito Penal Cibernético e Direito Digital. Universidade de São Paulo

Diana Prusova
linkedin.com/in/dianaprusova

Security Engineer at Accenture Cyber Fusion Centre, CVSS-SIG voting member, and great cyber security enthusiast. Loves unprecedented tasks which involve lots of mysteries and unpaved ways to solution, and therefore has been continuously developing skills in Computer Forensics, especially Linux memory forensics, reverse engineering, and OSINT. Immensely enjoys analyzing hardware memory units with her best friend Ghidra and playing with them using JTAG, JLink and other beautiful gadgets. Before she pursued her passion for cyber security, she worked in IT business development, taught business and management at universities, served as Observer of the European Commission in Arab countries, as well as Reporter in Czech Television.

Steve "Butchy" Bartimote
linkedin.com/in/stephenbartimote

Steve or Butchy as he is known, has a long-held interest and fascination in security and defense. He originally trained as a locksmith, however, for the last 25 years, he has worked within the IT Industry. As with many in this industry, Butchy initially followed the pathways of Web Development and IT Support. He has provided Server Administration (Windows and Linux) before developing greater skills in programming and software development. More recently, Butchy has developed his skill set as a 'solution architect' as well as his interest in cyber security. He continues to work with technology, including electronics, from one end of the spectrum to the other and has developed a passion for the 'Raspberry Pi platform'. In his away from technology time, Butchy is an avid martial artist and instructor.

Frederico Ferreira
linkedin.com/in/frederico-l-ferreira

He is a Cyber Security Enthusiast, currently working as a Senior IT Analyst. Experience and broad knowledge in a wide range of IT fields. Skilled in IT and OT systems with a demonstrated history of working in the oil & energy industry. Frederico is passionate about new technologies and world history.

Justin Casey
linkedin.com/in/justin-casey-80517415b

As a young but dedicated security professional who has spent the past number of years seizing each and every opportunity that has crossed his path in order to learn and progress within the industry, including extensive training in the Physical, Cyber, and Intelligence sectors. As an instructor & official representative of the European Security Academy (ESA) over the years, Justin has been involved in the delivery of specialist training solutions for various international Law Enforcement, Military, and government units. He has led both covert surveillance and close protection operations as well as previously putting in the groundwork here in Ireland as a security operative for Celtic Security Solutions and working in Dublin as a trainer for the International Center for Security Excellence (ICSE).

LaShanda Edwards CECS-A, MSN, BS
linkedin.com/in/lashanda-edwards-cecs-a-msn-bs-221282140
facebook.com/AbstractionsPrintingandDesigns

As a Cyber Defense Infrastructure Support Specialist and a Freelance Graphic Artist, her background is not traditional but extensive. Capable of facing challenges head-on, offering diverse experiences, and I am an agile learner. 11+ years of military service, as well as healthcare experience. Swiftly to study and master new technologies; equally successful in both teams and self-directed setting; and skillful in a variety of computer systems, tools, and testing methodologies.

Kevin John O. Hermosa

An aspiring cybersecurity professional who once was stuck in web and systems development. But his world turned upside-down one day has suddenly changed everything about his life and led him to newly found passions in Linux, Computer Networking, Electronics, and Cybersecurity. Kevin strongly holds to the importance of a strong stance towards cybersecurity in order to keep not only businesses and organizations safe but also to help the common citizen uphold their personal cyber safety for the sake of the greater good of the community. With this in mind, Kevin continues to grow his knowledge and skill in cybersecurity.

Mirjana Ivanic
linkedin.com/in/mirjanaivanic

Cybersecurity enthusiast, currently working as Network Specialist with 10 years in the IT field. I like to explore and with a great passion for new technologies.

Bonnie Betz
linkedin.com/in/bonnie-betz-ajp-rg-rga-1b60571

I was born at an early age.... Seriously, my story goes back quite a bit: worked for NSA in the U.S. Army Security Agency doing electronic covert operations; a Vietnam Vet; started my computer career with Digital Equipment Corp. and that lasted 28 years up to a systems Consultant before I left to own and operate my own computer consulting corporation for 10+ years working mostly in pharmaceutical infrastructure and finished up with Wyeth Pharmaceuticals and Pfizer Pharmaceuticals.

After that I started working on my second passion – "Gemology", becoming a Registered Gemologist & Appraiser and now I am back to my first great passion – IT and Cyber Security. A long way around the circle and back where I started 47+ years ago and no regrets and have always been happy I did the journey.

My enjoyments over the past years have been varied from Target Shooting, Owning and Maintaining a Corvette, doing presentations on the Science of Gemology, Teaching Computer Basics at a local college, and now just trying to relax in my home with my dog and continue to enjoy the adventure.

Luna Winchester
linkedin.com/in/luna-winchester

She is a Cyber Security enthusiast with a concentrated passion for protecting others from social engineering attacks. Luna is currently creating her consultancy to assist both people and businesses. When she is not studying and building her business, she is also advocating for neurodiversity, especially in the areas of ADHD and Aphantasia. She wants to help create a path for others to pursue their passions and create a new conversation at the table in regard to neurodiversity in the workplace.

Prabhu Rajasekar
MSc, MCA, MBA, LLM, (PhD)

Cyber Security Architect | Digital Forensics | Cyber Criminology | Fraud Investigation | Cyber Intelligence

Zack Jones
linkedin.com/in/zachary-jones-k4ako

Zack is a Capabilities Analyst and Threat Researcher that has 21 years of experience within the Department of Defense. While serving on Active Duty as a United States Marine, his areas of interest include UAS/Counter-UAS Systems, Electromagnetic Theory, Software Defined Radio, Cyber Threat and Open-Source Intelligence, and Geographic Information Systems. He is certified in ATT&CK® Cyber Threat Intelligence and is pursuing a Master of Science in Information Security Engineering.

Khadija Naz
linkedin.com/in/khadija-naz-b9207a20a

Cyber Security Expert| Ethical Hacker| Bug Hunter

Ed Cabrera

Ed Cabrera, President, and CEO, Argos – Applied Intelligence has more than 25 years of experience in various cybersecurity roles and currently serves as Chief Cybersecurity Officer at Trend Micro. Before joining Trend Micro and founding Argos-AI, Ed Cabrera was a 20-year veteran and former CISO of the United States Secret Service (USSS) with experience leading information security, compliance programs, and digital forensic programs. He was responsible for global forensic operations support for large-scale data breach investigations and program capacity building. Capacity building efforts for agents and USSS international partners included improving and delivering basic and advanced forensic training; equipping and setting policy for over 300 ECSAP agents and Network Intrusion Responder (NITRO) agents, and designing and delivering international cyber investigations training.

Andrea Martinez

Andrea is attending Florida International University (FIU) and working towards her bachelor's in Information Technology. Andrea joined FIU's IC-CAE Intelligence Fellowship program under the Cyber Threat Intelligence track, where she is completing a certificate in Cybersecurity Intelligence and Information Policy. Andrea is a current member of the Upsilon Pi Epsilon Honor Society and is part of the Cybercorps Scholarship for Service program. She has earned her CompTIA ITF+, A+, and Security+ certifications. Andrea is currently doing a pathway internship with the US Department of Agriculture/Agriculture Research Service as an IT Student Trainee.

Abel Mateo

Abel is a cybersecurity enthusiast looking for any possible reason to learn more about Infosec and privacy. Currently finishing his bachelor's degree majoring in the Internet of Things, Abel comes from a prestigious high school where he was able to complete a high school degree with an associate's degree. Abel gained knowledge in OSINT through practical application, which was later utilized in his internship at the Department of Energy, where he researched National Security Threats.

Nicole Consuegra

Nicole first graduated in 2016 from Florida International University (FIU) with a bachelor's in International Relations and Asian Studies. In 2020, Nicole joined FIU's Cyber Threat Intelligence Track alongside the Intelligence Community Centers for Academic Excellence, completing her Global Cybersecurity Policy Certificate in 2021. Nicole first acquired experience in conducting OSINT research and analysis when working as an intern for the Office of the Director of National Intelligence. She currently pursues additional knowledge in FIU as a continuing education student.

Jerry Hartsell

Certified Penetration Tester and Forever n00b with a passion for creating hip hop instrumentals, audio engineering, animals, and Quantum things.

Maria Segarra

Security researcher

Muhammad Abubakar

Security researcher

Syed Shayan Abbas

Security researcher

Umar Farooq
linkedin.com/in/umer-ufaqcorp101

Security researcher

Table of Contents

What is inside?

Cyber Secrets is a cybersecurity publication focusing on an array of subjects ranging from Exploitations, Advanced Persistent Threats (APT)s, National Infrastructure, (ICS/SCADA), **Darknet/Dark Web**, Digital Forensics & Incident Response (DIFR), Malware Analysis, and the gambit of digital dangers.

Cyber Secrets rotates between odd issues focusing on DFIR / Blue Team / Defense and even issues on Hacking / Red Team / Offense.

Cyber WAR *(Weekly Awareness Report)*

We have another publication *(Free)* called the Cyber WAR. It is an OSINT resource to keep you up to date with what is going on in the Cyber Security Realm. You can download or subscribe at:

InformationWarfareCenter.com/CIR

Doxing is NOT OSINT

Doxing or doxxing is the act of publicly revealing previously private personal information about an individual or organization, usually through the Internet. OSINT focuses on publicly available information. OSINT is NOT Doxing... Those that dox, will use OSINT techniques, and then add other methods such as hacking and social engineering attacks. Using sites like Grabify, you can send a fake link to a target to reveal their IP address and possibly their GPS location if you use the geolocation API within the browser AND location services are turned on. Doxing may be carried out for various reasons, including online shaming, extortion, vigilante aid to law enforcement and hacktivism.

Some jurisdictions have made doxing, especially against public employees, illegal.

The Epstein Data

What happens in Vegas no longer stays in Vegas, even if it is Epstein Island. According to the International Labour Organization's (ILO) latest labor report, there is an estimate of 40.3 human trafficking victims out there with 4.8 million (19%) persons in forced sexual exploitation.

There is a lot of data that gets stolen, leaked, or released every year. Aggregating this data can be a gold mine for both criminals and investigators alike. One such data set that is floating on the Internet are the flight logs from Jeffrey Epstein's private jet. This data the names of some of the most powerful and influential people in the world including Donald Trump, Bill Clinton, Prince Andrew, Kevin Spacey, Chris Tucker, and Bill Gates, among others. Add the "little black book" contacts list of 1,971 names and you have an interesting read.

This type of data is never a "smoking gun", but it does give probable cause to dig deeper. It also helps to provide a timeline while allowing an investigator to do link analysis for who knows who. When you add the allegations of what happened on Epstein Island, Epstein's alleged suicide, and the court's decision to seal the contacts book, there are a lot more questions that now beg to be answered.

The Ghislaine Maxwell trial reminded the public that there is a lot of data that linked a lot of people to some heinous activity. Many of the guilty will be looking over their shoulders for a long time hoping that their past won't catch up to them. People are creatures of habit and unfortunately, some of those that did commit criminal acts will probably commit them again. At least this the data already in the public domain can be used to show a pattern of activity and help prove malice and their predilections.

When analyzing data to prove or disprove a theory, if the hypothesis is correct, you will see a pattern emerge or lack thereof which is a pattern in itself. Many times, there is a consistency and there is a chance a guilty "person of interest" will make another mistake. One can only hope that the guilty get caught before anyone else gets hurt.

The problem that a lot of people have in this case specifically is that there is data in the public domain that many would consider a clear case of "probable cause" to start an investigation on some of the more powerful people in the world.

Now, some of the information you can find online allows you to take your cyber sleuthing one step further. For example, let's say you had the Tail Numbers of Epstein's planes when the activity was occurring. You could track each flight in real time using third party sites to track the planes in the air. Some of the sites will even allow you to look up the historical records.

The Epstein aircraft Tail Numbers:

- N68245
- N908JE
- N212JE

Images from Flightaware

Be very cautious when you start diving down the rabbit hole. Some sites may contain some very heinous images and content. Using a browser plugin like uBlock Origin and change the setting to block files larger than a few KB. This will limit your exposure to dangerous content. This is especially a concern when you find yourself on a private network or a Dark Web site. You need to decide if you want the red pill or the blue pill to see where in Wonderland the data takes you.

Epstein Data:

- https://epsteinsblackbook.com/flights
- https://epstein.flights/about
- https://epsteinsblackbook.com/pdfs/black-book-unredacted.pdf

Flight Tracking:

- flightaware.com
- flightradar24.com
- flightview.com
- planefinder.net

Resources:

1. http://www.ilo.org/global/lang--en/index.htm
2. https://www.stopthetraffik.org

Dark Web Corner

Tor Services V3

CSAM Dark Web Intelligence:
What is the Million-Dollar Question?
By: Carolina Christofoletti

If I could take a photograph of the Dark Web now, what would it look like? Does it simplify things if two events are occurring, at the same time, in very different places? A lot. First, the first question one needs to ask oneself is how is that possible.

Further than how it is possible, the next question is, whenever analyzing things together helps or rather damages and complicates the analysis. Even if things look absolutely the same, the different networks surrounding it can poison a great part of one's analysis. Especially, if one decides to give up on duplicate data. Let us keep what seems to be duplicated data for a while.

For example, the same criminal website operating in various addresses. Now the question one might ask is if we are thinking about resilience. Does it even make sense, for criminals, to create multiple copies of their crimes as a matter of resilience?

There is a second data point I am interested in. What can we learn about how often a criminal site appears on the Dark Web? Would the first instance, found nowhere else, be relevant? I believe so.

After all, in the Big Data Ocean of dark, dynamic data must be made static at some point. What questions are the crawlers expected to answer? That is the half-million dollars question and that goes to the academicals... On how one operationalizes that. Without questions, we do not crawl, without data we cannot research. Then we are stuck.

History Of OSINT

By: Syed Shayan Abbas

What is OSINT?

The phrase OSINT refers to the gathering, processing, analyzing, producing, classifying, and disseminating data received from various sources and by techniques that are both open to the public and legally accessible and able to be used by the general public in response to official requests national security considerations.

OSINT

Exploiting open data has a long history, dating back to the early days of intelligence as a tool for guiding a government's actions and decisions.

Foreign Broadcast Intelligence Service

OSINT concept was not common until the founding of the Foreign Broadcast Monitoring Service (FBMS), which developed out of a research endeavor at Princeton University, where the United States pioneered the institutionalization and professionalization of a capacity for observing foreign media. Following the Pearl Harbor attack, the FBMS gained rapid traction. The Foreign Broadcast Intelligence Service (FBIS) was created in 1947 and became renamed the Foreign Broadcast Intelligence Service (FBIS) in 1947.

Director of National Intelligence's Open Source Center

In the aftermath of the 9/11 attacks and the enactment of the Intelligence Management and Terrorism Prevention Act in 2005, FBIS was renamed the Director of National Intelligence's Open Source Center, including other research components (OSC). The OSINT operation has been in charge of analyzing, extracting, translating (therefore interpreting), and preserving knowledge and updates from all forms of foreign media sources since its start.

British Broadcasting Corporation (BBC)

With its Digest of Foreign Broadcasts, later known as the Summary of World Broadcasts (SWB) and now known as BBC Monitoring, the British government asked the British Broadcasting Corporation (BBC) to launch a civilian, and later commercial, service examining foreign print journalism and radio broadcasting in 1939. According to a BBC manual from 1940, the goal was to build a "new Tower of Babel," where "people listen to the voices of enemies with "exceptional concentration." By the middle of 1943, the BBC monitored 1.25 million broadcast words every day.

Federal Research Division

In 1947/48, the BBC and its American counterpart established a formal collaboration agreeing on a full production exchange. The US Library of Congress's research arm was founded out of the Aeronautical Research Unit in 1948 to provide specialized research and analytical services based on the library's extensive holdings. The Federal Research Division is now known as that (FRD).

OSINT in Cold War

Countries on both sides of the Iron Curtain developed open-source collecting capabilities during the Cold War, often integrated into their clandestine intelligence organizations. According to CIA analyst Stephen Mercado, open sources not just "formed a large portion of all intelligence," but also became "the primary source" of information about rivals' military capabilities and political intents, including early warning and threat forecasting. The East German Ministry for State Security (MfS, commonly known as the "Stasi"), for example, reviewed 1,000 Western publications and 100 books per month and summarized more than 100 newspapers and 12 hours of daily West German radio and television transmission.

OSINT and Private Sector

The private sector has made investments in OSINT collecting and analysis tools. In-Q-Tel, a venture capital firm in Arlington, Virginia, backed by the Central Intelligence Agency, helped companies create web monitoring and predictive analysis tools.

Eliot A. Jardines was appointed as the Assistant Deputy Director of National Intelligence for Open Source by the Director of National Intelligence in December 2005 to serve as the Intelligence Community's senior intelligence officer for open source and to provide a strategic plan, guidance, and supervision for the National Open Source Enterprise.

Mr. Jardines founded the National Open Source Enterprise and wrote Intelligence Community Directive 301. Mr. Jardines returned to the private sector in 2008 and was followed by Dan Butler, who was formerly Mr. Jardines' Senior Advisor for Policy and is now ADDNI/OS.

OSINT Importance

OSINT is valuable because its processing and exploitation methods and deadlines are less stringent than those of more technical intelligence disciplines like HUMINT, SIGINT, MASINT, GEOINT, etc. OSINT also captures a variety of viewpoints because it draws from a wide range of sources.

References:

- [1] https://miro.medium.com/max/1400/1*6KPY0TChucrl1mFK1U0Hog.png
- [2] https://en.wikipedia.org/wiki/Open-source_intelligence
- [3] https://avatars.githubusercontent.com/u/42422997?s=200&v=4
- [4] The Evolution of Open Source Intelligence (OSINT) by Florian Schaurer and Jan Störger
- https://www.afio.com/publications/Schauer_STorger_Evo_of_OSINT_WINTERSPRING2013.pdf

Cool Tool: ReconSpider

ReconSpider can be used by Infosec Researchers, Penetration Testers, Bug Hunters and Cyber Crime Investigators to find deep information about their target. It aggregates all the raw data, visualize it on a dashboard and facilitate alerting and monitoring on the data.

https://github.com/bhavsec/reconspider

Building Skills in OSINT
By: Prabhu Rajasekar

Open Source Intelligence (OSINT) is a collection of information that can be accessed from publicly available resources like Google search, news media, photos, maps, etc., to decide on OSINT methodology. OSINT is used by all, even by ordinary people without their knowledge. Intelligence agencies use social media and other information to track a person or system. Security personnel use information available on the web to find vulnerabilities in a system. Surveillance of a person before interacting with them is an example of OSINT. Open-Source Intelligence, more commonly known as "OSINT," is a technology that uses data from publicly available sources for data intelligence purposes. Even though similar intelligence technologies have been present over hundreds of years, OSINT has gathered momentum after the digital revolution.

Skills required in OSINT

Psychology Skills

Good Psychological skills are essential to excel in OSINT.

Communications / People Skills

Communication is critical for any career, but it's essential when studying human behavior. The ability to communicate with clients is imperative for psychologists to help them, while research psychologists need to effectively describe observations and portray their findings well.

Numeracy

Although it may not seem intuitive, psychologists must have a facility with numbers. Researchers, especially those involved in quantitative information, look at large amounts of data that must be interpreted. A good psychologist understands how to summarize these numbers using statistical tests and equations. Without these abilities, researchers could not begin to know what they observe and whether it is significant to the broader human population. Clinical psychologists would not understand the data and how to apply it to their practice.

Research

No matter your role in psychology, research will play a critical part. Whether you are conducting your experiments and want to see if they have been performed before or are trying to help a patient by seeing what other psychologists have experienced, knowing how and where to find the information you need is critical. There are thousands of scientific journals with details from decades of research. Being able to find the information you want, and evaluate it effectively, is crucial.

Ethics

As with any profession that takes care of people, psychologists have an enormous responsibility. They can change people's lives and frequently deal with people at their most vulnerable. Having a robust ethical code is essential to ensure the safety and well-being of your patients. And as a researcher, basing experiments on a solid moral foundation is critical to ensure you get unbiased, beneficial results without harming anyone.

Problem-Solving

Just as in every career, things in psychology do not always work as planned. Problems will arise, and they need to be solved. Good psychologists must have alternative strategies available and implement them quickly. Well-written research plans account for common issues that may hinder work. Sometimes unexpected things happen, and you will have to step in and make a change to save your work. It would help if you had a library of approaches ready to ensure that your career moves forward.

Legal Skills

The data security laws such as GDPR have only strengthened the use of a proper OSINT system.

- Law Enforcement Agencies
- INTERPOL
- National Security
- Intelligence Agencies
- UN Conventions
- Treaties
- TRIPS Agreement
- UNESCO and its Functions
- WIPO

Technical Skills

A lot of technologies such as machine learning, predictive analysis, and behavioral science have used the OSINT for better understanding the data subjects' behavior and patterns. According to the RAND model of OSINT, intelligence technology works in many steps concerning the information available on news, social media, and gray literature. These steps are:

- Collection
- Acquisition
- Retention
- Processing
- Translation
- Aggregation
- Exploitation
- Authentication
- Credibility Evaluation
- Contextualization
- Production
- Classification
- Dissemination

These steps allow the gathered intelligence to be more authentic and reliable. If machine learning or AI is implemented, collecting, and processing such complicated processes require more time and effort from the data scientists. As OSINT does thorough research and involves detailed analysis, there are a few challenges which you need to overcome while implementing OSINT. We will be discussing those OSINT challenges in this blog.

Patience

Results in psychology can often take years to see, whether in pure research or when working directly with patients. But for actual progress to be made, patience is imperative. It would help if you kept yourself motivated, even when results aren't immediately apparent.

Technology Skills

- Data Science
- Cloud
- Big Data
- IOT
- Cyber Security
- Digital Forensics

Software Tools and Techniques

- Kali, CSI Linux, Deft, CAINE
- Tools like Sherlock for OSINT and Social Media Intelligence
- Fake Persona in all social media
- OWASP ZAP for VAPT
- NMAP, ZenMAP for network
- FTK Imager, XWays, Encase for Data Imaging
- Mobile Forensics using tools like Itunes, Itunes Viewer, BackupTrans, MOBILedit for Android or licensed tools like Cellibrite, Oxygen Forensics
- Email Forensics tools like Email Backup Wizard, Intella, Paraben
- OSForensics tools for Windows and Computer Forensics

Conclusion:

Thus, we need to integrate all of these skills. You are combining Technology, Technical Skills in Tools & Techniques, Psychology, Global Politics, Law Enforcement Agencies of a country, National Security, Cyber Security Laws, Privacy Laws, Data Protection Laws, Intellectual Property Laws, Intelligence, Criminology, and much more. OSINT needs a collection of all these skills together molded to excel in a career. Reconnaissance is an integral part of OSINT. You start approaching your target by doing manual reconnaissance work on it. You gather as much information about the target as online and offline resources. Your search about the target on Google, Social media sites, News coverage, and Shodan, among others.

Pic Courtesy of The European Security Academy

Executive Protection: It's all about the detail

By Justin Casey

I want to go over two videos recently brought to my attention and the whole CP/EP world. Let's begin this one by discussing various types of threats that our principals may be faced, as those not involved in this line of work, a perception about an elaborate portrayal adopted from years of watching TV that we spend our time dodging bullets and driving "blacked out" Land Cruisers. Although this may be true to certain aspects of the job depending on the principal, environment, and task alike, typically, our role consists of long shifts spent on the road, entering, and exiting buildings, standing in corridors, liaising with onsite security, local law enforcement, personal assistants and finished up with studying routes, locations, checklists, and itineraries in a hotel room, being last asleep only to be the first ones awake. Many of us are fully aware that it is not a glamorous occupation, but when the job is done and goes smoothly, it is a rewarding one, nevertheless.

Generally speaking, in day-to-day operations, potential threats come in all sorts of mediums, from physical violence, Kidnapping, theft, the list goes on and on, but in reality, the likelihood of such incidents can be far and few between. Once a good security detail is in place, especially an overt point, the visual deterrent alone can often be enough for nefarious attackers with hostile intentions to recognize a hard target and retreat. With this in mind, the more common threats that principals may face can be PR related; our job is to protect not only the physical well-being of our principal but also include their reputation/ public image and try to keep them from embarrassment/or harassment.

For example, over the past few weeks, we have seen more than one scenario where CP teams have possibly been blind sighted by the idea of higher-level threats; this mindset may have caused the infamous 'tunnel vision' effect leading them to fail in identifying and countering non sophisticated attacks which ultimately led to complete PR disasters but yet still had the potential to have been severe!

If you haven't realized by now, I am referring to two incidents in particular which can be seen below; if you have not seen them yet, then I assume you do not work in the industry (which is perfectly fine) or live under a rock....

Case Study

Firstly, let's take a look at the case where an awaiting assailant in plain sight managed to throw a milkshake over Nigel Farage (again!!)

Ok, so some people might say, "No harm, No foul" fair enough, everyone loves a milkshake but let's think about this for a second, what if the attacker had a more sinister motive? That could have quickly been filled with a corrosive liquid such as acid. Then that split-second lapse in situational awareness would have been a drastically different outcome and could have potentially resulted in long-lasting scar tissue, severe respiratory issues, or even loss of sight!

My intentions here are not to mock or discredit the security detail in question but merely to highlight the little details to consider when conducting a threat assessment. On the day in question, local police requested that the sale of milkshakes be suspended in the surrounding fast-food chains as this method of attack was predetermined and deemed a credible threat due to similar prior incidents. I could, like many others in the industry, start to dissect the video and knit pick at the actions of the operatives. However, I think the video speaks for itself, so that I will leave that to your personal opinion. This style of PR attack is becoming a more frequent method of protest not just for Nigel Farage but several politically related figures. Only last month, I was leading a close protection team for a visiting speaker named Bernard Henry Levy (BHL), a well-known figure who has been referred to by The Boston Globe as "the most prominent intellectual in France today."

Levy was one of six Jewish public figures in Europe targeted for assassination by a Belgium-based Islamist militant group; however, the plot was foiled after the group's leader Abdelkader Belliraj was arrested on unrelated murder charges dated back from the 1980s.

BHL was accompanied by his personal protection team consisting of 2 agents focusing on reactive extraction. Our local operatives' role was to provide operational assistance (overseeing facility sweeps, access control, conducting inductive surveillance, and coordinating with onsite security, local law enforcement & diplomatic protection teams, which were present with foreign dignitaries who were there to hear BHL's seminar). Although we were aware of the active threats on his life, being supported by specialist covert armed Gardaí (Irish Police Force) to tackle that matter, we focused our attention on the more probable risk of hostile protesters as similar to Nigel Farage's array of milkshake loving protesters, BHL was known to be "Cream Pied" on more than one occasion, as he has traveled around the world several people have managed to strike him with cream pies as an act of protest. Thankfully the operation went smoothly, and no such incidents occurred.

The point I am trying to get across is that no matter how high profile the principal or task at hand is, you should always cover the basics, whether that means minimizing the risk of exposure to photographers, Journalists, unwanted members of the public, or good old fashioned cream pie protesters, The basics are what form a solid foundation of any protective operation.

TRUST THE CAPABILITIES OF YOUR TEAM

In this example, we will look at an incident in South Africa last month regarding Arnold Schwarzenegger.

Context: Arnold appeared at a public sports event and was accompanied by what I can see in the video as three 'Bodyguards.' The reason I use the word Bodyguards is that I think this term is outdated and doesn't accurately depict the role of today's Close Protection/Executive Protection Operatives. This being said, the gentlemen in question seem to be more 'Body' than 'Guards' in my opinion. Let's take a look at the video:

It doesn't take a CPO certification to establish the issue here; it looks to me that there was no active structure in place regarding the roles and responsibilities of this security detail. Typically, we train CPO students to understand and adapt to the systems of a CP team, including knowing the difference between TL, PPO, and CP, SD, RST, and Advanced team roles, to name a few. (The titles and Acronyms can vary depending on the organization; however, the structural elements generally remain the same).

For this example, lets me explain the following for those without a background in this work.

- **TL (Team Leader):** The TL's are often the most experienced on the team, and their role is to oversee the movements and duties of each element of a CP team and command the team.
- **PPO (Personal Protection Officer/Operative):** The PPO's primary responsibility is the principal alone; they are the member of the team who always maintains eye's on and generally is within arm's reach of the principal should an issue arise the PPO's main objective is to cover and take control of the principal.
- **CPO (Close Protection Operative):** Although technically all team members can be classified as CPOs, from an operational standpoint, the CPOs are those who protect within the inner cordon while static or maneuvering on-foot formations.

In the video, we can see oul'Arnie receiving what is essentially a dropkick by a member of the public, I am sure I am only stating the obvious here, but it seems clear to me that the security detail where all are focusing inwards toward the principal and therefore majorly limiting their field of view, totally abandoning their independent Sectors/A.O.R's (Area Of Responsibility).

This can happen when improper structures are put in place or when the ego comes into play. Each operative should be aware of their AOR plus understand and trust the abilities and sectors of their fellow team members.

I do not claim to be an expert in protective services or even close; my intention of this article is to share my *personal* views and opinions, and I hope that someone finds it to be interesting at the very least.

Thank you for taking the time to read this, it is very much appreciated, and I value any support with comments or shares extensively!

If you would like to find out more about Close Protection Operative Training, then head over to the European Security Academy's website via the link below:

Resources

- www.euseca.com/course/close-protection-operative/
- Alternatively, you can contact me directly via email at: Justin@euseca.com
- Also, to check out some great articles and insight into the security industry, visit security operative.ie
- For courses, Videos, and resources regarding information security, then visit: informationwarfarecenter.com

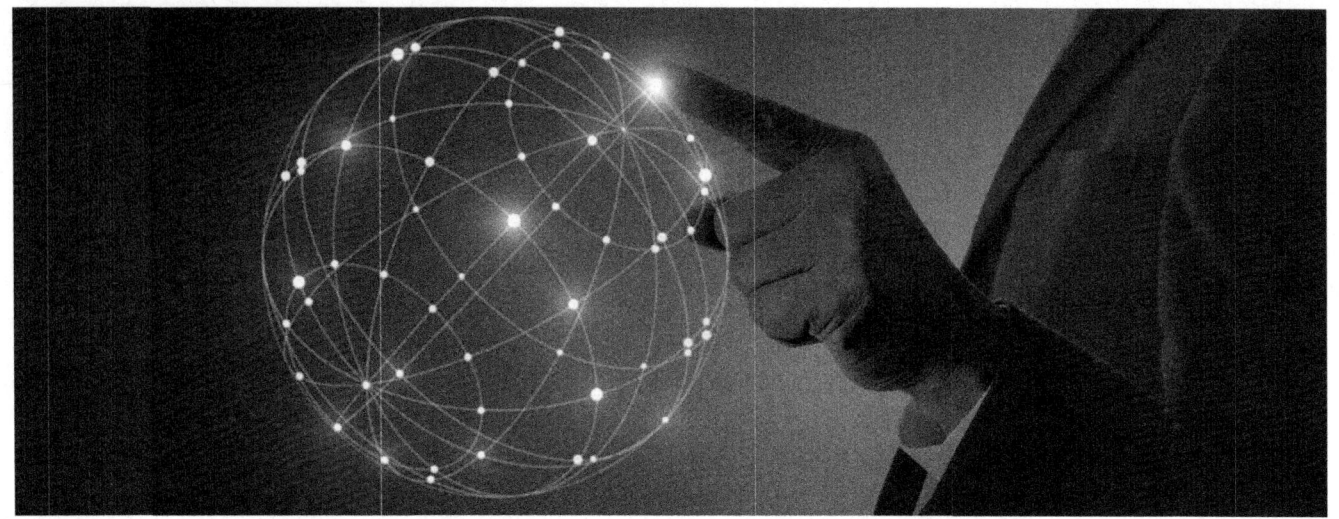

OSINT & Protective Intelligence:
In the digital age

By Justin Casey

The goal of this article is to open the minds of those who may be interested in learning more and encouraging them to conduct their research and find new and innovative ways to incorporate these aspects into their protective operations, as this is just a basic overview of just **some** ideas and in no way covers the vast number of resources out there at our disposal

I have written similar articles on various types of Intelligence categories in the past. However, I now want to hone in on applying protective intelligence analysis within the close protection and security Industry. Specifically, we will look at this from an OSINT perspective, and digital aspect as protective intelligence also includes HUMINT, SIGINT, Surveillance, etc.

We live in a digital age; the internet was once simply a means of entertainment and communication; however, it has become a crucial part of everyday life over the years. It has become so with the risks and vulnerabilities that were once inconceivable to those working in a protective role.

The threat landscape for clients and events is under constant review due to the dynamic nature of the world we live in today. Nevertheless, this also means that we have a growing arsenal of resources at our disposal regarding intelligence, precisely that which is Open Source.

Attack vectors within the executive/close protection industry have developed rapidly over the past number of years and continue to do so. No longer are physical weapons and aggression our only avenue of concern and/or defense as a Close Protection Operative (CPO).

What was once the product of Hollywood scripts and spy novels, Intelligence and counter-intelligence now play a hugely beneficial part in the everyday process of planning, preparation, and conducting of close protection operations?

The success of positive threat identification & mitigation can be increased tenfold with various "INT" resources. However, I am still surprised at the number of experienced and seasoned CP operatives who fail to fully understand the benefits and utilize passive Intelligence.

There are many forms of passive Intelligence, and the applications of each vary greatly depending on the sector in which they are required, however in 'my personal opinion' when it comes to Executive Protection there are four key categories that possess the most significant return:

OSINT: Open Source Intelligence

"Open-source intelligence (OSINT) is a multi-factor (qualitative, quantitative) methodology for collecting, analyzing, and making decisions about data accessible in publicly available sources to be used in an intelligence context. In the intelligence community, the term "open" refers to overt, publicly available sources (as opposed to covert or clandestine sources). OSINT under one name or another has been around for hundreds of years. With the advent of instant communications and rapid information transfer, a great deal of actionable and predictive intelligence can now be obtained from public, unclassified sources. It is not related to open-source software or collective intelligence." - Wikipedia

OSINT is the art of acquiring publicly available data and sieving through it to identify actionable intelligence. Historically OSINT first came to playback in the cold war when nation-state spies would collect political and geographical information from physical sources such as local newspapers, election campaigns, manuscripts, etc. Over time as technology evolved, so did the need for OSINT in non-governmental sectors such as investigative journalism, Humanitarian aid organizations, Corporate and protective sectors. Today with social media being so prevalent in day-to-day life, we have access to an abundance of publicly available information, often on a personal level of our targets, suspects, clients, and colleagues.

Let's look at some valuable methods and techniques we can leverage to give us a more significant advantage and hopefully a 'better hand' than our adversaries.

Client Based Analysis

ELYSIUM

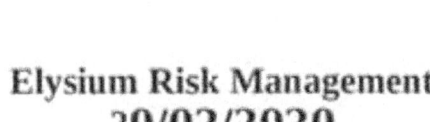

Elysium Risk Management
20/02/2020
Case Number 2020-███

Investigative Profile

Subject's Name: █████████
Assessment Type: Privacy
Case Investigator: Justin Casey
Assigned By (Client ID): 4104
Assigned Date: █████
Investigative Criteria: PII Scrubbing
Approved By: ████████

CASE SUMMARY	CASE # 2020-███

The Client has requested that we conduct an OSINT based investigation in order to identify their online footprint, assess exposure for negative content in relation to character and recommend counter measures as they wish to initiate a basic Greyman protocol focusing on PII scrubbing prior the acceptance of a new position with a prospective employer.

PEDIGREE INFORMATION		SOURCE
GENDER	Male	Provided
DOB	████████	Evidence - Link #0101
COUNTY	Dublin	Evidence - Link #0106
P.O.B	Dublin	Known
OTHER INFO	Partner: ████████ (Wife)	Evidence - Link #0114

HEIGHT	5'9''	WEIGHT	180lb	RACE	IC1	EYES	Brown	Height /weight = estimated

HOME ADDRESS	SOURCE
████████████ Ireland.	Evidence - Link #0103

PHONE NUMBERS		
NUMBER	TIMEFRAME	SOURCE
+003538████████	20██ - Present	Evidence - Link #0105
01-████████	20██ - Present	Evidence -Link #0104
Affiliated Phone Numbers: N/A		

When identifying the threat landscape of a new client or task, it is essential to consider their public persona, professional standing, logistics protocols, previous history of risk, etc. But it is vital that we also gain a greater understanding of their digital footprint so we can begin to assess what level of information an adversary could use to gather a profile on their target/your client.

I always like to begin using a technique known as 'Pivoting.' This is when you use one piece of information to lead onto another. For example, we can start by the typical google search of the client's name, although unlike the day to day 'googler,' we are going to refine our search queries by using what is known as

'Boolean Operators'

We are not going to go through the complete list of Boolean operators as that is an entire article, however, so let's look at some of the main ones we can use to our advantage.

- **Quotation marks** ("John Doe") - If we put John Doe into a google search, this could provide results that include both the name John and Doe. Still, using quotation marks tells Google that we want specific results that only have "JOHN DOE" in sequence as one full name rather than displaying results for both john and doe.
- Let's say for this example that results came back and included findings that stated john doe worked for NASA. We can use this information to pivot our search query to narrow in on JOHN DOE, who works at NASA.
- **PLUS SIGN (+)** - now we could search using quotation marks again by inputting "JOHN DOE" "NASA" but this would result in displaying findings for both john doe and NASA, so instead we can add the plus sign to tell google that we want anything that is related to john doe but includes direct reference with NASA, so our search query now becomes - "John Doe" + "NASA" giving us exact results.
- **SITE:** - The method above could give us back all results, including newspaper articles, interviews, etc. Bu t what if we wanted to find results from a specific website using our search query? We would now use the SITE: Boolean operator. If we're going to search for results solely from a particular website, we could adapt our search query to - "John Doe" + "NASA" Site: (Followed by the site we want results from).

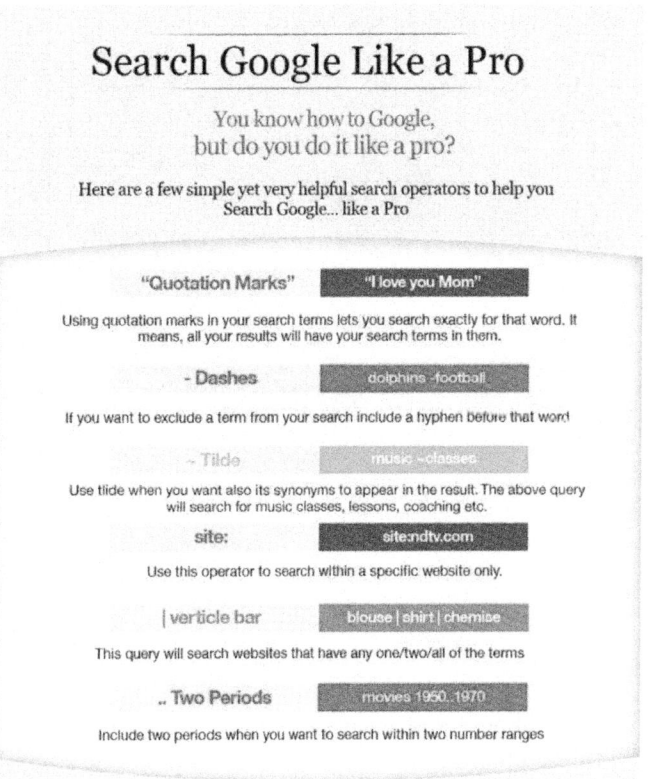

Search Google Like a Pro

You know how to Google, but do you do it like a pro?

Here are a few simple yet very helpful search operators to help you Search Google... like a Pro

"Quotation Marks"   "I love you Mom"

Using quotation marks in your search terms lets you search exactly for that word. It means, all your results will have your search terms in them.

- Dashes   dolphins -football

If you want to exclude a term from your search include a hyphen before that word

~ Tilde   music ~classes

Use tilde when you want also its synonyms to appear in the result. The above query will search for music classes, lessons, coaching etc.

site: site:ndtv.com

Use this operator to search within a specific website only.

| verticle bar   blouse|shirt|chemise

This query will search websites that have any one/two/all of the terms

.. Two Periods   movies 1950..1970

Include two periods when you want to search within two number ranges

Okay, let's now say we have used the above methods and found some information on the company website, including our client's email address. Now we can use this email address to pivot onto our next level of intelligence gathering.

There are many more advanced ways of analyzing a target's digital footprint, such as Maltego, but we will save this for another day.

Data Breaches

So, we now know the name, company, and email address for the target and possibly some other information such as background, age, and role from company bios, etc.

But now, we can use this email address to assess if an adversary could acquire personal information such as direct phone numbers, home addresses, IP addresses, and even personal passwords belonging to our client.

Instead of writing a whole section on this, check out this video as I have done a practical demonstration of how to do this:
 www.facebook.com/watch/?v=2841989819178270

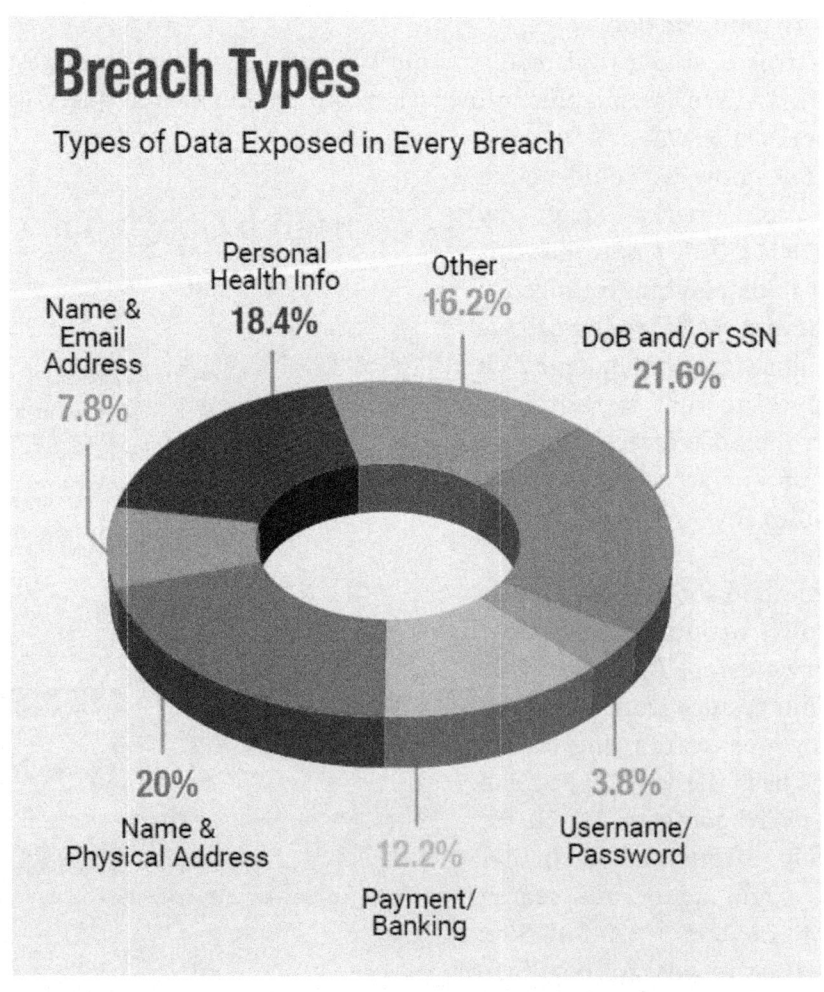

I don't think I need to explain how dangerous this information could be to our operations. The client's organization and reputation alike as if an attacker was to gain access to someone's email address, social media accounts, etc., 5then they could reap havoc and spread spyware, launch ransomware, or even embarrass them publicly.

These are just the tip of the iceberg when we consider just how deep the ocean of Open Source Intelligence is; one of the absolute best collections (in my opinion) of information and tools for OSINT is what is known as The OSINT Framework, it is a collection of links to various tools and resources available to our disposal, each is categorized into starting points based on the primary source/information we wish to pivot from so be sure to check it out, you will not be disappointed!

The OSINT Framework:

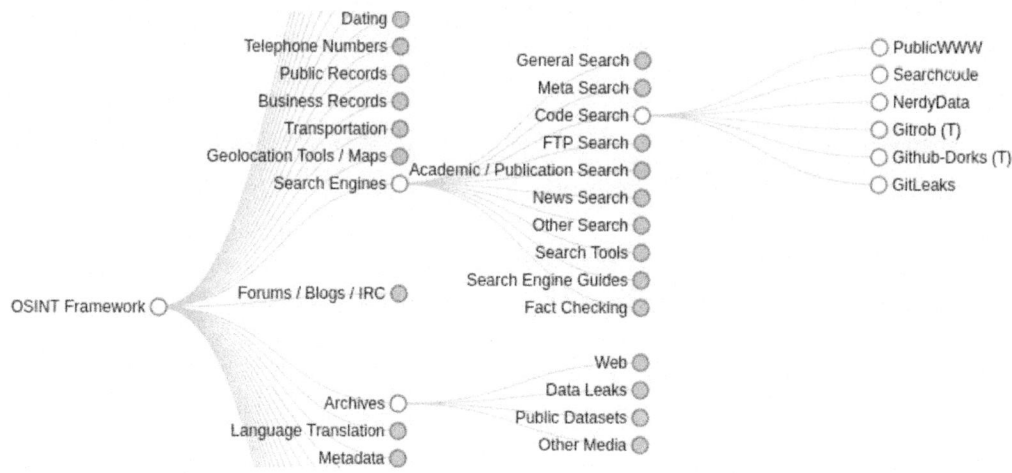

GEOINT: GEOSPATIAL Intelligence

So, we have all seen these cars driving around with roof-mounted 360-degree cameras for mapping out Geospatial data used for developing google street maps, etc. And we are familiar with Google Earth, but many don't realize the true potential of this technology and data sets in applying protective intelligence.

"In the United States, geospatial intelligence (GEOINT) is intelligence about the human activity on earth derived from the exploitation and analysis of imagery and geospatial information that describes, assesses, and visually depicts physical features and geographically referenced activities on the Earth. GEOINT, as defined in US Code, consists of imagery, imagery intelligence (IMINT) and geospatial information." Wikipedia

GEOINT covers data collection relating to geographical sources such as general maps, Google Earth, Streetview, etc. These can be vital in the work of an advanced team for planning and preparing routes, ingress, and egress points, and so on.

GOOGLE EARTH STUDIO

This is one of my favorite resources for pre-op planning and logistics. Yes, you can take a screenshot of the standard google earth imagery, but did you know that you can create interactive videos which include your own data sets?

These can be vital in our pre-op mission briefing as well as emergency planning as you can quickly develop clear and direct route planning with the use of its satellite and 3D imagery, making what was once a 20-minute presentation of route analysis into a 3-minute interactive video explaining every aspect of the logistics with in-depth and fluid visual detail breaking down each step of the operation. This is specifically helpful for auxiliary staff to understand who may not have a background in operational planning. It is also suitable for getting the 'Lay of the land' for those tasks that don't accommodate for pre-reconnaissance with an advanced team as the level of detail in the 3D mapping is extraordinary; it can provide details such as exits and entrances, including the fine details such as whether the door opens inwards or outwards, etc.

Explaining Google Earth Studios is also an article within itself, but I HIGHLY recommend checking it out and spending a few days getting to know just how powerful it is.

Here is a link to its website and a video clip of a basic example:

Google Earth Studio: earth.google.com/studio

For the more elaborate of tasks, there are various databases available online which offer unique insight into political and sociological ideologies of different regions, specifically those with political unrest and conflict zones, including ones such as:

- **Global Terrorism Database**
- **CIA World FactBook**

VIDEO

This method is also very useful in corporate security and for HR departments to monitor the activity of an individual.

Protective Intelligence and the use of OSINT can also be utilized during and throughout any protective operation, not just for High-Level CP/EP teams but also for security control rooms at mass capacity events to monitor activity for both proactive and post-incident response.

SOCMINT: Social Media Intelligence analysis

Social Media is the ultimate cash cow about both targeted and mass intelligence. It is important to remember that social media accounts are mainly free services, as the grim reality is that the users themselves are the commodity for the company. Every time we download a new app or join a social media account and even simply read an article on some websites first, we need to click that dreaded 'ACCEPT' button. We consent the company to gather and sell an abundance of data about us by doing this.

Here we will look at some more advanced methods of SOCMINT that do require some preparation; however, they can be well worth the effort!

Let's say we have been informed of a possible hostile who may have malicious intent towards our client or task.

The first step will be to gain a profile of this individual that includes basic information such as full name, a picture to use for PID (Positive Identification), etc. Then we might want to look through their social media posts to understand their psychological tendencies etc.

Again, here is an excellent video to save time writing. It will give a practical demonstration of a method used to identify the targets of various social media accounts, which may lead to other avenues of pivoting.

TWEETDECK

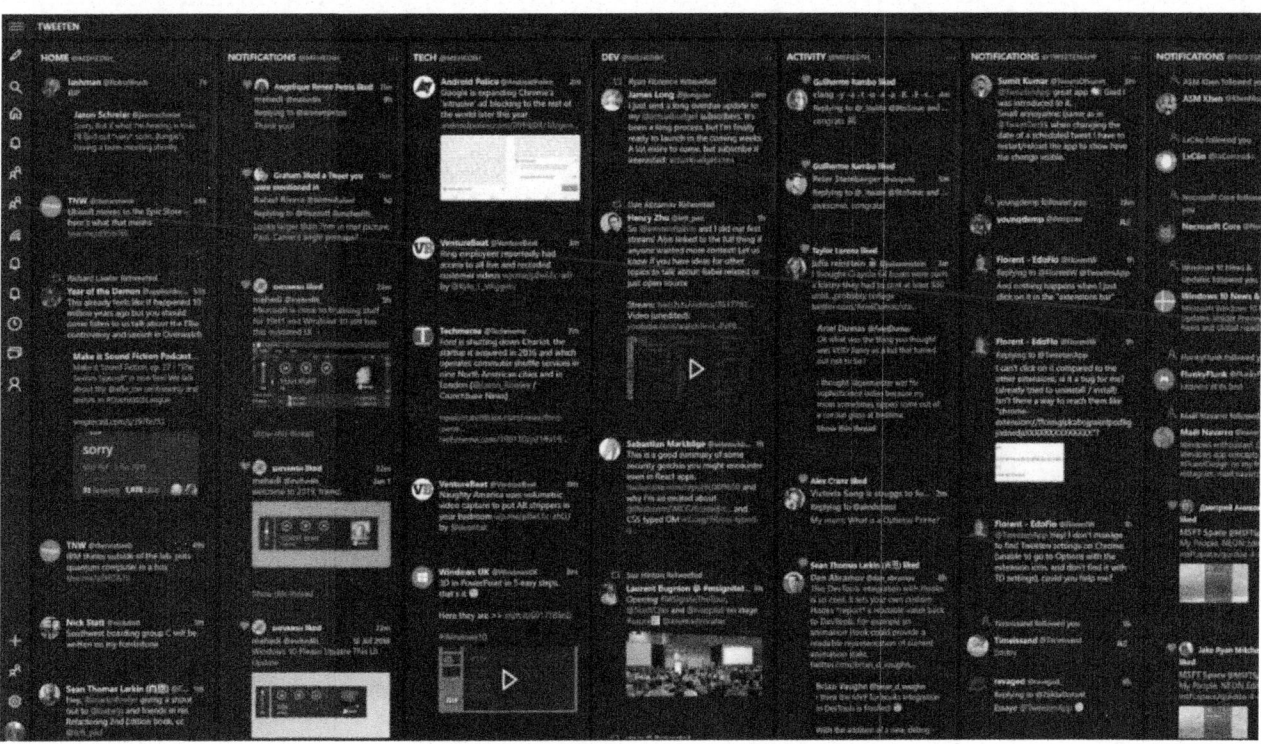

Tweetdeck was initially made by Open source developers, but once the big dogs realized its full potential, Twitter purchased it from the developers for 40 million dollars back in 2010.

Tweetdeck is, in 'my opinion' one of the best free Open source resources for active live monitoring, which can be a massive asset to security teams at all levels as it allows for accurate time monitoring and engagement of activity and has several advanced features which enable us to make use of its filters to acquire and monitor specific content associated to our threat landscape and the task at hand. (Con: It will only index content on Twitter and no other social media)

Filters include:

- **Content** - Tweets matching keywords, media type, dates and time, language, or including or excluding retweets.
- **Location**: Tweets geotagged in a specified location.
- **Users**: tweets from specific accounts, such as potential hostiles that we have identified and flagged via our pre-op intelligence gathering stage and included them as members of a monitor list.
- **Engagement**: tweets with a minimum number of retweets, likes, or replies.

Additionally, it allows us to set up alerts if tweets are posted with any specific keywords; this may include an extensive list such as our client's name, company, hate speech keywords, or words that suggest hostile intent such as dead, kill, fuck, knife, etc. There is no limit to this other than your imagination. However, it is essential to note that the most significant risks can be what we call 'information overload,' meaning that if we add too many keywords without direct parameters, this can inundate us with too much information and therefore reduce our identification and response times to actual valid, actionable intelligence.

Yet again, we could do a whole article on this, so take it for a test ride in a controlled environment and get to know it before deploying it in the field.

ECHOSEC:

Yes, this article covers free open source methods, although it would not be complete without mentioning paid professional services such as **ECHOSEC"**.

ECHOSEC is a highly professional OSINT software platform used by corporate, diplomatic, and government agencies for open source threat intelligence. If you have a high-net-worth client and a healthy budget, then maybe this is precisely what you are looking for, visit the website to learn more.

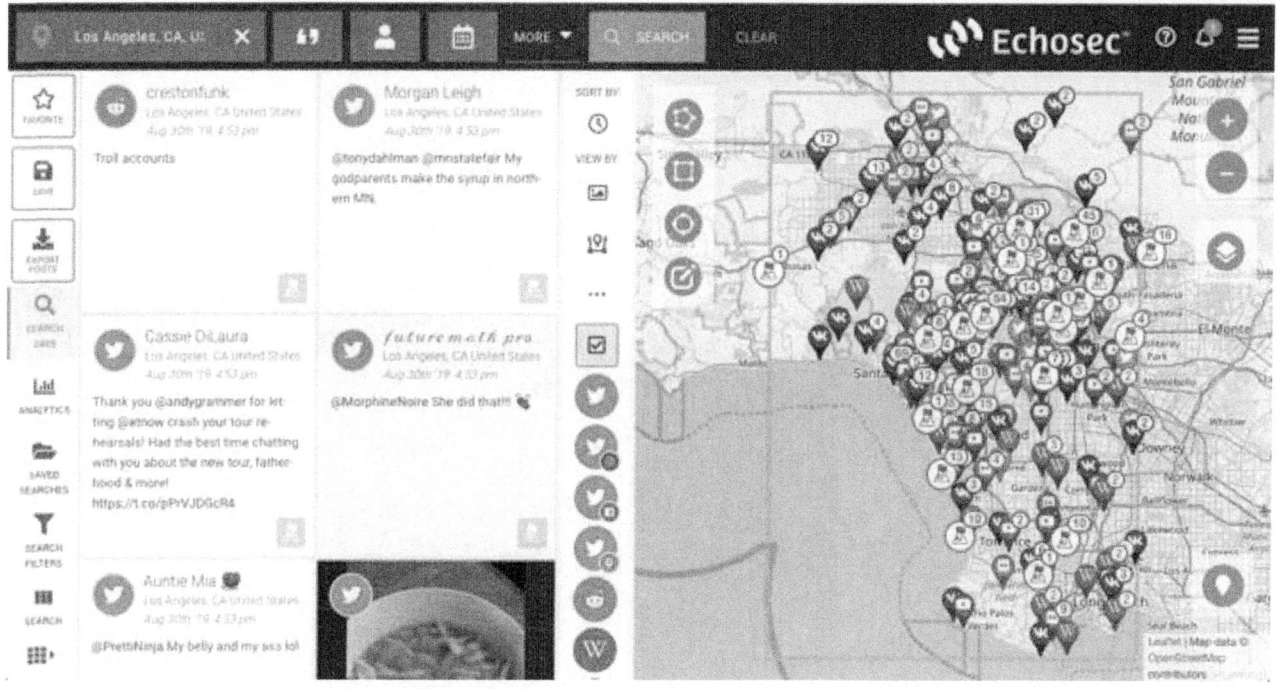

Cool Tool: MISP

MISP Threat Sharing (MISP) is an open source threat intelligence platform. The project develops utilities and documentation for more effective threat intelligence, by sharing indicators of compromise. There are several organizations who run MISP instances.

Developed by a team of developers from CIRCL, Belgian Defense, NATO, and NCIRC, Malware Information Sharing Platform (MISP) is an open-source platform that allows sharing, storing, and correlating of Indicators of Compromise (IOCs) of targeted attacks, threat intelligence, financial fraud information, vulnerability information or even counter-terrorism information.

With in-built sharing functionality to ease data sharing using different models of distributions, MISP can automatically synchronize events and their attributes. Its filtering functionalities can be utilized to meet an organization's sharing policy and the user interface allows end-users to create and collaborate on events, attributes, and indicators. The STIX-supported MISP stores data in a structured format and is equipped with a free-text import tool that enables the integration of unstructured reports into the platform. In addition, users can automatically exchange and synchronize events with other parties as well as import and integrate MISP feed, OSINT feed, or any threat intelligence from third parties.

The platform's API allows integration with an organization's solutions and its PyMISP, a Python Library, helps to collect, add, update, search events' attributes, and study malware samples. With an adjustable taxonomy, MISP users can classify, and tag events based on their existing taxonomies or classification schemes. Bundled with a unique intelligence vocabulary called MISP galaxy, malware, threat actors, ransomware, RAT, or MITRE ATT&CK can be linked with events in MISP.includes several scanners."

github.com/dark-lbp/isf

Cool Tool: AlienVault OTX

 WHAT IT IS

 AlienVault Open Threat Exchange (OTX) is the world's largest open threat intelligence community that facilitates the gathering and sharing of information about new or ongoing cyberattacks and threats.

HOW IT WORKS

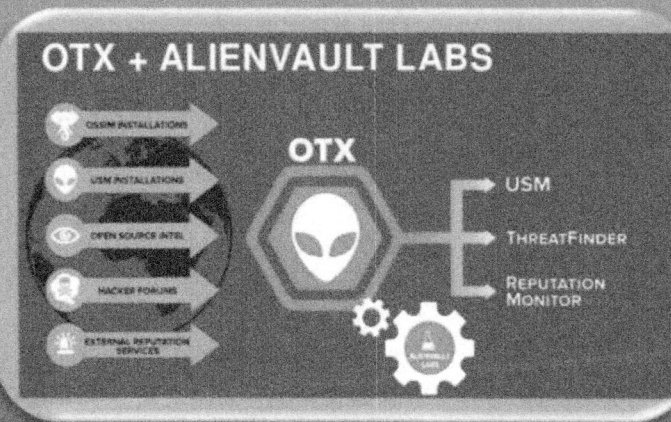

https://image.slidesharecdn.com/otxintro

AlienVault OTX's information for sharing information is configured in the form of pulses. Pulses provide a summary of the threat, a view into the targeted software, and the various related indicators of compromise (IOC) that detect these threats.

 **WHY IT'S USEFUL**

Security research is oftentimes not openly shared for several reasons such as
- a lack of trust,
- internal business policies,
- or the simple inability to distribute information.

AlienVault OTX helps to solve this issue by allowing users to subscribe to a variety of pulses in the community. In doing so, AlienVault OTX provides open access to a global community of threat researchers and security professionals, thereby narrowing the intelligence gap for government agencies and businesses alike.

References: AlienVault Open Threat Exchange (OTX) | UnifiedThreatWorks.com. (n.d.). UnifiedThreatWorks. https://www.unifiedthreatworks.com/OTX.asp

First steps into the world of OSINT

By Justin Casey

This article aims to help direct those looking to dip their toes or dive into the world of Open-Source Intelligence. Specifically, the theme is surrounding the OSINT community rather than the practical applications of OSINT gathering.

There are hundreds of tools, resources, and services applicable to any investigation. Still, the key message I try to instill to any of my OSINT students is that it is a mindset and a way of thinking as each investigation differs based on the objective, scope, and available sources, in terms of the line of inquiry, there is no definitive 'blueprint' or set outline as to where to begin and how to proceed.

Typically, the fundamental principle is to identify opportunities to pivot from source to source while still maintaining relevance to the scope and objective at hand. Without a certain level of discipline, we can find ourselves falling down a rabbit hole, leading the course of our investigation further and further away from where we need to be. This usually happens gradually, but instant realization can hit us that we are way too far off the scope. Hence, it is about finding that sweet point between creative curiosity and a clearly defined scope.

Let's say we have one single case assigned to multiple analysts; even though each of them may arrive at the same conclusion, often each analyst would have taken separate paths, using different tools and methods to collect and analyze the data, which in my opinion is the beauty of OSINT and why the Open Source community is so important as a fresh set of eyes can often be an effective tactic when you hit a 'roadblock' on an investigation.

So, let's ignore the tools, training, and services, etc., for this article and take a look at some links to help you submerge yourself into the incredible and supportive community of OSINT.

My first recommendation would be, begin with, a fresh Twitter profile!

Twitter, in my opinion, is one of the best mediums for interaction with the community and those within it. Also, an excellent point to make is that you can easily switch between multiple profiles within the Twitter app.

For example, I have multiple Twitter accounts under various pseudonyms/handles; each one themed specific such as one that just posts and follows others associated with OSINT, one themed around infosec, and then my account for friends and family. This means that I have constant topic-specific feeds that are updated all the time with new articles, points of interest, resources, etc.

If you wanted to go 'all out,' you could establish additional categorized themes such as each account themed around those who specialize in individual elements of OSINT, be that GEOINT, SOCMINT, Imagery, Corporate, Extremism, etc.

THE Dutch OSINT guy is exactly what it says on the tin 😊 He is a Dutch guy with a wealth of experience within OSINT Investigations, OPSEC, OSINT Resources

So, let's look at some heavy hitters in the world of OSINT and some great places to start!

@OSINTJustInCase:

Full disclosure this is my OSINT related Twitter handle :) feel free to follow and use your OSINT skills to go through my list of those I follow as they are all OSINT related, so go check them out; I promise you won't regret it as it includes over 300 profiles that will help. To shape your OSINT network!

Inteltechniques

Michael Bazzell is an ex-FBI agent with incredible insight into Privacy, Security, and OSINT; his website hosts multiple resources, including a blog and a very knowledgeable podcast which I highly recommend; he is also the author of a range of books that can be purchased on Amazon covering topics such as OSINT and Extreme Privacy.

Website: inteltechniques.com
Podcast: soundcloud.com/user-98066669
Books: inteltechniques.com/books.html
Twitter: @Inteltechniques

OSINTCURIOUS

These guys are some of my favorites! It is a collection of industry-leading professionals who all come together to share their abundance of collective experience with anyone willing to listen; their regular webcasts can be found at their YouTube channel as well as various ten-minute tips videos, they also invite other special guests onto the show to share insight on multiple aspects.

Website: osintcurio.us
Youtube Channel: www.youtube.com/channel/UCjzceWf-OT3ImIKztzGkipA
Patreon: www.patreon.com/osintcurious
Twitter: @OSINTCurious

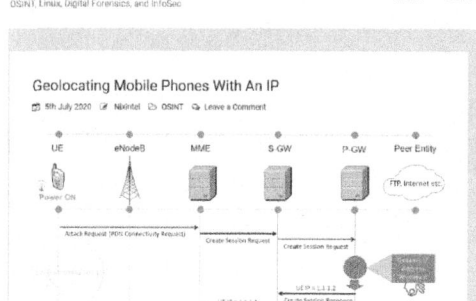

NixIntel

NixIntel is the handle for one of the members of the OSINTCurious project who has proven to be a worthy addition to the team as his blog hosts in-depth articles of various case studies, techniques, and methods of OSINT; I have seen this guy successfully conduct some of the most difficult Quiztime challenges there is, his investigative process is incredible!

Website: nixintel.info/
Twitter: @Nixintel

MW-OSINT

Matthias is a formidable player in the industry. Being a former SIGINT team lead in Germany's foreign Intelligence agency, he has been involved in many "mission critical" operations throughout the middle east throughout his career. His blogs and posts are incredibly insightful and an excellent opportunity to learn.

Website: www. key findings. blog
Twitter: @MWOsint

Dutch OSINT guy

Dutch OSINT guy is exactly what it says on the tin 😊 He is a Dutch guy with a wealth of experience within OSINT Investigations, OPSEC, and Security Investigations, and operational background in counterterrorism.

Website: www.dutchosintguy.com
Twitter: @dutch_osintguy

Sector035

The sector is one of my favorites when it comes to Geolocation; he is one of the main coordinaTors of the Quiztime challenges. Although his background is somewhat of a mystery as his OPSEC game is strong with a catchy handle, it is difficult to identify who is behind the persona but what is evident is that he is seriously talented and knowledgeable in this field!

Blog: www.medium.com/@sector035
Twitter: @sector035

OSINT Techniques

OSINT Techniques is a perfect association to follow; they host a goldmine of helpful links to categorized resources and writing and sharing some detailed articles via their blog!

Website: www.osinttechniques.com
Blog: www.osinttechniques.com/blog
Twitter: @osinttechniques

WebBreacher

Micah is the 'Godfather' of the OSINTCURIOUS project; that term does not reflect his young age, but because he was the initial brains and founder of the OsintCurious project, he has helped to align all of these experienced pros under the same roof (figuratively speaking). You can check out Micah's blog on his website below.

Website: webbreacher.com
Twitter: twitter.com/WebBreacher

Technisette

Technisette has over a decade of experience in OSINT research and offers a free comprehensive library of external resources via her website, as well as being a member of the OSINTCurious team.

Website: www.technisette.com/p/home
Twitter: twitter.com/technisette

Benjamin Strick

Hello. I am **an investigator.**
I come from a small town in a very remote place.
I write about open source, security and data.

See My Work

Ben is personally one of my favorite investigative journalists to follow in the world of OSINT. He has worked alongside Bellincat and some incredible investigative work with BBC Africa Eye. Ben's analytical mindset is fascinating, so much so that when teaching OSINT, I find Ben's work to be some of the best case studies to cover as they help provide a clear and detailed example of the importance of OSINT in today's world and how it offers a reputable level of transparency specifically within global conflict and international journalism.

Website: benjaminstrick.com
Bellingcat Articles: www.bellingcat.com/author/benjaminstrick
Twitter: twitter.com/BenDoBrown

Bellingcat

Bellingcat Is an Independent collection of Investigative journalists who specialize in using OSINT during their investigations. They have helped to bring the world of OSINT to the global table and be taken seriously in the eyes of international media outlets, so much so that they have almost single-handedly backed the Russian Intelligence service into a corner on more than one occasion!

Website: www.bellingcat.com
Podcasts: www.bellingcat.com/category/resources/podcasts
Documentary: www.bellingcatfilm.com
Elliot Higgins (Founder): twitter.com/eliothiggins
Twitter: twitter.com/bellingcat

Loránd Bodó
@LorandBodo

#OSINT Producer @NBCNews | Interest in #terrorism & #environment | co-founder @osintcurious | from ▮

Loránd Bodo

Loránd Is another heavy hitter and member of the OSINTCurious team. He specializes in Terrorism and offers excellent resources and articles via his Start. my page.

Start. Me page: radter-osint.com
Twitter: twitter.com/LorandBodo

Alternative sources

Ok, so I really could go on for days and include hundreds more influential people within the OSINT Community. Still, I think those I have mentioned are a great starting point and opportunities to pivot onto more and more as you fall down the OSINT community rabbit hole.

There are also some alternative sources for articles that can help shape your knowledge and improve your investigative skills and be creative creatures; let's use some google dorks to try to find some more.

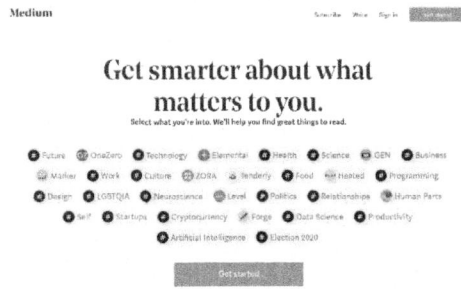

Medium

Medium is an excellent platform within the community which allows you to share articles without the need for your website to host them.

Google-Dork: "OSINT" Site:medium.com

Start.me

Start. I am another incredible platform that allows users to create and share a dashboard hosting links to all sorts of good stuff such as external tools, programs, resources, articles, etc. There is an abundance of great OSINT themed dashboards, so take the time to go through them, and you can start your dashboard use it to save some of your favorite valuable links you find on other dashboards.

Google-Dork: "OSINT" site: start.me

NullByte

I first came across Nullbyte on YouTube several years ago, starting in Infosec and Pentesting. However, he has covered various OSINT based tutorials, so they are worth checking out.

Website: null-byte.wonderhowto.com
Youtube: www.youtube.com/channel/UCgTNupxATBfWmfehv21ym-g
Twitter: twitter.com/nullbyte
Google-Dork: "OSINT" Site:null-byte.wonderhowto.com

NOTE: There should be enough within medium and start.me to keep you busy for weeks, if not months! But as always, get creative and tweak the google dorks to find more specific categories such as "SOCMINT," "GEOINT," etc.

So, the OSINT community is not just a one-way street; you can also help out and get involved in several different ways.

Open Source Leads
@OpenSourceLeads

Ideas - some practical, some not - for open source investigations.
with it. Account collaboratively ran by @bellingcat investigators.

Twitter: twitter.com/OpenSourceLeads

OpenSourceLeads

OpenSourceLeads Is the outreach arm of Bellingcat. Often during their investigations, they can appeal for some help from community members. So feel free to lend a hand if possible and help them continue carrying out the fantastic and vital work they do.

Europol: Stop Child Abuse - Trace an object

This is a project set up where Europol appeals to the community to help identify or trace an object in the background of child exploitation images online.

Website: www.europol.europa.eu/stopchildabuse

TraceLabs

TraceLabs is an organization that hosts CTF (Capture The Flag) Style competitions that try to aid Law Enforcement in the search for Missing People. They also offer some great prizes for teams with the top results.

Website: www.tracelabs.org

CSI Linux Training

The people that brought you CSI Linux now have a free OSINT starter course called CSI Linux Basics that covers some basic OSINT techniques and some of the unique features only found inside the CSI Linux platform, including the Case Management system, a GEO Location app, and an online video/streaming content application. This makes some of your OSINT searching a bit easier and captures the evidence inside a case folder for you to use. It even hashes all the evidence for you to make the preservation and validation of evidence a bit easier.

Website: training.csilinux.com
TuTorials: csilinux.com/tutorials
Threat Intelligence feed: informationwarfarecenter.com/Cyber_Intelligence_Report.php

Fun ways to practice and improve your skills

Verif!cation Quiz Bot
@quiztime

Join us and verify yourself through a little series of quizzes that we post daily on Twitter. Learn about the main tools and collaborate with others.

Twitter: twitter.com/Quiztime
Medium: medium.com/quiztime

QuizTime

This is one of my favorite ways to keep skills relevant and learn new and exciting ways to geolocate images and answer other challenging questions; the Quiztime platform is a way for everyone to get involved, it also offers a great example of how OSINT is a mindset as you can see how many others conducted their investigations in different ways but came out the same.

Website: ctf.cybersoc.wales/

CyberSoc Wales: Cyber Detective CTF

This is a fantastic collection of Cyber related CTF-style challenges. Create an account and start trying your hand at the multitude of challenges available on the platform. Some of the tasks are more digital forensically focused, although many are OSINT based. You will really enjoy this, trust me, it is exciting and informative!!

OK, I think I best stop there as, as I said before, the OSINT Community is a vast ocean of supportive and creative people and resources, so dive in and begin to network, learn and most importantly, enjoy!

To anyone I have not included, please forgive me as there are so many more I would love to include but feel free to begin a thread in the comments and include anything you think may help others get started with our amazing community.

On a personal note, I would like to thank everyone who has contributed to the community, be it with tutorials, videos, articles, or even simply sharing a link. Let's continue to support each other in using OSINT to help make the world a better place.

It's Not Stalking When It Is Public Record

By: Zack Jones

"A body of men holding themselves accountable to nobody ought not to be trusted by anybody." - Thomas Paine

In "The Rights of Man," Thomas Paine made a point about accountability.[1] While Mr. Paine was not speaking on record keeping, it is the fundamental reason public records exist. Public records provide accountability for the functions and daily transactions of government. From a legal standpoint, the definition of a public record, as defined by The People's Law Dictionary, is "any information, minutes, files, accounts, or other records which a governmental body is required to maintain, and which must be accessible to scrutiny by the public".[2]

From an OSINT perspective, public records provide a treasure trove of information. They can be used as a starting point to collect known data points to expand upon or validate information obtained during the research. The records are reliable and can be independently validated. Searching these records can be very discreet and, often, provide a great "Return on Investment" (ROI). We will cover some US-centric resources, but each country has its own public/government records they can access.

What Records are Public Record

As mentioned earlier, public records are "information, minutes, files, accounts, or other records which a governmental body is required to maintain." Some examples include:

- Company Filings
- Property Records
- Tax Records
- Voter Registration
- Court Records

While not an exhaustive list, the examples above are common and easily obtainable examples of public record types. Municipalities could fill volumes to detail on all the various record types across all the myriad of federal, state, and local. Not to mention international records outside of the United States. To this end, consider any government record as a public record. You can request anything. Whether or not you get what you request is a matter of legislation and legal opinion.

The Freedom of Information Act

There are **instances** in which records are not easily obtainable. In the United States, the Freedom of Information Act (FOIA) has provided the public the right to request access to records from any federal agency since 1967.[3]

Applicable to only the federal government, federal agencies are required to disclose any information requested under the FOIA unless it falls under one of the following nine exemptions:

Exemption 1: Information that is classified to protect national security.
Exemption 2: Information related solely to the internal personnel rules and practices of an agency.
Exemption 3: Information prohibited from disclosure by another federal law.
Exemption 4: Trade secrets or commercial or financial information that is confidential or privileged.
Exemption 5: Privileged communications within or between agencies, including those protected by the:
Deliberative Process Privilege (provided the records were created less than 25 years before the date on which they were requested)
Attorney-Work Product Privilege
Attorney-Client Privilege
Exemption 6: Information that, if disclosed, would invade another individual's privacy.
Exemption 7: Information compiled for law enforcement purposes that:
Could reasonably be expected to interfere with enforcement proceedings
Would deprive a person of a right to a fair trial or an impartial adjudication
Could reasonably be expected to constitute an unwarranted invasion of personal privacy
Could reasonably be expected to disclose the identity of a confidential source
Would disclose techniques and procedures for law enforcement investigations or prosecutions, or would inform guidelines for law enforcement investigations or prosecutions if such disclosure could reasonably be expected to risk circumvention of the law
Could reasonably be expected to endanger the life or physical safety of any individual
Exemption 8: Information that concerns the supervision of financial institutions.
Exemption 9: Geological information on wells.

Additionally, there are special protections for three narrow categories of law enforcement and national security records. These special protections are known as Exclusions and are not subject to the requirements of the FOIA.

Exclusion 1: Protects the existence of an ongoing criminal law enforcement investigation when the subject of the study is unaware that it is pending, and disclosure could reasonably be expected to interfere with enforcement proceedings.

Exclusion 2: Limited to criminal law enforcement agencies and protects informant records when the informant's status has not been officially confirmed.
Exclusion 3: Limited to the Federal Bureau of Investigation and protects the existence of foreign intelligence or counterintelligence, or international terrorism records when the presence of such records is classified.

Making a FOIA request is straightforward if you know what information you want and what agency has the information. Each federal agency handles its record requests and has Points of Contact (POC) listed on its website. For more information on FOIA or to make a request visit www.foia.gov. The figures below illustrate the process of making a FOIA request

Step 1: Search for the Agency with the information you are requesting.

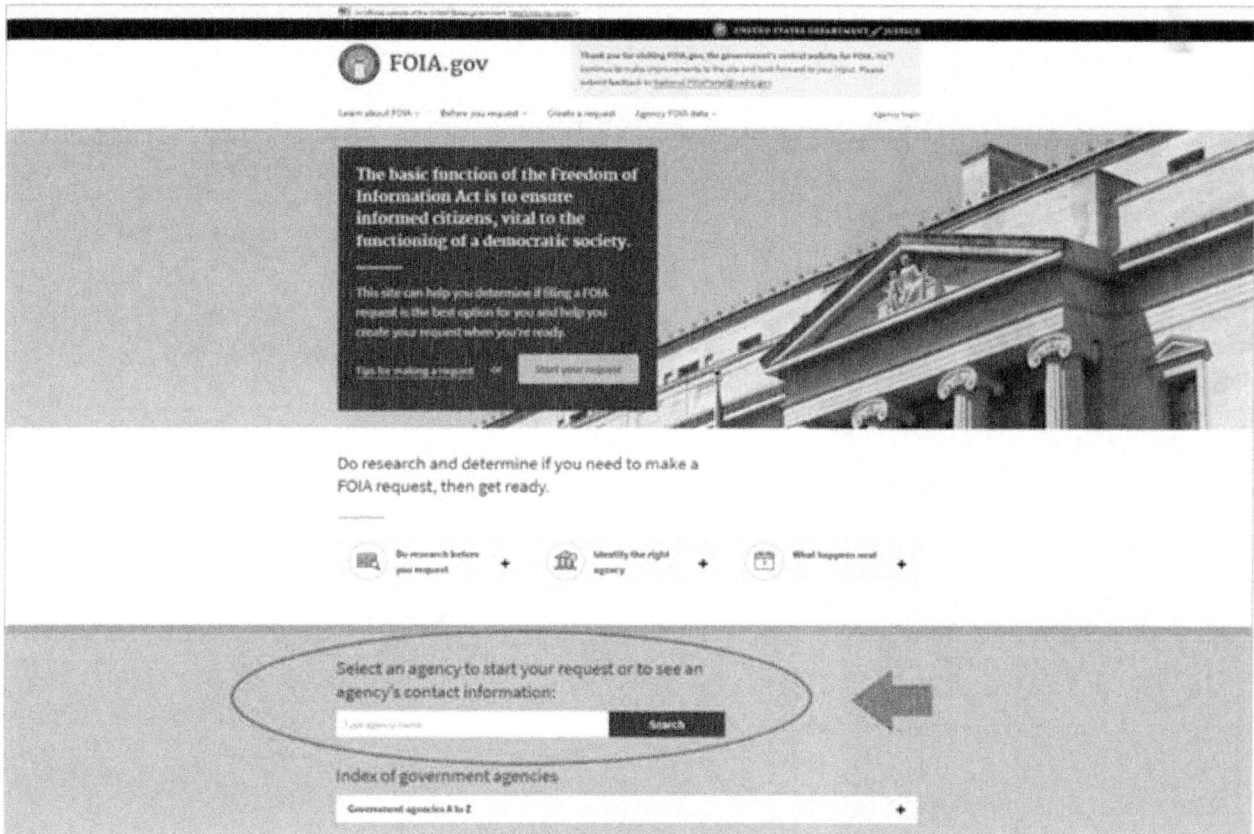

Figure 1. Agency Search

Step 2: Select "Start FOIA request."

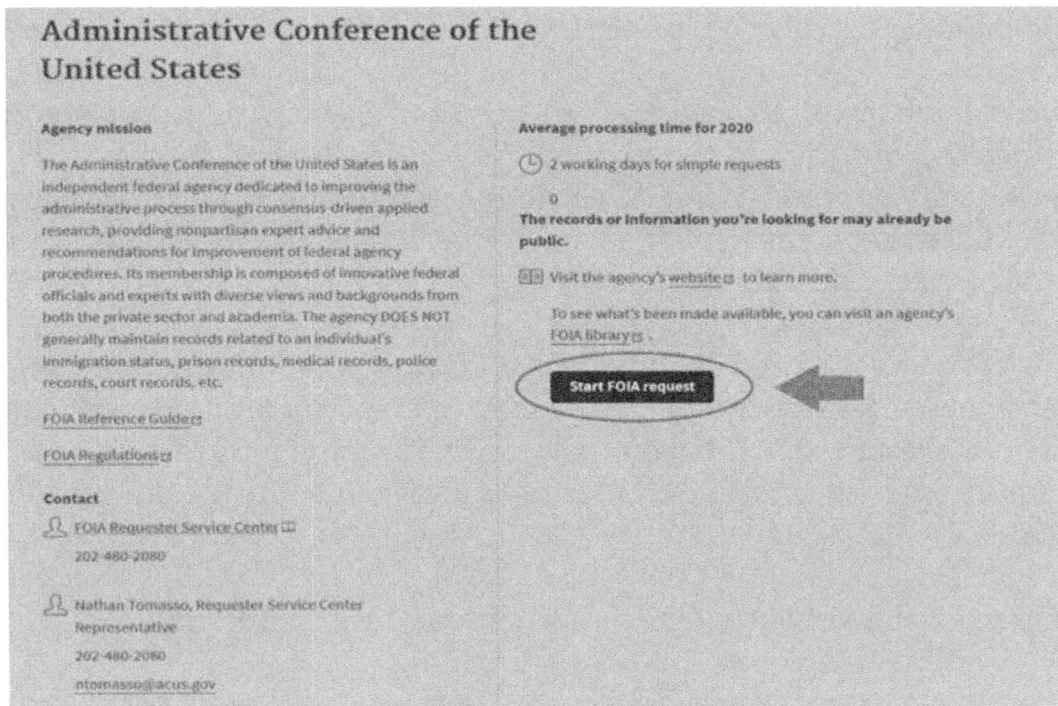

Figure 2. Agency Info Page

Step 3: Follow the instructions and make your request.

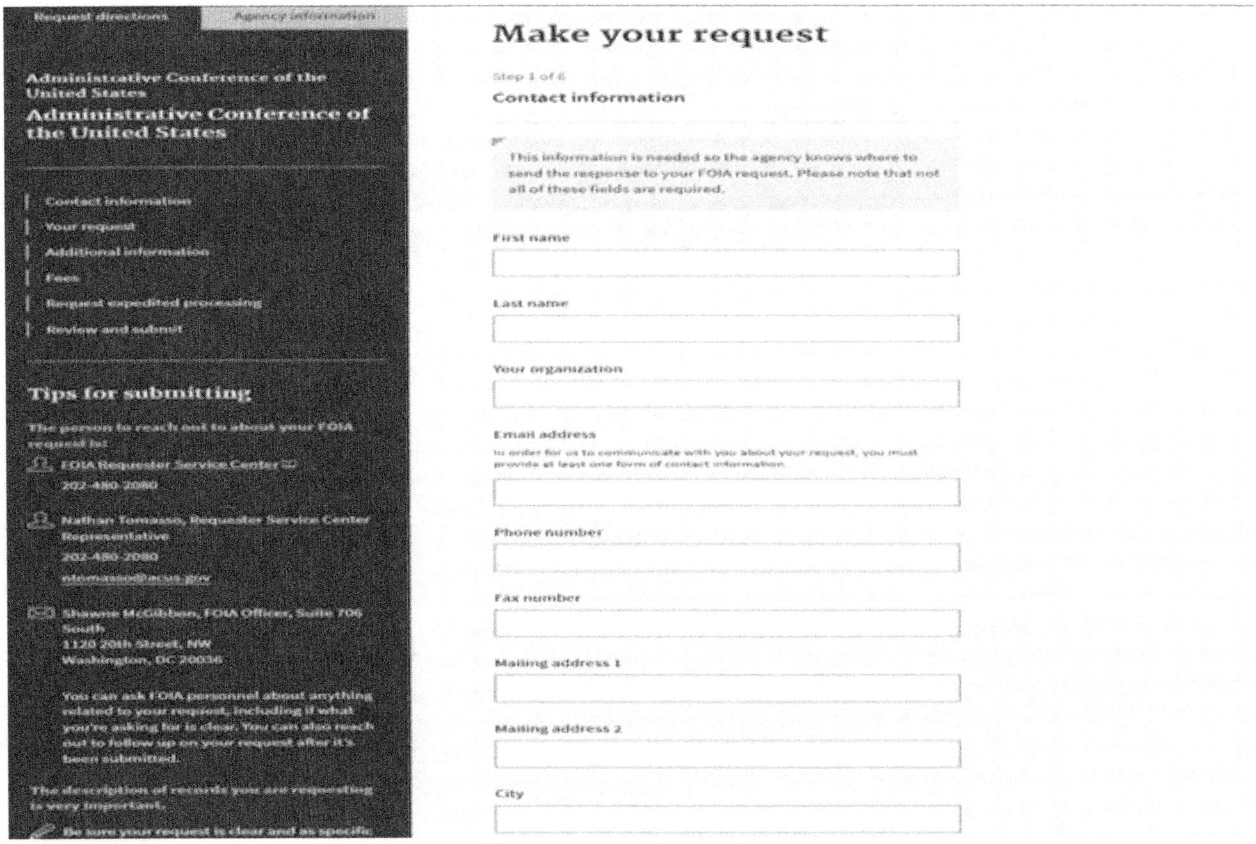

Figure 3. Agency Request Page

When making these requests, be as specific as possible. Do the research and make your request clear and concise. Requesting all email correspondence from agency "X" will likely not result in a favorable response. However, requesting email correspondence from [Person "A"] to [Person "B"] between [Date "X"] and [Date "Y"] will likely get better results. Imagine if someone requested all your email correspondence. You would probably want them to be more specific in that request to ensure they got what they needed. Keep in mind that you will be navigating layers of bureaucracy and red tape designed to "protect" the system of government. If you request controversial information, that red tape will be an easy excuse to kick back your request. Make it hard to say no.

Tools, Tactics, and Procedures (TTP's) for Public Records

Searching for Public Records is a straightforward process if you know where to look. Federal, State, and Local municipalities have various data sources and laws governing public records. The Reporters Committee for Freedom of the Press has an Open Government Guide to aid in this endeavor but is not inclusive.[4] The guide can be found at: www.rcfp.org/open-government-guide.

Below are a few sources of public records and how to use them.

Company Filings

All "Public" companies, foreign and domestic, are required to file registration statements, periodic reports, and other forms electronically through the U.S. Securities and Exchange Commission's EDGAR (Electronic Data Gathering, Analysis, and Retrieval) system. Anyone can access and download this information for free or query it through various EDGAR public searches.[5]

Use EDGAR and navigate to [sec.gov/edgar/searchedgar/companysearch.html] and utilize the various options to refine your search. The current EDGAR search form is shown in Figure 4.

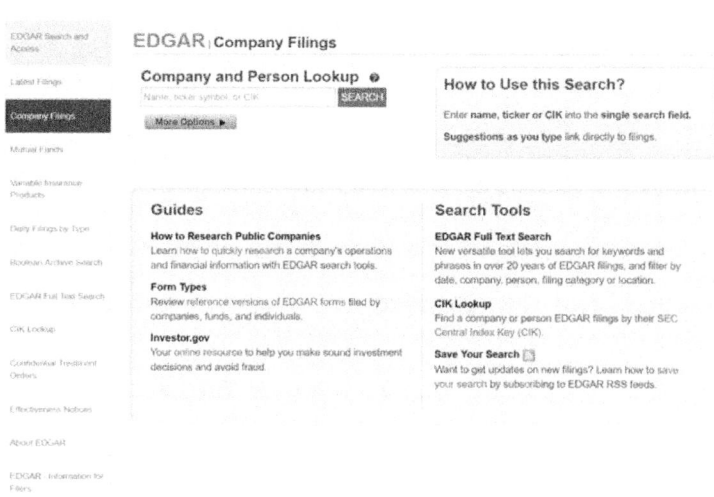

Figure 4. EDGAR

The search methods will depend on the information you seek—figure 5. Shows the results for an investigation against the stack symbol "AAPL." The result shows the company information, latest filings, and selected filings such as the annual 10-K report and ownership disclosures. This rabbit hole can go deep, so be sure you have plenty of caffeine at the ready when digging into financials. This is, after all, Warren Buffet reading material.

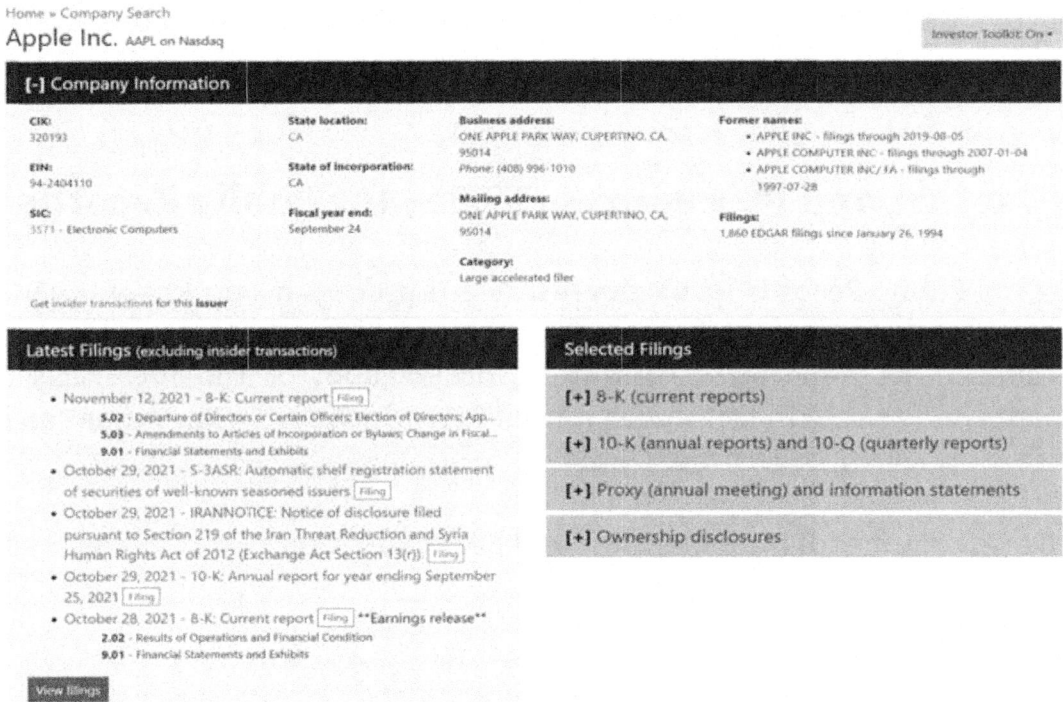

Figure 5. AAPL

Not all records are searchable through EDGAR (typically those dated before 1996) but can still be requested in one of three ways at the time of this writing.

1. Filling out a Request Records form.
2. Send a fax to: (202) 772-9337
3. Submit a written request to:

> U.S. Securities and Exchange Commission
> Office of FOIA/PA Operations
> 100 F Street N.E.
> Washington, DC 20549-2736

Private Business Records

There are times when research is required for a non-public company or business. This is more difficult but possible. You will not find the same level of scrutiny for these entities and will require knowing what state the industry was formed in. Each state has its process for registering a business. Figure 6. shows the business registration search for North Carolina.[6] Figure 7. Shows the results of a business search.

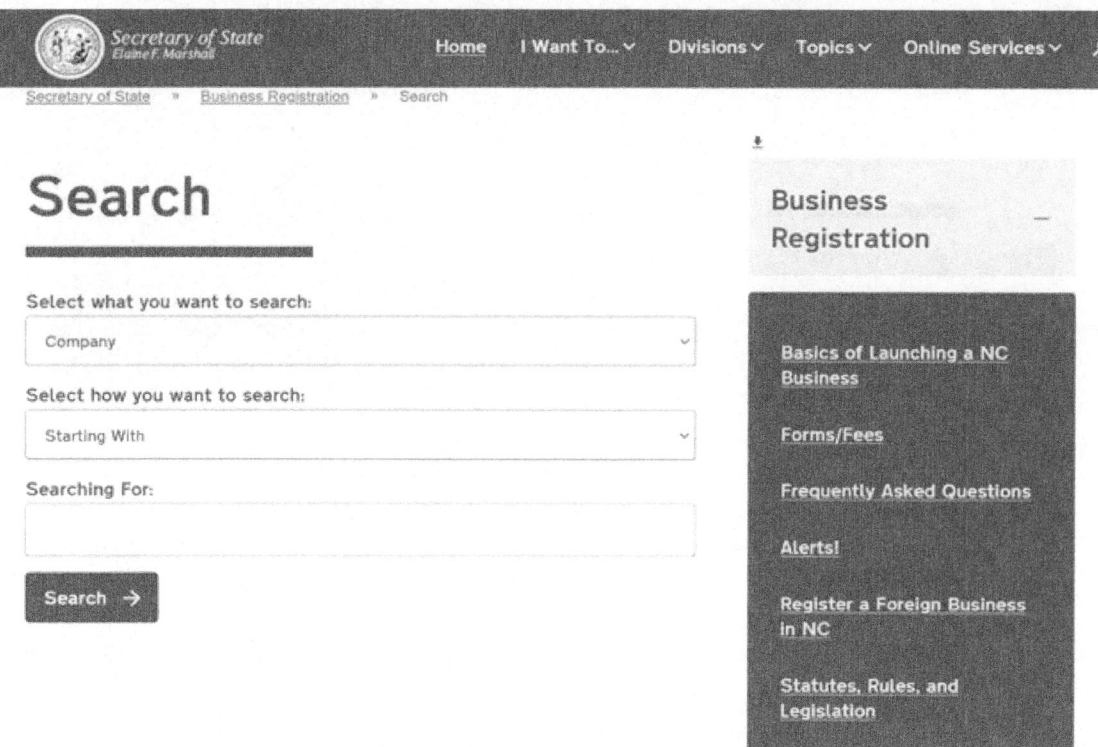

Figure 6. NC Business Registration Search

In Figure 7. And Figure 8., notice the types of information obtained from a search (actual results redacted).

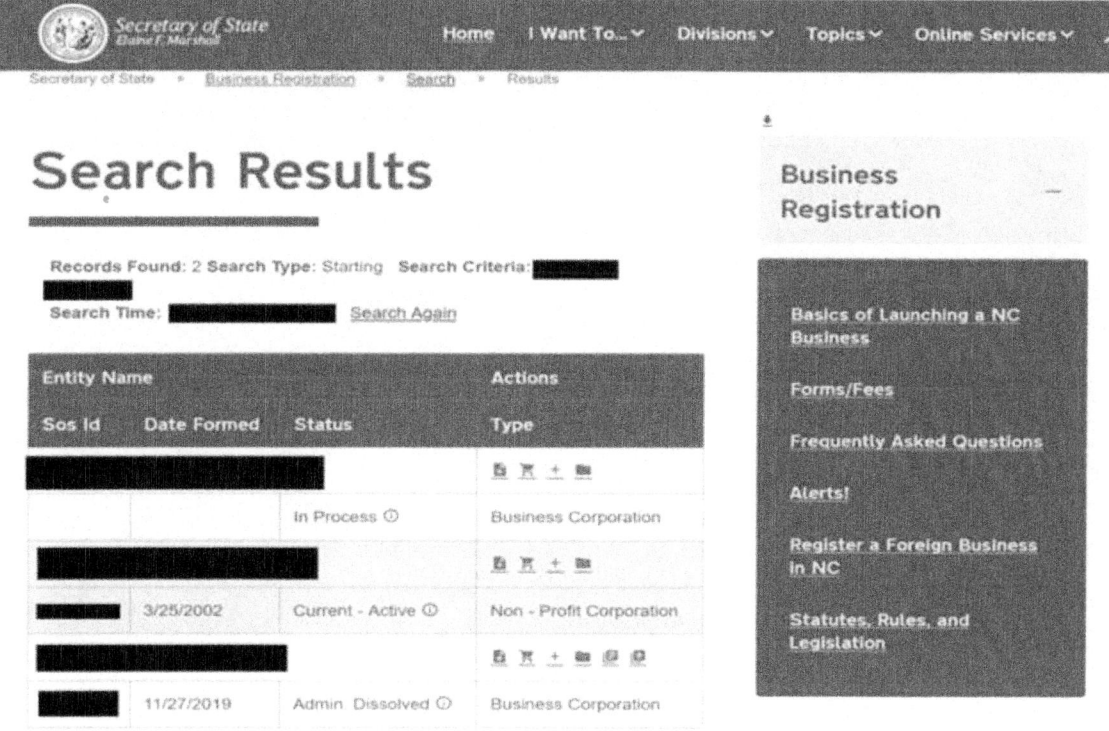

Figure 7. Business Search Result

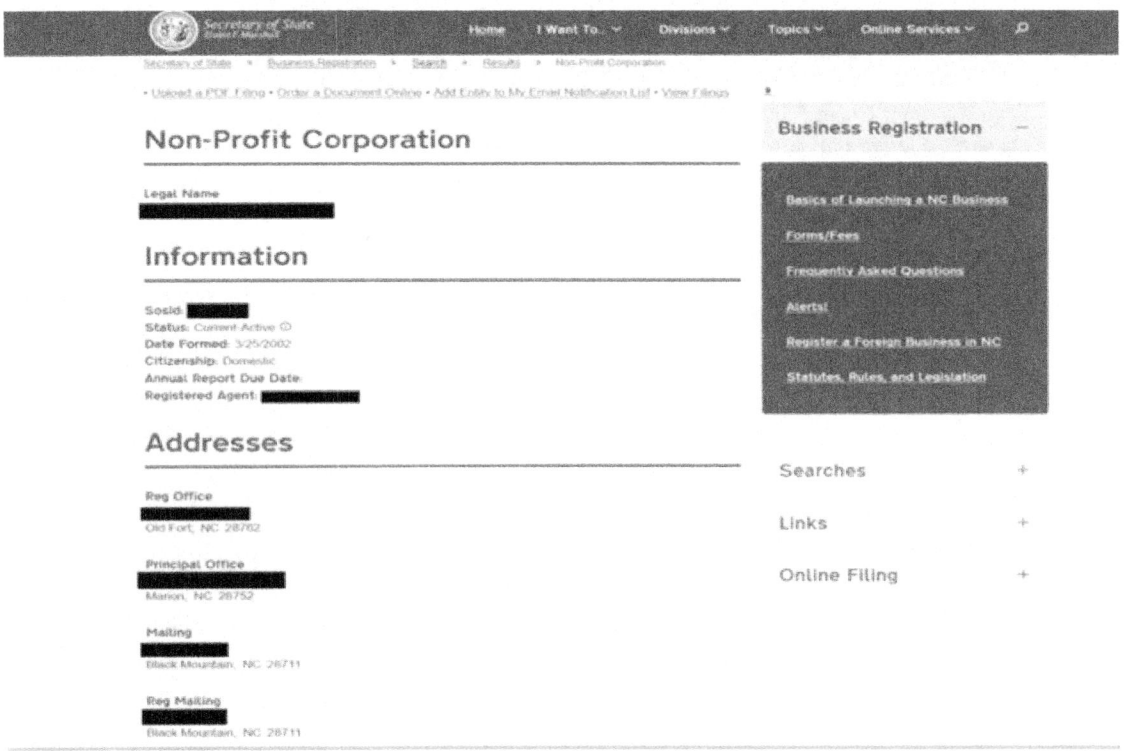

Figure 8. Detailed Report

Secretary of State List

Here is a list of links to the Secretary of State websites, current as this publication.

State	URL
Alabama	sos.alabama.gov
Alaska	state.ak.us
Arizona	azsos.gov
Arkansas	www.sosweb.state.ar.us/corps/incorp
California	sos.ca.gov/
Colorado	www.state.co.us
Connecticut	www.state.ct.us
Delaware	www.state.de.us
District of Columbia	os.dc.gov
Florida	www.sunbiz.org/search.html
Georgia	sos.ga.gov
Hawaii	www.state.hi.us
Idaho	sos.idaho.gov
Illinois	www.ilsos.gov/corporatellc
Indiana	secure.in.gov/sos
Iowa	www.state.ia.us

Kansas	www.sos.ks.gov
Kentucky	www.sos.ky.gov
Louisiana	www.sos.la.gov
Maine	www.maine.gov
Maryland	sos.maryland.gov
Massachusetts	www.sec.state.ma.us
Michigan	www.michigan.gov/sos
Minnesota	www.state.mn.us
Mississippi	www.sos.ms.gov
Missouri	www.sos.mo.gov
Montana	sosmt.gov
Nebraska	sos.nebraska.gov
Nevada	www.nvsos.gov/sos
New Hampshire	sos.nh.gov
New Jersey	www.state.nj.us/state
New Mexico	www.sos.state.nm.us
New York	dos.ny.gov
North Carolina	www.sosnc.gov
North Dakota	www.state.nd.us/sec
Ohio	www.ohiosos.gov
Oklahoma	www.sos.ok.gov
Oregon	sos.oregon.gov
Pennsylvania	www.dos.pa.gov
Rhode Island	www.sos.ri.gov
South Carolina	sos.sc.gov
South Dakota	sdsos.gov
Tennessee	sos.tn.gov
Texas	www.sos.state.tx.us
Utah	secure.utah.gov
Vermont	sos.vermont.gov
Virginia	cis.scc.virginia.gov
Washington	www.dol.wa.gov
West Virginia	sos.wv.gov
Wisconsin	sos.wi.gov
Wyoming	sos.wyo.gov

Property and Tax Records

Property and Tax Records can be obtained from the State regional municipality office known as a County, Parish, or Borough (naming convention depends on the State). Each regional municipality has its unique system, and while some are easier to navigate than others, most offer the same functionality. Figures 9. And 10. show the results used from the business address returned in the search from figure 8. Notice the various information types and levels of detail resulting from the search (identifying info redacted).

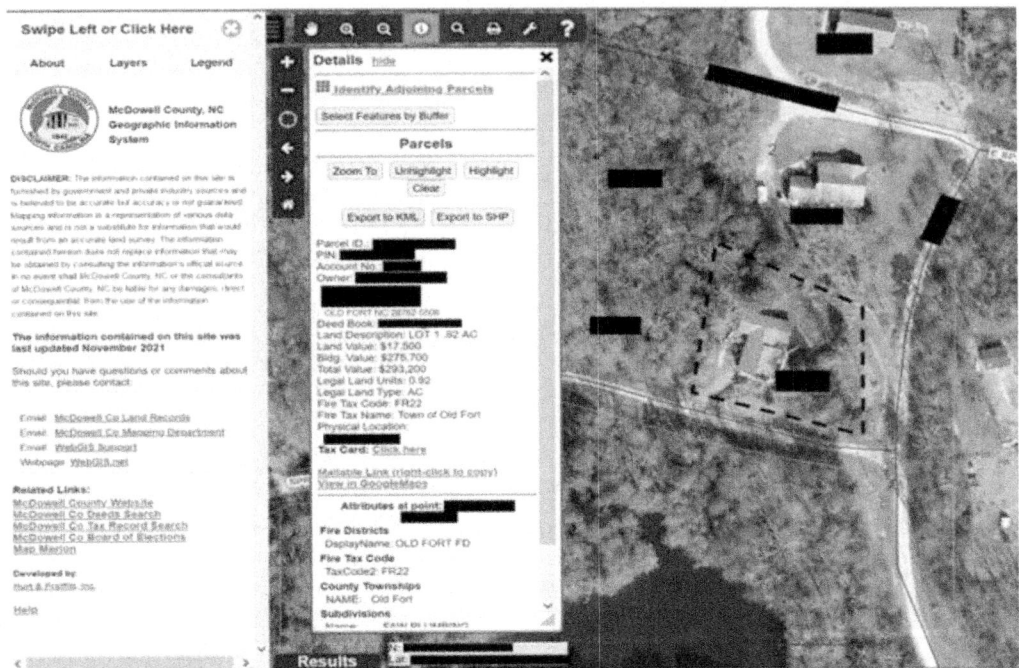

Figure 9. Property Record

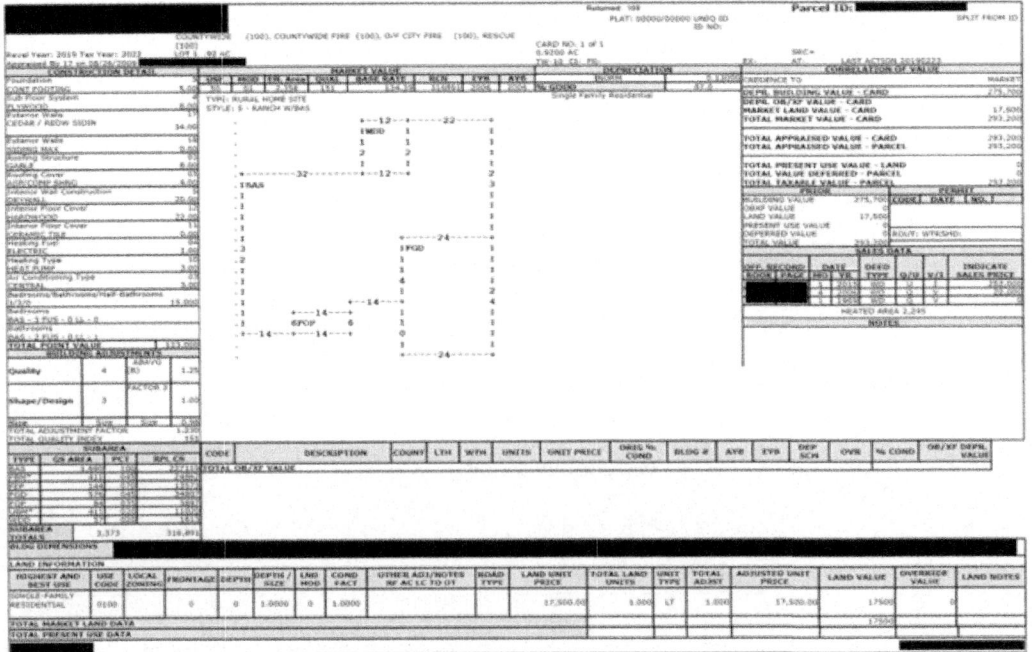

Figure 10. Tax Card

44

Voter Registration

Voter Registration records can be obtained through the State Board of Elections. Each state has its system and information detail available. Expanding on our business owner search and supporting information gathered from our Property Record search, Figures 11 and 12 show our business owner as white, male that is unaffiliated with any political party that voted Democrat in 2008 and Republican in 2016 during the Primary elections (identifying information redacted).

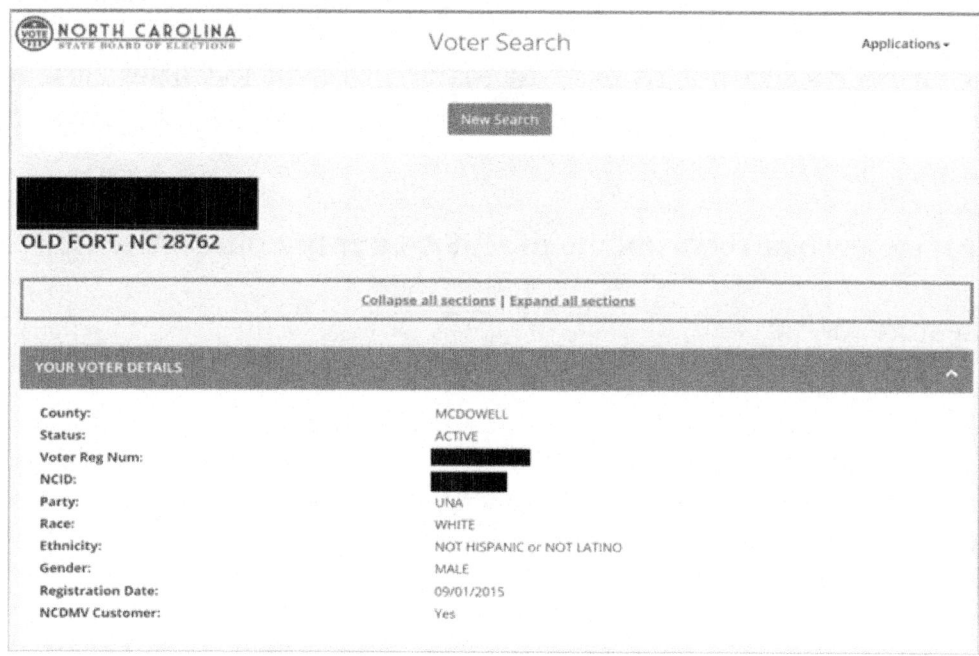

Figure 11 Voter Demographic

If this section is blank, we do not have a record that you voted in a past election in North Carolina.

Election	Voted Method	Voted County	Primary Election Ballot
11/03/2020 GENERAL	ONE-STOP EARLY VOTING	MCDOWELL	
11/06/2018 GENERAL	ONE-STOP EARLY VOTING	MCDOWELL	
11/08/2016 GENERAL	ONE-STOP EARLY VOTING	MCDOWELL	
03/15/2016 PRIMARY	IN-PERSON ELECTION DAY	MCDOWELL	REPUBLICAN
05/06/2008 PRIMARY	ONE-STOP EARLY VOTING	BUNCOMBE	DEMOCRATIC

Figure 12. Voting History

Court Records

Court records are handled differently by Federal, State, and Local Municipalities. Federal Court records can be searched through Public Access to Court Electronic Records (PACER) at the following website [pacer.uscourts.gov/]. PACER is a service of the Federal Judiciary. Its mission is to provide the public with the broadest possible access to court records and foster a greater public understanding of the court system.[7] It is free to make an account, but pricing is set at $0.10 per page. However, effective January 2020, if a user accrues $30 or less in a given quarter, those fees are waived.

State and local courts are not as easy to search. Not all localities host a searchable database online. Black Book Online is a valuable tool to help find State and local court records.[8]

The website is [www.blackbookonline.info/USA-County-Court-Records.aspx].

A quick search of an individual in North Carolina resulted in numerous pending cases. Figures 13 and 14 show an example of the North Carolina system (identifying information redacted).

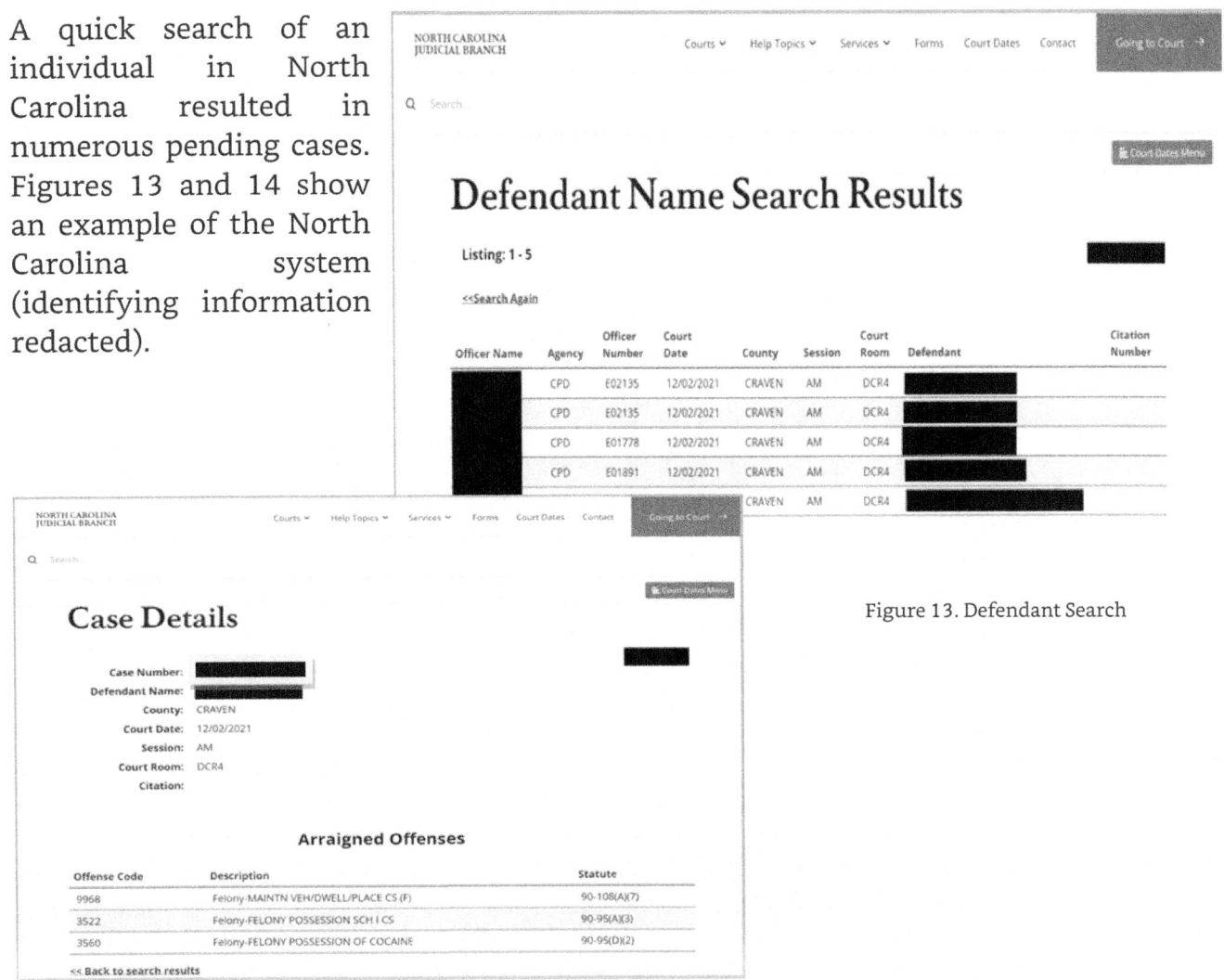

Figure 13. Defendant Search

Figure 14. Case Details

Onward to The Rabbit Hole

Many more types of information are a matter of public record. So much that an entire book could be written about finding and researching the various record types, this "rabbit hole" can go deep while providing an Investigator with some of the most cost-effective information available. Additionally, public record searches are a "low signature" research method. In most instances, the subject of an inquiry will be unaware of the collected information.

Learning to navigate the government bureaucracy and record management practices is essential for an OSINT practitioner. Luckily, the proliferation of technology access and data storage architectures are forcing government agencies to modernize their record management practices which make for an ever-evolving landscape of record sources. Mastering this art allows for information obtained via other means to be confirmed and supports a hypothesis but at the low cost of free.

References:

1. Thomas Paine, "The Rights of Man," USHistory.org, Feb. 9, 1792, Accessed Nov 9, 2021, www.ushistory.org/paine/rights/c1-016.htm.
2. Gerald and Kathleen Hill, "Public Record," The People's Law Dictionary, Accessed Nov 2, 2021, dictionary.law.com/Default.aspx?selected=1684.
3. United States Department of Justice, "Frequently Asked Questions," FOIA.gov, Accessed Nov 2, 2021, www.foia.gov/faq.html.
4. Reporters Committee for Freedom of the Press, "Open Government Guide," rcfp.org, Accessed Nov 2, 2021, www.rcfp.org/open-government-guide/.
5. U.S. Securities and Exchange Commission, "Accessing EDGAR Data," sec.gov, Accessed Nov 3, 2021, www.sec.gov/os/accessing-edgar-data.
6. North Carolina Secretary of State, "Search," sosnc.gov, Accessed Nov 8, 2021, www.sosnc.gov/online_services/search/by_title/_Business_Registration
7. PACER, "About Us," pacer.uscourts.gov, Accessed Nov 3, 2021, pacer.uscourts.gov/about-us.
8. Black Book Online, "Select State for Free County Court Records" blackbookonline.info, Accessed Nov 8, 2021, www.blackbookonline.info/USA-County-Court-Records.aspx.

TEAM TNT

WHO ARE THEY?

Team TNT is one of the most prevalent cryptojacking threat actors attacking Linux & Windows servers right now.

BACKGROUNG

 **Active Since October 2019**

 **Targets: Cloud and containerized environments**

 **Malware: Hildegard, Black-T, LaZagne, MimiPenguin**

EVENTS

August 2020

Created a Crypto-mining Worm that Stole AWS Credentials

Worm use tools such as:
- Masscan   -Punk.py
- XMRig
- Tsunami IRC Backdoor

May 2021

Team TNT Attacked Exposed Docker API to Spread Malicious Images

Tools and Techniques used:
- TNTfeatB0rg -Zgrab
- XMRig   -Deploy Container
- User Execution: Malicious Image

September 2021

Team TNT Hackers used Open-Source Tools to Steal Usernames and Passwords

Tools used:
- Masscan port scanning
- ProcessHider -7z
- B374k
- LaZagne

References:
- Doman, C. (2021, October 8). Team TNT – The First Crypto-Mining Worm to Steal AWS Credentials. Cado Security | Cloud Native Digital Forensics. https://www.cadosecurity.com/team-tnt-the-first-crypto-mining-worm-to-steal-aws-credentials/
- Lacework Labs. (2021, July 8). Taking TeamTNT's Docker Images Offline. Lacework. https://www.lacework.com/blog/taking-teamtnt-docker-images-offline/
- TeamTNT, Group G0139 | MITRE ATT&CK®. (2021, October 1). MITRE ATT&CK. https://attack.mitre.org/groups/G0139/
- TeamTNT with new campaign aka "Chimaera." (2021, February 23). AT&T Alien Labs. https://cybersecurity.att.com/blogs/labs-research/teamtnt-with-new-campaign-aka-chimaera

Using Sock Puppet Accounts for OSINT

By Jeremy Martin

"A sock puppet is an online identity used for purposes of deception. The term, a reference to the manipulation of a simple hand puppet made from a sock, originally referred to a false identity assumed by a member of an internet community who spoke to, or about, themselves while pretending to be another person." – Wikipedia

Both sides of the cyber game use these fake social media accounts. You can find hackers, scammers, bots, and other cyber criminals on the dark side while journalists, penetration testers, and Investigators on the other. Like any proper tool, it can be used for good and evil.

Why would YOU want to create an undercover account? It is always a good idea to separate your real identity from the initial investigation when investigating. You increase the likelihood that the target will get suspicious. You also run the risk of being identified and doxed, harassed, and in the absolute, worst-case scenario, targeted for lethal retaliation. Depending on the suspect, you always need to take the appropriate countermeasures to protect your organization/agency, yourself, and even your family.

Another thing to consider is that many social media sites have a Terms of Service (TOS) that specifically cover fake or investigation accounts. Organizations like Facebook actively look for these accounts, even if law enforcement and ban them.

REMINDER!!! DO NOT YOU YOUR PERSONAL OR BUSINESS ACCOUNTS TO DO INVESTIGATIONS!!!

The importance of Anonymity and Security

It would be best to connect to a public WiFi access point and only use VPN or Tor as a last resort. The reasons are that VPNs and Tor are sometimes tracked, blocked, or marked as questionable by websites when creating an account. This means the likelihood you will make the account without having an actual phone number decreases drastically. Public WiFi tends to look a bit more "normal."

More about Tor

I love Tor and always have. Tor is great at offering some of the best anonymity available, and the best part is that it's free. The mechanics of Onion routing is that you are essentially moving through several different proxy servers, which minimizes trace evidence that can be used to tie the traffic back to its original source. You can easily set up a hidden service with a ". onion" address. This allows us to communicate securely with other Investigators, informants, or even suspects. The downside of using Tor is that criminals commonly use it, and many of the websites we need to investigate may be blocking traffic from Tor or red-flagging it. So, even though it offers many benefits, Tor is not always good for Surface Web investigations.

VPN Value?

There has been a ton of advertising for Virtual Private Network (VPN) services that claim that they will protect your Internet traffic. This is only partly true and mostly false. A VPN is a Point-to-Point encrypted tunnel that allows one network to talk to another through an encrypted tunnel.

Think of it this way. You are using a third-party VPN service; your traffic is very secure when connecting from your system to the third-party network. The traffic then routes from that server through their Internet connection. The other thousand people using the same service will also share that gateway IP address. That sounds fine. Well, after you leave that service provider, your traffic is back on the Internet for everyone else to see. This means it is naturally less anonymous than Tor.

The providers may also be watching everything you do in the name of "Marketing." Free VPNs and cheaper ones are the most significant risks. The services that claim they DO NOT STORE LOGS are also usually lying or not telling you the whole truth. Within networking, there will always be logs. They are required to troubleshooting when things fail. Logs will be there; it is just a matter of how long and how they are destroyed.

Some of the websites are red-flagging the popular VPN services.

Creating a persona

Some people make these accounts from scratch. The more content and backstory you create in the beginning gives you more direction to make the account look like a natural person's account.

Use a password manager to keep track of everything you create for these accounts, including the user/pass info, and keep notes. KeePassXC is a great free solution that is cross-platform that will allow you to share your password management database among multiple computers and different operating systems.

Character/Persona generators

Creating an account can take some time, effort, and creativity if you are short on any of those for whatever reason. Anyone that has played role-playing games like D&D, WARHAMMER, or other games where you need to generate a character to play, has a step up because they have done this before. You can leverage a few resources to help speed up the process and spit out a "character" with many random attributes and content. Below is a list of resources you can use when generating your Sock Puppet persona. Just remember that all information generated is fake. You can change the data to fit your narrative.

- Generator (fakepersongeneraTor.com)
- Random Name Generator (www.elfqrin.com/fakeid.php)
- Random Character Generator (random-character.com)
- Personality Generator (rangen.co.uk)
- Trait Generator (rangen.co.uk)

Image generators

Generating images that have consistency to them can be a challenge. You want to create is a realistic person with history and consistency. It is important to NEVER use pictures of friends or family. This can put the investigation at risk and possibly them at risk.

- This Person Does Not Exist (thispersondoesnotexist.com) – GitHub project available
- AI-Generated Faces (boredhumans.com)
- Gallery of AI Generated Faces (Generated. photos)

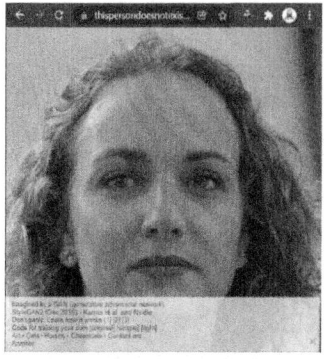

Emails

Creating an email is the basis for setting up your undercover investigation account. This will be used for setting up social media accounts and communications with a Person of Interest.

- Tutanota.com
- Protonmail.com
- GMX.com
- Mail.com
- Yandex.Mail
- Etc... Almost any email service will work.

Note: All email providers must comply with the laws in the country they reside in. For example, Proton Mail is in Switzerland, and they must abide by Swiss Law, while Tutanota is in Germany and must abide by German law.

Read this statement from Proton. protonmail.com/blog/climate-activist-arrest/

Burner Phones

A burner phone is handy and may be required to create accounts on certain websites and create a history for the persona. The reason is that the sites are trying to prevent fake accounts from being made and send an SMS validation message to a phone. Bots rarely have their phone numbers. In some countries, you do not need to tie your ID or Passport to buy a SIM card or burner phone. If you are in one of these countries, it is suggested to use cash only and let the phone sit for 2+ months before you activate it with a sock puppet email. Sometimes SIM cards can also be purchased on Amazon.com. Keep an eye out for deals and trial offers. Phone emulators can also work.

VoIP Phone

Generate a Voice over IP (VoIP) account with an online vendor. This will be useful to add another layer of separation. Many online services like Google Voice require an actual phone number to tie to your account. This makes your burner phone that much more critical.

Pre-Paid Credit Cards and Gift Cards

In some cases, you may need to use a credit/debit card for purchases, account setups, and account verifications. If you are in a country or area that allows you to purchase these cards (VISA/Mastercard), use good OPSEC to minimize links back. You can also use a privacy.com masked credit card.

Cryptocurrencies

If your investigation requires cryptocurrencies for transactions, you can use prepaid cards on most crypto services. Exodus.com is a wallet that allows you to trade many different currencies and their Desktop software is cross-platform compatible.

An example of needing cryptocurrencies during an investigation may include fraud cases on sites like Facebook Marketplace, Instagram's Shop Now, Craigslist, etc. You may also find them helpful when purchasing content and buying services.

Social Media Accounts

When creating a social media account, you want to look like 'normal' as possible to the website because many of them are trying to stop people from creating fake accounts. Make sure you are not breaking the law or violating terms of service when doing this. Now things to look at when building your OSINT undercover accounts...

1. Use public Wi-Fi and do NOT use a VPN
2. Pick a social media site to focus on
3. Use your persona's "real" phone number for verification
4. Save the information in a password manager like KeePassXC
5. Keep Operational Security (OPSEC) in mind
    a. Use a solid password for the password manager access
    b. Use a different password for each account
    c. Never cross over accounts with your real-world or personal accounts
6. Go into the settings of the account you just created and change the phone number to a VoIP number
7. When you are done, log out of the account
8. Log back in and start adding information to your account relevant to your persona
9. Go back to step 2 for the rest of the sites you want to try

Note: You may burn UC personals when creating accounts. Just be patient and persistent. This process takes time and effort.

Aging the Account

The account needs to be "aged" like a fine wine or good whiskey; the account needs to be "aged." This means creating content and history. This will minimize the likelihood of the account getting flagged as a fake by the service provider and deleted. Become the persona. Go to the same public WiFi you created the account with to log in and generate activity. Like posts, make comments, share things, and grow your connections. Log out when you are done. This is very important and ties into OPSEC. Not logging out can leak other networks and information out for Big Data if you are not careful. The goal is to train the site that you are a natural person by doing real person things.

Try to add content and history following the personality of the fake character. This includes finding banners with image searches. Think of banners for your social media pages, memes, pictures from the location your persona is from. Build your account pages how you believe your sock puppet would have. Add enough information to make it look real. Over time, keep logging into the account and add content to build history and the trustworthiness that the account is a "real" person.

Learn from your Investigations

"Operations security (OPSEC) is a process that identifies critical information to determine if friendly actions can be observed by enemy intelligence, determines if information obtained by adversaries could be interpreted to be useful to them, and then executes selected measures that eliminate or reduce adversary exploitation of friendly critical information." - Wikipedia

Things constantly change, and you must keep improving to keep up. Make it a habit of using good OPSEC. There is a saying with Investigators. The suspect needs to be lucky every time, but you only need to be lucky once. The other side can use the same Tactics, Techniques, and Procedures (TTP) as you do, which flips the table on you. Now, you need to be lucky every time, and they only need to be lucky once.

Resources

- Protonmail.com: climate-activist-arrest
- Creating Research Accounts for OSINT Investigations – We are OSINTCurio.us
- Dark Side 116: Sock Puppets. What if I told you not all fake social…
- DeBot: Twitter Bot Detection via Warped Correlation
- How to Make Sock Puppet Accounts for OSINT in 2021 | Hacker Noon
- The Art of The Sock (secjuice.com)The Ultimate Sock Puppets Tutorial for OSINT Operators - Ehacking

Cool Tool: Dradis CE

Dradis CE is an extensible, cross-platform, open source security project framework for collaboration and reporting that'll save you hours on every project.

This collaboration platform is:
- Platform independent
- Markup support for the notes: text styles, code blocks, images, links, etc.
- Integration with existing systems and tools:

Brakeman, Burp Suite, MediaWiki, Metasploit, Nessus, NeXpose, Nikto, Nmap, OpenVAS, OSVDB, Qualys, Retina, SAINT, SureCheck, VulnDB, w3af, wXf, Zed Att0ack Proxy, …

https://github.com/dradis/dradis-ce

VPNs vs Proxies vs Tor
What are These & How Can They Hide Your Location?
By: Bonnie Betz

In this day and age, we are more than ever concerned about our business and personal privacy and greater anonymity as we rely more and more on our connections with the world via the Internet. One of the most famous pieces of software marketed to provide privacy and increased anonymity for users who use the Internet is the Virtual Private Network or VPN. But two other methods need to be considered when looking for a solution. These are Network Proxies and Tor.

This article will attempt to understand better these three (3) solutions available to add a much greater level of privacy and anonymity into our Network and Internet Infrastructure. This article will focus on these three (3) viable hardware/software service solutions for a greater level of security, privacy, and anonymity. The article provides:

1) What is each service is and how does the service work?
2) How secure are they, and can they hide your location?
3) Pros and cons of using each solution.

Virtual Private Network (VPN)

What is a VPN? How does it work?

A Virtual Private Network or VPN is a software service that will change your IP address and encrypt your Internet data.

This allows you access to the web safely and privately. VPNs are good at preventing government intrusion and surveillance; ISP imposed online censorship because your Internet Service Provider (ISP) is prevented from seeing what you are up to on the Internet and organizations or individuals blocking website(s) access and traffic.
Websites cannot see either your actual IP address or who your Internet Service Provider (ISP) is. All they see is the IP address of the VPN server, and because this address is usually shared among many users, this further protects each user or network environment.

A VPN utilizes a software client installed on a network's endpoints (see Note below) and created a secure connection via an "encrypted tunnel" to a VPN hardware server. The hardware server passes user data to the Internet, isolating the endpoint client. Kind of simple, but let's see how that is accomplished.

Note: In the world of Information Technology (IT), an endpoint is any device (i.e., laptop, phone, tablet, desktop, or server) connected to a secure business or personal network. When you connect to a network, you are creating an endpoint. Every endpoint is vulnerable, and cybercriminals can take advantage of this fact and exploit it by using phishing attacks, spyware, Trojans, or other forms of malware. Endpoint protection is the business of securing endpoints against possible cyberattacks, but not the business of VPNs. A VPN can enable you to scale your endpoint security capabilities, but by itself does not secure endpoints! This article will not look at Endpoint Protection as it is a separate article.

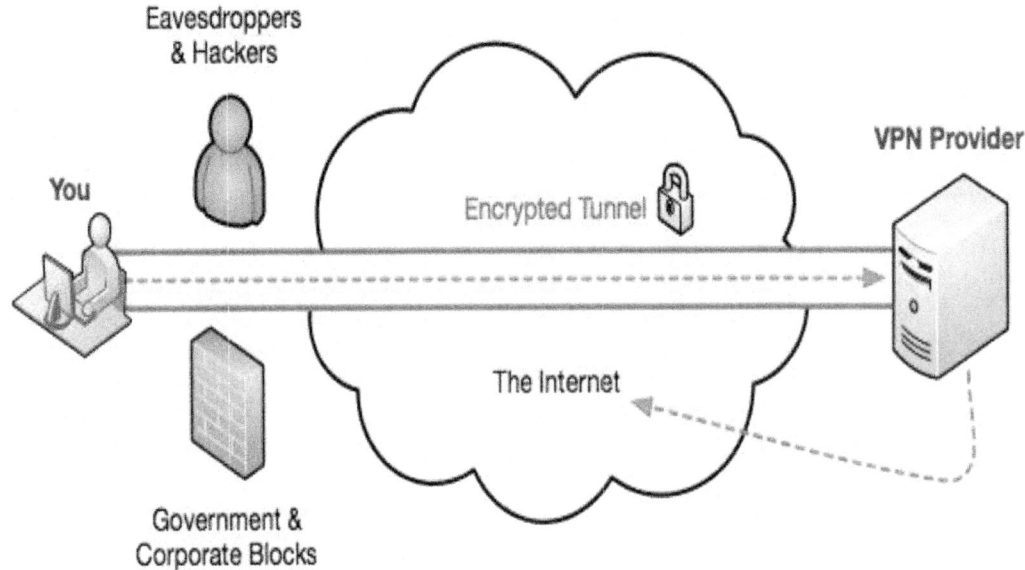

Figure 1 – Basic Layout of a VPN [1]

When a user initiates a connection with a website for data transmission, the following occurs:

1. The VPN client (software/service) on their endpoint encrypts the user data, even before the Internet Service Provider (ISP) or the WiFi provider (even public WiFi) sees it.
2. The data is then sent via software constructed "Encrypted Tunnel" to the VPN-hosted server.
3. From the VPN server, the data goes to the Internet and to the online destination the user requested initially.
4. The online destination sees the user data coming from the VPN server and its location, but not from the users' endpoint and their location, including an IP Address associated with the VPN server and not the user.
5. The user data is encrypted because the VPN service is being utilized. The data left the user endpoint already encrypted even before it got to the users' ISP and remains encrypted to the VPN Server. Think of the VPN Server as the third party involved in data transfers to the Internet.
6. This solves privacy and security concerns and provides greater anonymity for accessing the Internet. The destination site sees the data's origin being the VPN Server, not you. Since the information is encrypted, all they see is encrypted data, even if someone captures it.

There are different combinations and techniques a VPN can use for Encryption, and these can be better understood when someone knows the "Types of VPNs Available,"

"Protocols a VPN might use," and "Encryption Internal Basics." All of this is covered in the following section.

How secure is a VPN? How does a VPN Hide User Location?

Because VPN companies have varied offerings of service and security, the technology used by a particular vendor as well as how it is utilized to hide data and who the user is and their location to provide the privacy and a level of anonymity for the business or individual should be looked at when a VPN is going to become an integral part of any business or individual infrastructure.

A VPN uses different combinations and techniques for Encryption, which can be understood when you know the types of VPN and the protocols used for Encryption and security. Critical components of VPN technology will be introduced to understand better how a VPN functions to provide the protection needed and how a user is hidden.

Types of VPNs Available

"Site to Site VPN"

This type of VPN is mainly found in office environments and is called a "Router-to-Router VPN." Companies sometimes need to connect one office to another office remotely and maintain privacy and security.

This is achieved by installing this type of VPN. The VPN builds a private encrypted tunnel and provides a secure connection between office sites. The use of the name "Router-to-Router VPN" is more appropriate because one router acts as a VPN Client, and the other router serves as a VPN Server. This type of VPN can provide privacy, security, and anonymity to offices in different geographical locations if needed.

"Remote Access VPN"

This type of VPN can provide an Internet connection to remote users from the site or central office into the company's private network—Used mainly by users residing in their homes or when traveling to connect to company servers. It functions similarly to any other VPN Client by creating a secure virtual tunnel between the remote user and the VPN Server.

Home users on their private network usually use this type of VPN to remove the geo-restrictions and access blocked websites in their region.

In contrast, office employees use it whenever they want to access company servers from a different location.

IP Address - Hide User & Location

One of the first vital components a VPN should offer is the ability to hide a user's location and make it difficult to correlate data with a specific user or business entity. VPNs offer this privacy and a greater level of anonymity by making it appear that the data on the Internet is coming from the VPN server and not the actual user endpoint to anyone on the Internet who might be tracking the data.

By simply using the VPN Server as the final link in the chain of user data to the Internet, any observer monitoring user activity will see the VPN Server's IP Address and not the user address. IP Addresses are closely tied to a geographic location, so hiding them prevents observers from figuring out a user's location. A business or user location can also spoof by connecting with a VPN Server residing in a different country.

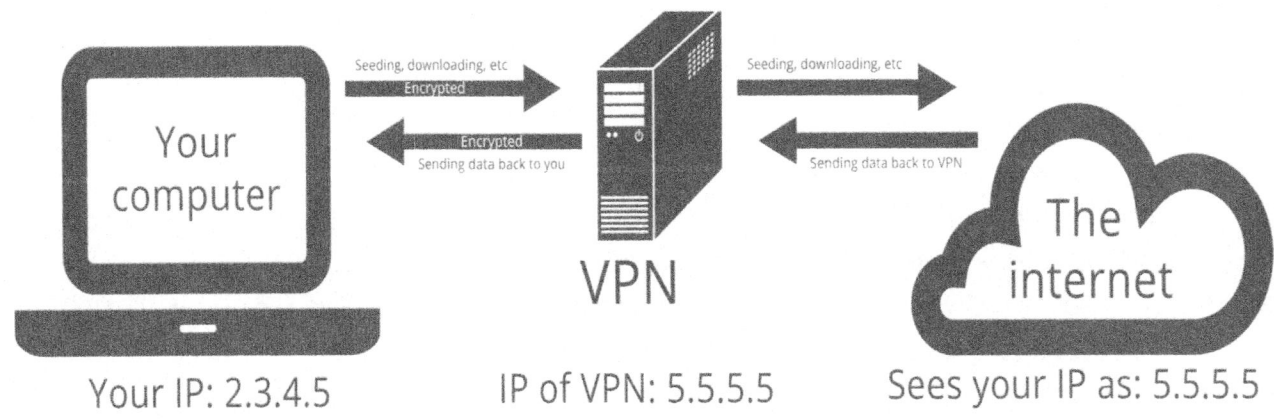

Figure 2 – IP Address Sequence with VPN [1]

VPN Protocols

"Protocols"

Defines how the VPN service handles data transmission over the VPN. The most common protocols are PPTP, L2TP, SSTP, IKEV2, and OpenVPN.

Note: Most VPNs allow you to choose the protocol to use, and the more secure the protocol used, the more secure the entire data transmission will be for the user.

Brief Protocol Overview –

- **PPTP (Point-To-Point Tunneling Protocol)** – One of the oldest protocols in use today and was a Microsoft design. It works well on older model computers and is part of the Windows O/S. It is becoming less widely used since faster and more secure protocols are available. By today's standards, it is barely safe.
- **L2TP/IPsec (Layer 2 Tunneling Protocol)** – Combination of PPTP and Cisco's L2F protocol. The sound concept uses keys to establish a secure connection on each end of the VPN Encrypted Tunnel. When added to the IPsec protocol, which authenticates and encrypts packets of data sent over the Internet, this addition of IPsec improves security. Some think that the NSA can break this protocol and view the data, so this protocol should be considered with that in mind.
- **SSTP (Secure Socket Tunneling Protocol)** – Offers a connection with some SSL/TLS encryption, a de-facto standard for web encryption. SSL and TLS are built on symmetric-key cryptography, in which only 2-parties involved in the data transfer can decode the data.

Note: Built by Microsoft and fully integrated into the Windows operating system and is considered a very secure protocol.

- **IKEv2 (Internet Key Exchange, Version 2)** – Jointly developed by Microsoft and Cisco, it is an iteration of Microsoft's previous protocols and much more secure. The protocol itself is a component of IPsec and is used to set up security associations and perform authentication. Offers better authentication and stability even during network hopping. Not as popular as other protocols, but available as part of IPsec on Windows XP, Windows 2000, Windows Vista, Windows Server 2003, Windows Server 2008, and Windows 7 and some open-source implementations released for Linux and OpenBSD. It delivers better speed than PPTP, SSTP, and L2TP, since it does not have the overhead associated with Point-to-Point protocols (PPP).
- **OpenVPN** – One of the most common implementations for a VPN solution. It implements techniques to create secure point-to-point or site-to-site connections in routed or bridged configurations and remote access. It is based on SSL/TLS, an open-source project. Because of the open-source, it is constantly being improved by many developers. It secures the connection and thus the data by using keys known only by the two parties participating in the data transfer on either end of the transmission. Can run over User Datagram Protocol (UDP) or Transmission Control Protocol (TCP) tunnels. This makes web traffic impossible to differentiate from standard HTTP over SSL traffic. Very difficult to detect, let alone block.

Note: It is the most versatile protocol and has perfect security, but because it is open-source and can be administratively controlled from an external program through a TCP or Unix domain socket and designed for developers who would control it remotely for programming reasons, there have been recent concerns of its vulnerability by hackers who could access it remotely and execute malicious code execution. This is just a note of caution in an otherwise perfect protocol.

Generally, most VPNs allow the choice of protocol a user wants to implement. Unfortunately, not all devices will enable the use of all these protocols. Most of these protocols were designed and built by Microsoft. You can use them on all Windows-based systems. Apple devices will come across some limitations. An example of these limitations is the iPhone, which uses L2TP/IPsec as the default protocol. In the case of an Android phone, you may encounter problems of its own, which we will not get into in this article.

Take heart, though; most VPN service providers offer iOS VPN apps and VPNs for Android users. However, finding support for less popular mobile operating systems may be challenging.

Encryption

"Encryption Defined"

It is a method used to enhance sensitive data or information security and privacy and cannot be read by any random individual or organization. Encryption converts the actual data and information to an unreadable/coded format protected by an encryption key set by the authorized user "Only." Data can be decrypted when received by an authorized user who correctly enters the appropriate key. The encrypted data is only readable by someone with the original key used to encrypt the data.

"Encryption Basics"

VPN Encryption is the process by which a VPN hides user data in a coded format unreadable by anyone trying to access your data. The VPN encrypts data when it enters and passes through the VPN Tunnel and then decrypts it at the other end of the VPN Tunnel, where the VPN Server connects the user to the requested website. In contrast, all login and data details are kept secure and hidden by VPN Encryption.

"VPN Encryption Algorithms"

AES (Advanced Encryption Standard): Is a secure algorithm used in symmetric key encryption. The key works on the premise that the longer the critical size, the stronger the encryption. Longer key sizes come with a caveat: processing takes more time, resulting in slower connection speed. Some features of AES are as follows:

- Symmetric key symmetric block cipher
- 128-bit data, 128/192/256-bit keys
- Stronger and faster than other standards

AES utilizes at a minimum a 128-bit algorithm. Many of the VPNs out there use a 256-bit AES encryption algorithm. The block schematic diagram of AES structure follows:

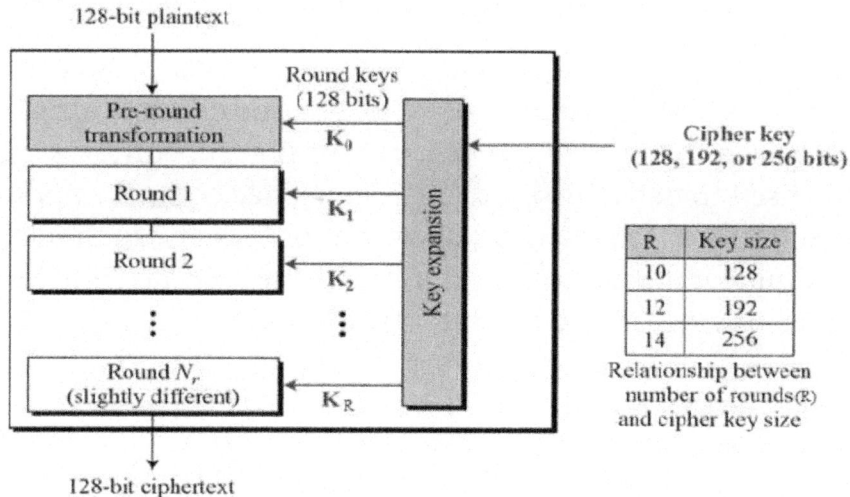

Figure 3 – Advanced Encryption Standard [1]

RSA: The name is derived from the first letter of the surname of three men who proposed it in 1977. A public key cryptography system is used to secure data transmitted over an Internet connection. It is mainly used in creating and establishing an SSL/TLS session and by the OpenVPN and SSTP protocols and sometimes the IKEv2 protocol.

It is used in an asymmetric public key system, which means a public key is used to encrypt the data, but a different private key is used to decrypt the data.

Note: When someone sends an encrypted message, they can pull the intended recipient's public key from a public key Directory and use it to encrypt the message before sending it. The message recipient then decrypts the message using their related private key. RSA key exchange involves sharing a public key derived from the private key at the time of generation, and anybody with access to the private key can create the public key. Now here is where it gets interesting with this type of encryption. Due to the complexity of the mathematical system utilized, deriving the private key from the public key is impossible. The public key can be shared over the Internet to establish a connection between client and server, which must occur before ever sharing encrypted data. This handshake or "key exchange" must occur so both client and server can agree on the keys to encrypt data.

Many protocols rely on asymmetric cryptography, including TLS (Transport Layer Security) and SSL (Secure Sockets Layer) protocols, making HTTPS possible.

RSA, in many instances, is part of the overall encryption methodology because it is prolonged due to its asymmetric nature. RSA is not usually used for bulk data encrypted transfers to establish the means for sharing encrypted data using faster symmetric encryption algorithms like AES.

SHA (Secure Hash Algorithm): Created by Cisco, this algorithm is very secure and robust. It requires both the sender and receiver to implement this algorithm while encrypting and decrypting messages or data traveling through a VPN Encrypted Tunnel.

"Hashing" is a cryptographic process used to determine the authenticity of various inputs and is also used to validate the integrity of files, documents, and other data on the Internet. It is used to determine if data received has come from a genuine source. A "Hash" is the result of a mathematical algorithm or "Hash Function" (see Note below) that converts a simple data input into an unreadable format. This simple data can be text, picture, audio, or video converted into a string of characters.

Note: The hash function works as a "message authentication algorithm" with which all your data is authenticated on SSL connections (including OpenVPN). Its sole purpose is to protect a user from active attacks. SHA creates a unique print of a valid SSL certificate that any OpenVPN client can authenticate. If that particular certificate is interfered with in any manner, no matter how small, it will be detected, and the connection will be refused and terminated immediately. SHA is also used in Passwords, coding languages, and SSL certificates.

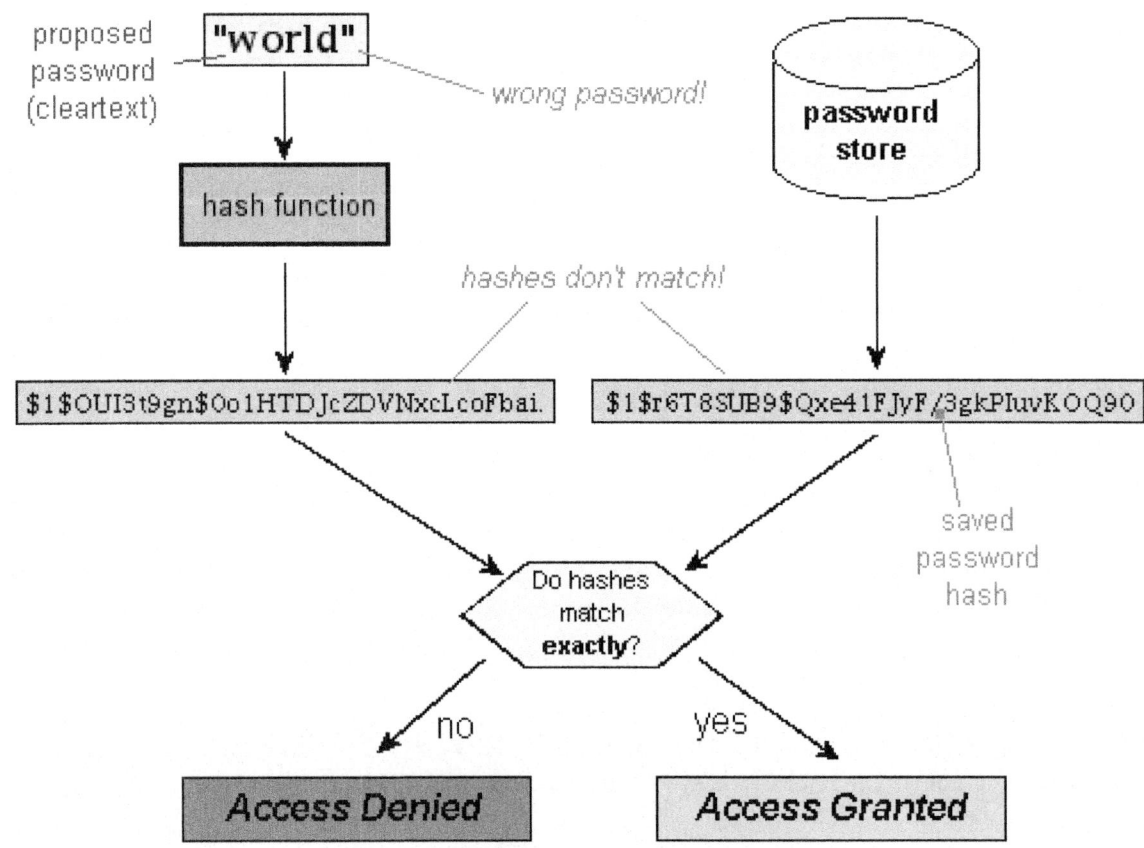

Figure 4 – Basic Diagram of Password Authentication [1]
(A wrong password entered flow)

"SSL/TLS VPN Encryption"

Secure Sockets Layer (SSL) VPN Encryption: A security protocol is commonly used to establish an encrypted link between a web server and a web browser. This encrypted link will provide security and privacy for all data between a web server and a browser. SSL cryptography provides a securely encrypted tunnel between VPN Clients and VPN Servers. This VPN configuration is commonly called an SSL VPN.

SSL vs. TLS: Before 2015, all VPNs used Secure Socket Layer encryption, but since that time, VPNs have adopted the Transport Layer Security (TLS) protocol. TLS encrypts all data packets traveling between an Internet-connected device and an SSL VPN Server. This is accomplished by providing "end-to-end encryption (E2EE)" between VPN Client and VPN Server. Similar to the encrypted link between a server and a browser, TLS encryption now ensures that "all data" passed from a VPN Client device to a VPN server is private and secure.

A significant advantage of SSL/TLS is third parties cannot intercept or "sniff" the encrypted data stopping ISP's, governments, employers, local network administrators, and cybercriminals from being able to "packet sniff" what a packet contains. It protects against "man in the middle (MitM)" attacks. TLS successfully stops eavesdropping and tampering by ensuring data integrity between the VPN Client and the VPN Server.

TLS has largely replaced Secure Socket Layer Encryption as it is more secure since vulnerabilities have been discovered in the SSL protocol. Secure SSL VPNs now implement TLS as SSL can no longer be trusted to ensure data integrity, security, and privacy.

"Multi-Protocol Label Switching (MPLS) VPN Encryption"

Note: MPLS is briefly described here to make the reader aware of this form of encryption and not treat it as another form of VPN Encryption, but encryption is different as it does not encrypt the data. A brief overview follows:

Encryption Methods are unique and are different from what a VPN is thought to be. VPNs referred to as; "Point-to-point (Pseudowire)," "Layer 2 (VPLS)," or "Layer 3 (VPRN)" are these unique look-alike VPN imitators. This is due to MPLS. It is a protocol routing technique or method designed to speed up and shape traffic flows across "Enterprise-Wide Area" and "Service Provider" networks.

MPLS takes different customers' traffic and ensures a packet from one customer cannot be received by another customer by adding an MPLS 32 bit header to the packet between Layer 2 and Layer 3 of the OSI Model.

VPN Security, Privacy and Anonymity Conclusion

We have given you an overview of how a VPN provides for a user's privacy and a greater level of anonymity when using the Internet and how a VPN secures the data being transferred by the user through the various methods to encrypt the data. Some people can consider VPNs the Cadillac of software services to ensure data security, user privacy, and a much greater level of user anonymity when users wish to use the Internet to communicate data.

Your impression of whether a VPN is indeed the Cadillac of security, privacy, and anonymity solutions is yours alone. We hope that we have provided information that can be used to make an informed decision when a business or individual wishes to incorporate VPN technology into their business and private network infrastructure for the purpose of Security, Privacy, Anonymity.

Proxies

The Meriam-Webster dictionary defines the word "proxy" as *"authority or power to act for another."* In the computing world, the definition takes on a slightly different meaning. It is typically associated with the phrase "proxy server," which is defined as a computer system that facilitates data exchange between users on a network.

Every computer on the Internet needs to have a unique Internet Protocol (IP) Address, which allows Internet traffic to ensure that the correct data goes to the right computer by using this IP Address. Proxy Servers are computers on the Internet with their IP Address, and only specific other computers know that IP Address. Think of proxy servers as your very own avenue to the Internet and the wealth of data on the Internet.

What is a Proxy? How does it work?

In computer networks, a proxy server is a server that acts as a gateway or intermediate system between a client requesting a resource and the server providing that resource on the Internet. A proxy accepts and forwards connection requests, then returns data for those requests. Instead of connecting directly to a server that can fulfill the request for a resource (i.e., file, webpage, etc.), the client directs the request to a proxy server, which evaluates the request and performs the required network transactions. The proxy server provides a method to simplify or control the complexity of the request or provide additional benefits, such as load balancing, privacy, or security.

Note: This is a basic definition of a proxy, which is quite limited because there are quite a few unique proxy types with their distinct configurations.

Proxies make up our websites, online services, and other networks. Proxies are used for a multitude of things.

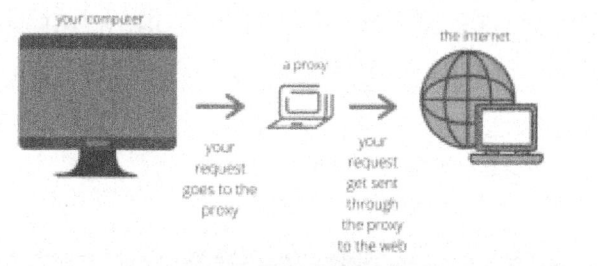

Figure 5 – Example of a Proxy [1]

You can use proxies for:

- Avoid geo-restrictions
- Web scraping/web crawling
- Ad verification
- SEO
- Changing your IP Address (most proxies change your address to provide user security, privacy, and anonymity)
- Copping sneakers (so weird, they have proxies available to allow someone to buy limited-edition sneakers)
- Working with automatic tools/bots for social networks

Proxy servers are tools for working on the Internet as they can keep your data secure and keep your browsing on the Internet with greater privacy and anonymity.

Both Windows and Linux offer a proxy server to be utilized within their respective operating systems. Installation differences are as follows:

- Windows O/S does not require any software to be installed. Having a proxy server running on a Windows computer can be quickly and relatively painless. The figure below depicts the Network & Internet window, which provides a setup section for setting up a proxy.

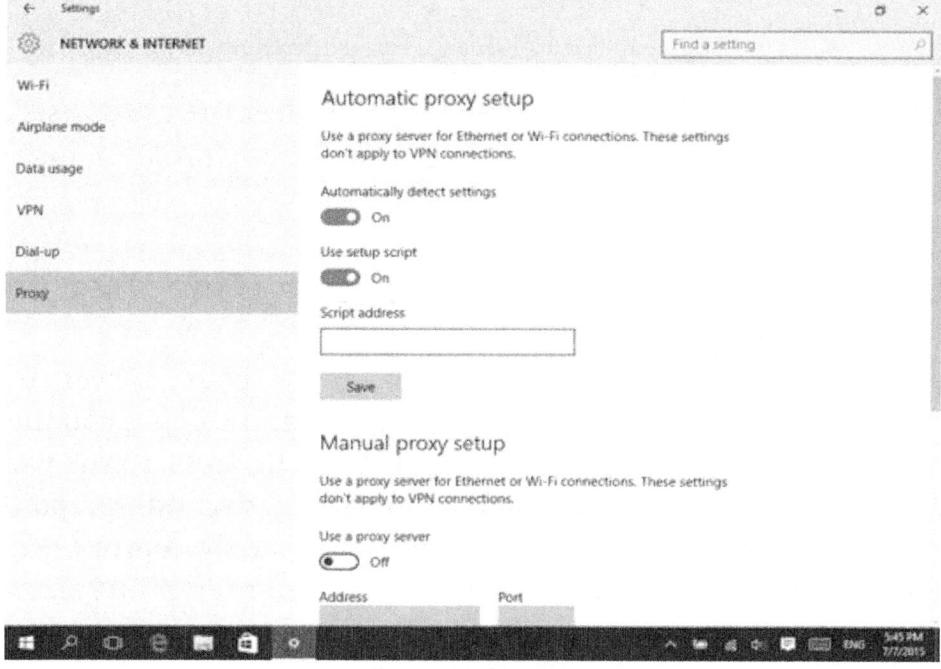

Figure 6 – Network & Internet Setup Window 10 [2]

To install a proxy on a Linux computer, you need to install the "Squid" proxy software as depicted in the following figure. This figure provides the steps for installing a Debian/Ubuntu Linux system.

```
$ sudo apt update
$ sudo apt -y install squid
```

When the installation is finished, you may now run the following system control commands to enable and start the Squid daemon on your system.

```
$ sudo systemctl start squid
$ sudo systemctl enable squid
```

Figure 7 – Installation Steps for Installing a Proxy on Debian/Ubuntu Linux [2]

There are many different Proxy Server providers who offer their proxy servers as a full-service package, making setup relatively easy for these proxies. Just follow their instructions.

How secure is a Proxy? How does a Proxy Hide User Location?

When you send a web request, your request goes to the proxy server first. When the proxy server forwards, it can change the data you send and still get you the information you expected to see. A proxy server can change your IP Address, so the web server does not know where your exact location in the world is, and depending upon the proxy, it can also encrypt your data, so your data is unreadable. Lastly, a proxy server can block certain web pages based on IP Addresses. Proxy servers are not "one size fits all" when enhancing security, privacy, and anonymity. Proxy Servers do not just hide a user's location by only showing the server IP Address and not the user's IP Address like many businesses, and individuals think.

Types of Proxy Servers Available

A proxy server may reside on the user's local computer or at any point between the user's computer and the destination server on the Internet. There are two types of proxies: Forward Proxies (or a tunnel (see note below) or gateway) and Reverse Proxies (used to control and protect access to a server for load-balancing, authentication, decryption, or caching.

Note: Tunneling transmits private network data and protocol information through public networks by encapsulating the data. HTTP tunneling uses a protocol of higher-level (HTTP) to transport a lower-level protocol (TCP) by specifying a request method called CONNECT. This is how a client behind an HTTP proxy can access websites using SSL: (i.e., HTTPS, Port 443)

- A "Forward Proxy" is an Internet-facing proxy used to evaluate the outbound user request and take action on the request before relaying the request to an external source and then retrieving data from a wide range of sources anywhere on the Internet. An "Open-Proxy" is a forwarding proxy server accessible by any Internet user. This is one of the most prevalent proxies on the Internet in use.

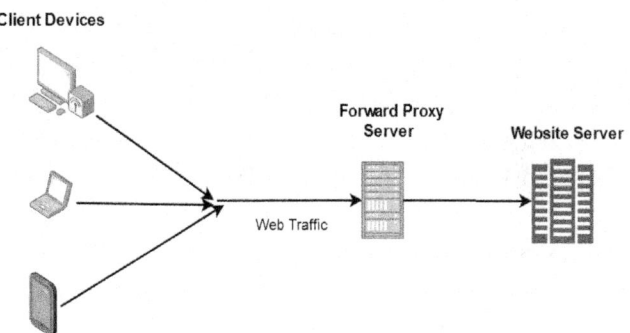

Figure 8 – Basic Diagram of a Forward Proxy [1]

- A "Reverse Proxy" is usually an Internal-facing proxy used as a front-end to control and protect access to a server on a private network. This server sits between a business or personal network and multiple internal resources. For example, an extensive website might have dozens of servers that collectively serve requests from a single domain. To accomplish that, these servers will forward client requests to one or more ordinary servers that handle the request. The response from the proxy server to the client is returned as if it came directly from the original server, leaving the client with no knowledge of the original server. This type of proxy also performs other tasks such as "authentication," "decryption," and "caching."

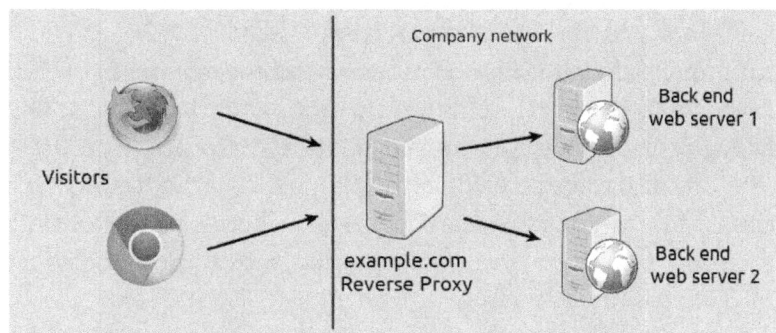

Figure 9 – Basic Diagram of a Reverse Proxy [1]

There are several reasons for installing reverse proxy servers, as listed below:

- "Encryption/SSL" Acceleration" – When secure websites are created, SSL is often done by a reverse proxy equipped with SSL acceleration hardware rather than the webserver.
- "Load Balancing" – The reverse proxy can distribute the load to several web servers, with each web server serving its application area.
- "Serve/Cache Static Content" – A reverse proxy can offload the web servers by caching static content like pictures and other static graphical content.
- "Compression" – The proxy server can optimize and compress the content to speed traffic.
- "Spoon Feeding" – Proxy reduces resource usage caused by slow clients on the web servers by caching the content the web server sent and slowly "spoon feeding" it to the client. This can benefit dynamically generated pages.
- "Security" – The proxy server is an additional layer of defense and can protect against some O/S and web server-specific attacks. It does not protect from attacks against the web applications or service itself, which might be considered the more significant threat.
- "Extranet-Publishing" – Reverse proxy server facing the Internet can be used to communicate to a firewall server internal to an organization. This can provide "extranet" access to some functions and keep the servers behind the firewalls. This method requires additional security measures for the remainder of the infrastructure in case the server becomes compromised.

Some unique "Proxies:

- "Anonymous Proxy" – Server reveals its identity as a proxy server but does not disclose the originating IP Address. It is easily discoverable, but since it hides users' original IP Addresses and geo-location, it might prove beneficial to some users.
- "High Anonymity Proxy" – The server does not allow the original IP Address to be detected, and no one can see it is a proxy server.
- "Suffix Proxy" – This type of proxy server appends the proxy's name to the URL of the content that has been requested to the broker. This proxy does not preserve a higher level of anonymity. Used for bypassing web filters.
- "Distorting Proxy" – Generates an incorrect original IP Address of the client once a proxy has been detected. Using HTTP headers to maintain the confidentiality of the Client's IP Address.
- "Tor Onion Proxy" – This proxy is, in reality, a software service that aims at online anonymity to the user's personal information. It routes traffic through various networks worldwide to make it difficult to track users' addresses and prevent anonymous activities. For this, it uses "ONION ROUTING." In this type of routing, the information is encrypted in a multi-fold, layer-by-layer process. At the destination, each layer is decrypted to prevent the data from scrambling or getting distorted. Also, cheap as it is open-source and free to use.
- "I2P Anonymous Proxy" – An anonymous network enhanced version of the Tor onion proxy, which uses encryption to hide all the communications at various levels. This encrypted data is then relayed through various network routers in different locations. I2P is a fully distributed proxy that aims at online anonymity. It also implements "garlic routing" (enhanced version of Tor onion routing). This type of proxy can be run on a client's node. I2P finds other peers to build an anonymous identity to protect the user's personal information. It also resists censorship, and again like Tor, it is open-source and free.
- "DNS Proxy" – Unlike other proxies, this type of proxy takes requests in the form of DNS queries and forwards them to the Domain Server, where they can also be cached, and the flow of requests can be redirected.

Proxy Server Protocols

Proxy Servers use different protocols (set of rules) to operate. Proxies dictate essential traffic rules, such as the size of data packets, destination management, and data security. These data transmission protocols are vital benefits that proxies provide the user.

"HTTP Proxy Protocol" –

The HTTP or HyperText Transfer Protocol proxy was explicitly built to provide a proxy for one-way web requests to web pages using HTTP protocols. It is usually the best choice for accessing HTTP:// or HTTPS:// addresses. It is widely used and supported by all browsers and most HTTP client software.

"FTP Proxy Protocol" –

This type of proxy server caches FTP requests and traffic and uses the concept of relaying. FTP or File Transfer Protocol is used to move files on the Internet. It is unique in that it uses two different connections. The control connection sends commands between the FTP client and the FTP server. File transfers are sent on a separate connection called a data connection. The FTP Proxy handles active and passive FTP sessions, and it also protects the FTP server and restricts FTP protocol commands between the client and server.

"SSL Proxy Protocol" –

SSL stands for Secure Sockets Layer, and the "S" in HTTPS also stands for "Secure." HTTPS protocol combines HTTP and SSL/TLS (Transport Layer Security). The HTTP protocol is a layer in a data transmission structure, so SSL (or HTTPS) is an additional layer below it, enabling a proxy to transfer data securely and anonymously between client and server. The SSL layer encrypts the data against access by third parties, including Internet Service Providers (ISP).

"SOCKS Proxy Protocol" –

The SOCKS protocol ("Socket Secure or Secure Socket," whichever you fancy) is commonly used to transmit data between the client (your endpoint) and server (usually a website) through a proxy, which shields your endpoint computer's identity. SOCKS proxies are generally used by installing them as a browser extension or configuring a Torrent client to use a VPN provider's proxy server.

An essential aspect of SOCKS proxy is it works with more protocols. For example, HTTP Proxy only works with the HTTP protocol, but SOCKS has no restriction.

It can operate with many protocols, including HTTP. The SOCKS protocol is low-level, meaning it is not as specialized software-wise as other protocols. Because it is not specialized, it has more comprehensive applications and, not being specialized, can handle more protocols. As a result, SOCKS is best for taking other protocols like POP for email.
-

TCP (Transmission Control Protocol) collects and reassembles packets of transmitted data within the SOCKS content, while the IP (Internet Protocol) ensures that data reaches the intended network target. These two protocols enable digital devices to communicate over long distances.

SOCKS does not have to go through the same routes as HTTP traffic. As such, if there is a firewall monitoring HTTP ports, SOCKS can skirt around this restriction even if it is using HTTP. This allows for browsing restricted content without the firewall blocking the websites.

There are two versions of SOCKS:

- SOCKS4 – handles client/server transmission efficiently, but without authentication, so not always appropriate depending on the project.
- SOCKS5 – Most recent version can handle voice and video and supports authentication methods.

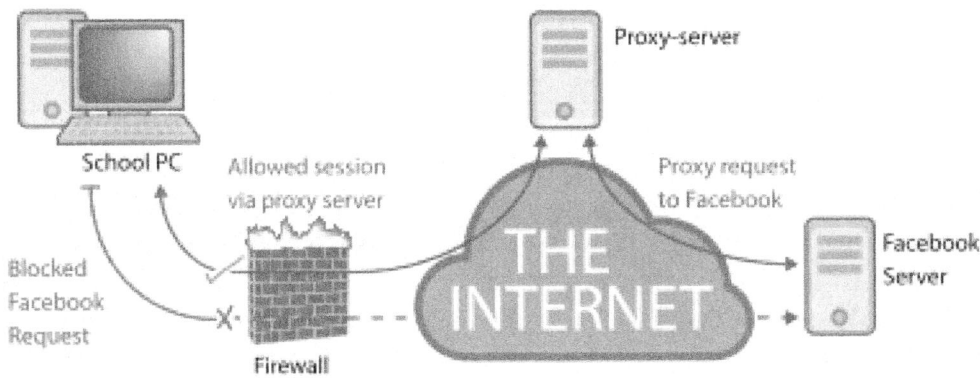

Figure 10 – SOCKS Browsing of Restricted Site Example [1]

Proxy Security, Privacy and Anonymity Conclusion

The overview of the information provided in the previous pages related to Proxies has given the reader insight into another solution available to provide a user with enhanced privacy and greater anonymity when using the Internet. Many businesses and individuals have thought that a proxy only provides a level of privacy because they can only change the original user's IP Address to hide the user and their location. As we have seen, this is not necessarily accurate. We have provided various types of proxies that can be an integral part of an infrastructure to provide data security and keep a user private and anonymous.

There is definitely a place in a business or an individual's network infrastructure for a proxy. Again, as with the VPN, we hope that we have provided information that can be used to decide how to make infrastructure more secure and improve privacy and anonymity.

ATTENTION:
Malware Companies in the VPN Game

Once a leading alternative to internet privacy, the VPN world is no longer be as secure as it once was. This is especially the case with the advent of malware companies in the VPN game. Kape Technologies, in particular, has been buying VPNs since 2017, with Express VPN being the most recent purchasing takeover.

VPN Takeovers

VPN	Year Bought	Price
CyberGhost VPN	2017	$10 Million
Zenmate VPN	2018	$5 Million
Private Internet Access VPN	2019	$127 Million
ExpressVPN	2021	$936 Million

Kape Technologies has indeed contributed to malware and adware distribution in the past. Despite not directly creating malware, the company instead made its cross-browser development platform easy for 3rd party abuse. What's more, Kape Technologies was also a leading player in the ad injection industry by offering monetization options that were in turn used by ad injectors.

While it must be noted that Kape Technologies shut down this program in 2016 and underwent significant leadership changes in addition to transitioning to the privacy and security industry, the fact persists that the company's recent actions remain highly questionable.

In 2021, for instance, Kape Technologies also bought several VPN review websites, changing VPN rankings and omitting not only their part in VPN ownership, but their past history as well. This lack of transparency leaves VPN users oblivious to the real owners of the VPN they're using. As a result, there remains an ongoing threat of data abuse for millions of VPN users.

https://restoreprivacy.com/kape-technologies-owns-expressvpn-cyberghost-pia-zenmate-vpn-review-sites/

Tor (The Onion Router)

If you are interested in online privacy and anonymity, then you've probably heard about "Tor." Tor (formerly an acronym for "The Onion Router") is often touted as a way to browse the web anonymously. Tor is used especially by activists evading governmental restrictions or less than stellar individuals selling their products on the "Dark Web" marketplaces, "Tor is a popular way to gain significantly more anonymity" than what you would typically expect online. At the same time, Tor is not perfect, so it can provide a false sense of security if used incorrectly.

Tor has been developed with the help of the U.S. Navy and other military organizations to perform anonymous communication and is maintained and upgraded by the "Tor Project" and remains to this day as part of their group of solutions to provide enhanced security, privacy, and anonymity. We will look at what Tor is really and what it can do. We will make comparisons with a VPN and a Proxy.

What is Tor? How does it work?

Tor is free and open-source software for enabling anonymous communications. It directs Internet traffic through a free, worldwide, volunteer overlay network, consisting of more than 7000 relays for concealing a user's location and usage from anyone conducting network surveillance or network traffic analysis. Tor's intended use is to protect its users' privacy and make it more difficult to trace the Internet activity of any user that uses the Tor network.

Note: Tor is not meant to completely solve the issue of anonymity on the web, but instead to reduce the likelihood for sites to trace actions and data back to a user.

Tor enables its users to surf the Internet, chat, and send instant messages anonymously and is used by various individuals for both legal and illegal purposes.

Using the Tor Browser is like using any other web browser. Still, the actual process of starting the browser differs from web browsers like "Chrome" or "Firefox" because Tor must configure a connection to the Tor Network before the browser can start and then making the browser quite intuitive.

The main difference with this browser is that when a user browses the web with Tor, the user's real IP Address and other system information is obscured and will hide this information even from an Internet Service Provider (ISP).

The primary uses for Tor are:

- Bypassing censorship and surveillance
- Visiting websites anonymously
- Accessing Tor Hidden Services (.onion sites)

As was previously mentioned, the browser uses the Tor network, a worldwide network of servers. When a business or individual operates the browser, their data is routed through multiple randomly-chosen Tor relay servers (or nodes) before accessing the destination website.

The traffic is heavily encrypted and slowly decrypted one layer at a time at the different nodes, so the traffic data is being encrypted and decrypted multiple times by each relay. Hence, the relay servers only know the last and next relay, not the request data contents or the entire circuit. The network request finally exits the Tor Network at an exit node to the requested website. From the perspective of this website, you are browsing directly from the exit node. This means that whoever identifies the user based on network traffic will just stumble on the last server the data passed through (exit node). This means that the browser makes it impossible or, at the very least, highly difficult to identify the user(s).

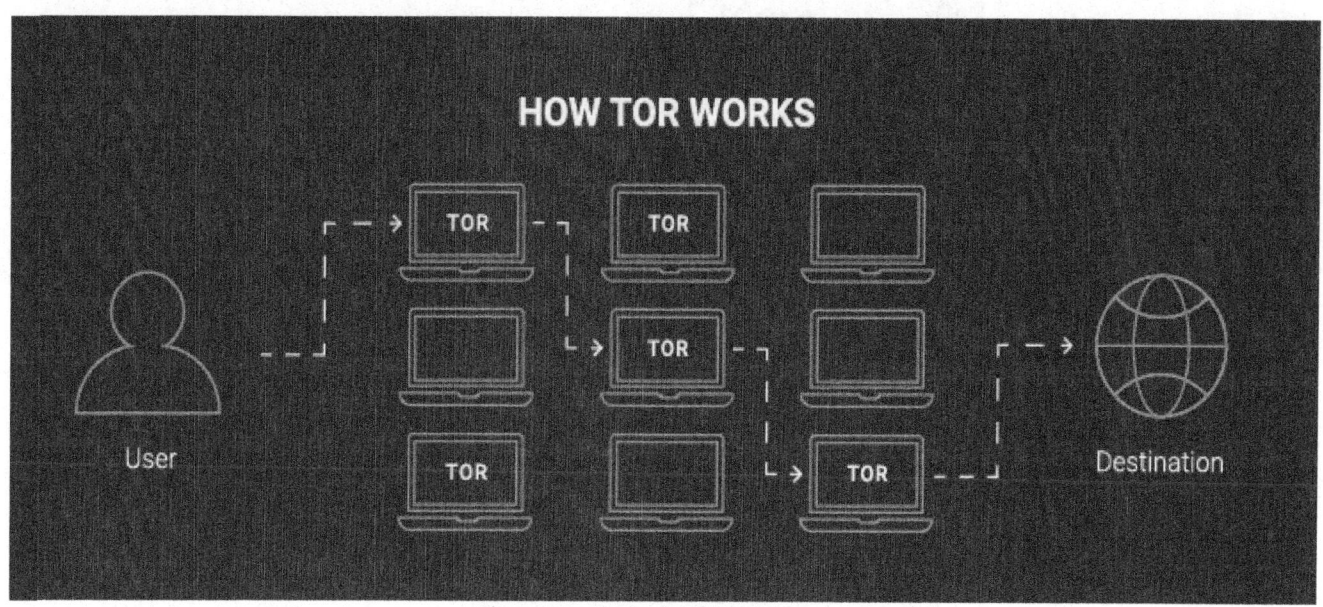

Figure 11 – Example of Tor Network Relays [1]

To access the Tor Network, you simply need to download the browser. Remember, it is open-source and, of course, free. The Tor Browser is a modified version of Mozilla Firefox that connects via the Tor Network. The browser also bundles several extensions that help users maintain their privacy. While using the Tor Browser, everything you do online will automatically be encrypted and "anonymized" in the above-stated process.

How secure is Tor? How does Tor Hide User Location?

As we have seen, Tor requires the Tor Network, which is a conglomerate of relay servers that encrypt/decrypt traffic data in multiple layers, much like the way an onion has various layers. Tor uses a technique called appropriately "Onion Routing." Onion routing is a technique for anonymous communications over a computer network. In a network based on "onion routing" and properly referred to as an "onion network," messages are encapsulated in layers of encryption analogous to layers of an onion. The encrypted data is transmitted through a series of network nodes called (wait for it…) "Onion Routers," and each of these nodes or servers will decrypt ("peel" away) a single layer uncovering the data's next destination. When the final layer is decrypted, the message arrives at its destination.

The sender remains anonymous because each intermediary knows only the location of the immediately preceding node and the following node. Since the destination has no idea of the sender, the original sender has become hidden. The destination does not see the original sender's IP Address and does not know its geo-location.

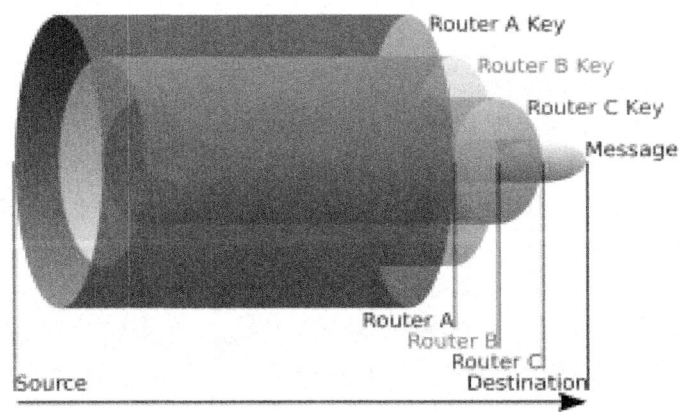

Figure 12 – Basic Diagram of Onion Routing and Tor Network [1]

The Tor Browser aims to make all users look the same, making it challenging to fingerprint-based on browser and device information. MULTI-LAYERED ENCRYPTION is a feature of Tor and is what makes it so private. Your traffic is relayed and encrypted three times as it passes over the Tor network. Other features offered by Tor to increase security, privacy, and anonymity are:

- Blocks Trackers – third-party trackers and ads can't follow data. Cookies are automatically cleared when done
- Defend Against Surveillance - prevents someone watching your connection from knowing your website visits
- Resist Fingerprinting – aims to make all users look the same
- Browse Freely – free to access sites your home network may have blocked

74

Tor Hidden Services

Tor Hidden Services, "onion services," or "Tor websites are websites that are only accessible from within the Tor Network. All hidden service domain names end in .onion and consist of a very long, seemingly random set of characters. Collectively, "Tor Hidden Services" are sometimes referred to as the "Dark Web."

These websites are not indexed and won't appear on search engines likes Google. Instead, several user-created Directories of hidden services allow you to find the sites you are looking for.

The term "Dark Web" generally creates a mental image of criminals selling illegal services through less than reputable Tor-based marketplaces. In reality, many reputable websites use the Tor network. An example would be sites like Facebook, DuckDuckGo, and the New York Times running versions of their sites with .onion addresses for journalists and activists living within an oppressive regime. Also, many extremely privacy-conscious individuals set up blogs and websites only accessible through Tor Hidden Services. This keeps their real-life identity secret.

The U.S. government is constantly improving its methods and technologies for catching criminals who frequent the "Dark Web" for illegal purposes. Tor is vulnerable to "timing attacks" and other advanced techniques that only a government can implement.

Still, the use of Tor is perfectly legal. Still, just a reminder that illegal activity goes on frequently involving Tor, so be sure to observe, so you don't end up accidentally on a somewhat sketchy .onion site. EXERCISE CAUTION!

Tor over VPN vs. VPN over Tor – Which is Better?

For privacy-conscious people, it is possible to combine these two services. There are two main ways in which it is possible to use "The Onion Router" and a VPN together. Although a VPN and Tor share similar purposes as they are both intended to protect the anonymity and security of your online traffic, the two settings produce different results. They each suit different requirements, so the right solution for your needs is essential, so you choose the better one.

"Tor over VPN"

Opting for this solution, you first connect to one of the servers offered by your VPN provider, which will encrypt your entire online traffic. Then the encrypted traffic is redirected through the Tor Network using a few Tor nodes before it finally reaches the Internet. This configuration is easy to achieve; you simply need to connect to your VPN before accessing Tor.

The VPN masks your IP Address and encrypts your online activity preventing your Internet Service Provider (ISP) from finding out that you are using Tor. With this setup, your encrypted data is protected from your VPN provider because it is sent over Tor. All your VPN provider sees is that you are connecting to Tor.

When connecting to a VPN server first, your IP Address is changed, meaning that the Tor entry node won't see your actual IP Address as the address will be the one assigned to the VPN server.

Making Tor the last gateway before connecting to the Internet allows Tor's Hidden Services and websites with the .onion suffix.

Lastly, the Tor over VPN configuration is considered a better option in terms of security.

There are downsides as listed below:

- Traffic that leaves the Tor exit nodes is not encrypted, making it vulnerable on the Internet.
- Since many Tor exit nodes are blocked, you may end up with a bad exit node without an Internet connection
- You need to trust your VPN provider, and this configuration only works if your service is reliable
- If the VPN provider keeps logs, then you can be linked back to your actual IP Address
- If you plan on hiding your Tor traffic with this configuration, be aware if VPN connection drops, your ISP could access your Tor traffic

"VPN over Tor"

In this configuration, your data can be encrypted by the VPN when it enters and exits the Tor nodes before being routed to the Internet. Your VPN provider won't be able to see your actual IP Address, just the one connected to the Tor exit node. With VPN over Tor, your Internet Service Provider (ISP) won't find that you are connected to a VPN. It will only see that you are connected to a Tor node.

Some websites block known Tor exit nodes, but these restrictions can be defeated because your VPN will hide that a Tor exit node is in use.

Since your actual IP Address is hidden by the Tor exit node, you can reduce the risk of your VPN provider logging your data since the IP Address connected to the VPN would be the Tor exit node.

The VPN over Tor setup allows you to select the server location that works better for you. This configuration provides better anonymity overall.
Again, there are downsides to this configuration:

- This setup does not allow you to access Tor's Hidden Services
- Does not protect Tor exit nodes that may monitor you and your ISP can see that you are using Tor
- Your VPN works as a fixed endpoint, which makes you vulnerable to global end-to-end timing attacks

"Tor with VPN Wrap-Up"

It is difficult to say which you should use, but enough data has been provided for a business or an individual user to make an informed decision. Tor through a VPN, you enjoy higher security, while VPN via Tor can be better for anonymity.

To use both together, you need to be sure of the reliability of your VPN provider's commitment to privacy and that they won't keep logs, then "Tor over VPN" would be an ideal configuration.

Tor and a Proxy Server – What differences?

You may also choose to increase your privacy and online security by using a Proxy Server. Proxies generally work well for specific purposes and situations. Many think that a Proxy is less effective and less secure than both Tor and a good VPN. How does a Proxy differ from Tor?

"Proxy vs. Tor"

Like Tor (or a VPN), a Proxy Server is another way to guide your online traffic through a different server that stands between a user endpoint and the data's destination server. A proxy server simply provides to the Internet a "fake" IP Address rather than the original user IP Address.

People tend to like proxies because many are free to use. However, Proxy Servers only offer a certain degree of anonymity and online security. Brokers must be chosen wisely because to have data encrypted by a proxy, you must select a specific proxy that offers data encryption.

Tor provides anonymity by hiding a user's IP Address and geo-location like a proxy and encrypts the user data without any specialization required.

As mentioned, choosing a Proxy Server has to be done carefully as the server host can see precisely what is happening online. In theory, they could log all your information, creating a vulnerability to your security, privacy, and anonymity. Proxy Server does not offer the level of privacy and security as Tor and Tor provide a much greater level of anonymity.

Pros and Cons – VPN & Proxy

We have already provided differences between Tor and a VPN and Tor and a Proxy, but we have not touched on differences between a VPN and a Proxy. This section will look at the Pros & Cons of a VPN vs. Proxy.

Note: This section has been put here so anyone wishing to enhance their online security, privacy, and a greater level of anonymity can see the differences and make a better-informed decision concerning these three (3) solutions.

What are the Pros & Cons of a VPN?

Using a VPN brings many benefits:

- All network traffic between the user endpoint and the VPN server is encrypted, making it impossible to see what websites a user visits or what services are used on the Internet
- VPNs hide the real user IP Address. Websites and Internet services only see the VPN Server IP Address
- VPNs hide the users' accurate geo-location. The Internet thinks that your location is, in reality, the location of the VPN Server
- Using a VPN Server can help bypass geographical restrictions. You can access data from restricted countries or regions when you use a VPN Server in that country or region
- Network traffic cannot be sniffed because of its full data encryption
- Plenty of Free and Paid VPN providers exist to choose from

Less than Positive Features of a VPN:

- Since VPN Servers encrypt all Internet traffic, it takes a toll on performance and speed
- Data is decrypted on the VPN Server, so a VPN provider knows information about the user, and if the provider keeps logs of user activity, the provider knows quite a bit about the user, and others can also get that log data
- Trustworthy VPN services tend to cost more than a perfect Proxy Server. All that encryption power comes at a cost for both the provider and is most likely passed on to the user or client
- Many Free VPNs are not trustworthy and, in some cases, dangerous

What are the Pros & Cons of a Proxy Server?

Advantages of using a Proxy Server:

- It hides a users' IP Address from basic checks
- It also hides the user geo-location; the destination sees the Proxy Server IP Address
- Depending on the configuration, Proxy Servers can improve security by blocking malicious websites that might distribute malware because Proxy Servers can, under the proper configuration, check for malicious content before forwarding it back to the user
- Proxy Servers can be used to access geographically restricted Internet services
- Many public and free Proxy Servers are available on the Internet, and some do provide reliable services

Negative Aspects of Proxy Servers:

- Proxy Servers don't encrypt your Internet traffic by default. Only specialized Proxies can encrypt data or can be configured to encrypt user data
- IP Address and Location of a user is not truly hidden from advanced detection techniques
- All user Internet traffic goes through a Proxy Server when in use. This means that a malicious Proxy Server can see and control everything that the user would be doing on the Internet
- Proxy Servers usually monitor and log user activity, which is an easy way of identifying the user
- If a Proxy Server is not configured correctly, unencrypted data can be sent to the user endpoint so that others can sniff data
- Many public and free Proxy Servers out there are not reliable, and in fact, some free Proxy Servers are downright malicious

VPN, Proxy & Tor Quick Comparison Chart:

Comparisons of a VPN vs. Proxy vs. TOR			
	Proxy	**VPN**	**TOR**
Does it hide original user IP Address from basic checks?	Yes	Yes	Yes
Does it hide original user location from basic checks?	Yes	Yes	Yes
Does it hide IP Address from advanced detection techniques?	No	Yes	Yes
Does it hide location from advanced detection techniques?	No	Yes	Yes
Does it encrypt Internet traffic by default?	No	Yes	Yes
Can it be configured to encrypt traffic?	Yes (certain proxies Only)	Yes (always encrypts)	Yes (always encrypts)
Does it keep logs of original user web browsing activity?	Yes (usually)	Provider Dependent	No

Figure 13 – Comparison Chart of VPN, Proxy & Tor [2]

Final Thoughts on Security, Privacy, Anonymity

This article has been put together to provide business entities and individuals with information to be utilized when making an informed decision on how each specific IT infrastructure should be configured to provide a greater level of Security, Privacy, and Anonymity for users when using Internet services or simply connecting business sites or allowing remote users connect to their company's business IT environment.

In the case of an individual on a private network, the luxury of knowing that their Internet use, whether browsing or using Internet services, is being given a greater level of security, privacy, and anonymity by using one of these solutions as described in this article.

We have chosen to provide both the positive and negative aspects of each solution and make some comparisons to assist in any decision. All three (3) solutions offer their specific level of support for securing Internet data and giving the user a level of privacy and anonymity when the user accessed the Internet that would not be there if not one of these solutions was utilized.

We hope that we have provided interesting facts about each solution and whether you choose a VPN, Proxy, or Tor for your specific needs, we wish you good fortune and best wishes in all your Internet endeavors. We hope you stay "SECURE" and lead a very "PRIVATE" and "ANONYMOUS" life on the Internet.

References

- [1] From open Internet searches for various diagrams
- [2] Developed by Bonnie Betz

Cool Tool: OpenCTI

OpenCTI is a free to use and Open Source product developed by volunteers. The first purpose of the OpenCTI platform is to provide a powerful knowledge management database with an enforced schema especially tailored for cyber threat intelligence and cyber operations.

The structuration of the data is performed using a knowledge schema based on the STIX2 standards. It has been designed as a modern web application including a GraphQL API and an UX oriented frontend. Also, OpenCTI can be integrated with other tools and applications such as MISP, TheHive, MITRE ATT&CK, etc.

https://www.opencti.io/

Teasing Identity & Moneylaundering Warfare Story

By: Diana Prusova

Sometimes, life can bring us very near to crime-related assets, people, institutions, activities – and their victims. Without us even realizing it and without having to deep-dive into the abyss of the darknet. The flashing red crossing lines between the surface web, deep web and dark web can be incredibly melted to the extent that we may not have enough information, resources or abilities to step back in time, re-think our decisions, carry out the necessary research and move futher away from the unclear boarders dividing the underworld of dark-minded actors who tamed their victims to serve as most powerless slaves and the happier world of those who either do not know or do not WANT to know that dark forces exist and pursue their intentions in mere vicinity of their happy homes. No matter if anyone denies it, the two worlds co-exist side-by-side in the same towns, the same streets, the same playgrounds, the same churches, the same mosques, the same houses, the same restaurants, the same banks. Members of the happier part of society may find themselves dining in a fancy restaurant next to a teen sex slave sold on the darknet to an ill-minded criminal offering her to just another abuser she must smile to and lead a cheerful conversation with unless she wants to risk the most severe punishment of being drugged or raped.

While doing my research on the darknet and tracing the huge flows of Bitcoin rivers, I could not ignore the goods offered and sought for certain – sometimes very surprising – amounts of the recently-so-much-celebrated cryptocurrency. I inevitably came accross appaling child pornography (CP) featuring children from 2-15 years and videos being valued as little as 0.0006 XBT, i.e. 33 USD and even less for unlimited 24-hour access - while the damage on the children's and babies' soul and body will last forever. Among other goods on the market, the darknet openly offers murders to be watched live on-line or carried out, including ritual murders of kids to be watched live on-line, rapes of children to be watched live on-line or carried out, banned machine guns and the heaviest drugs to be produced or transitted or distributed, stolen identities, and malware of all kinds. All that can be paid for in Bitcoin (XBT and BTC are both widely used tickers for Bitcoin with just a slight difference between the two) or Monero (XMR).

Of all the hellish goods offered on the dark market, I chose CP for my research, as the products can directly be downloaded and the path to them is pretty straightforward including the payments, so principles of dark web financial and identity paths can be demonstrated. In the gun and drug industry the path from the seller to the buyer is more adventurous, passing through several nodes to hide traces on the way using the so called layering during the money- and identity-laundering process. Layering in money-laundering is actually identical to the multiple-node pathway the TOR browser uses to make the user land on the destination IP address while gradually reducing his/her trace.

Let's see the typical financial and identity flows in the CP industry – both leading criminals to a safe shelter of anonymity and investigators to a blind street. The two following TOR CP websites demonstrate a step-by-step process the seller and buyer has to undergo in order to sell and buy the goods:

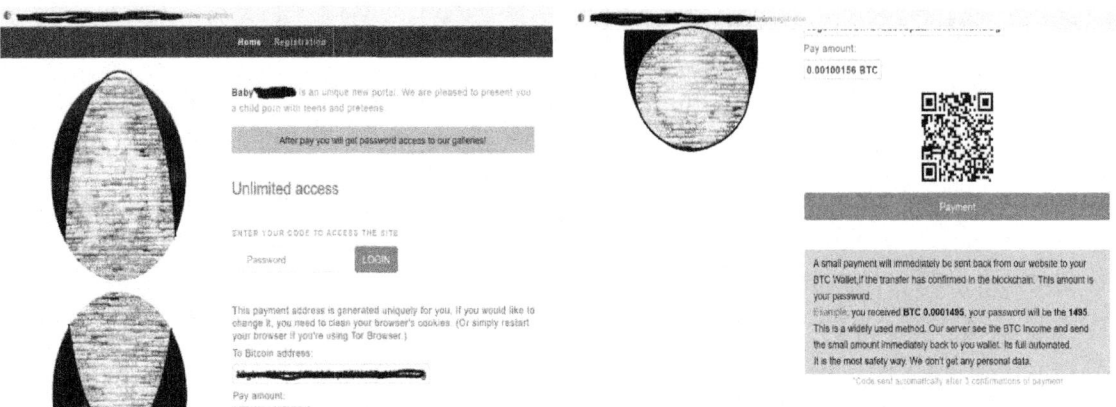

Both the seller and the buyer need to be in possession of a Bitcoin wallet. The seller provides the buyer with a unique one-time payment address which represents the only link to the seller. However, since dark market actors use anonymous cryptocurrency wallets that will be discussed later, this link is useless for criminal investigations. Neither the payment address nor the QR code leave a trace. As is clearly stated in the instructions provided to the buyer, the seller avoids any use of email or other forms of traceable communication by sending a very small amount of BTX back to the wallet of the buyer once the payment from the buyer has been received. The small amount sent back then represents the credential data the buyer uses as a login or password to enter the full-scope web page where he/she can download pictures and videos. Moreover, the entry onion web page is always active for a limited amount of time, usually 24 hours, to reduce the likelihood of successful investigations, such as face analysis or place recognition. After this time, another so called mirror web page is launched elsewhere on the dark web.

Here the process is even a little easier, as the seller's server just automatically adds the Bitcoin address of the buyer on a login whitelist once the payment from the buyer has been received. The buyer then uses his-her own Bitcoin address as a login:

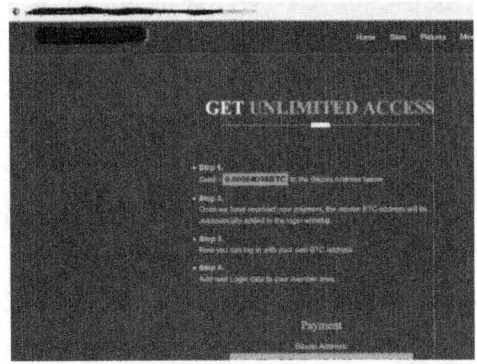

In order to understand the process of melting identity, we need to go deeper into the Bitcoin wallet issue. There are three types of Bitcoin wallets:

- those provided by legal crypto-brokers,
- the so called anonymous wallets of two kinds: software and hardware,
- XMR wallets.

The first type of the wallet is just a usual account where you can store your digital currency and operate transactions. In case the provider's seat is under the jurisdiction of a country requiring proper know-your-customer (KYC) and anti-money-laundering (AML) procedures to be in place, your indentity as well as all transactions will be clearly traceable. In the opposite case where the provider resides in a jurisdiction not requiring implementation of KYC and AML measures (see the up-to-date country blacklists at the end of the chapter), you will be required to provide entry data such as your name, address, email and bank account from which you will transfer deposits, but you may expect your transactions not to be examined.

Anonymous Bitcoin wallets do not require any personal information from you and creating one is extremely easy:

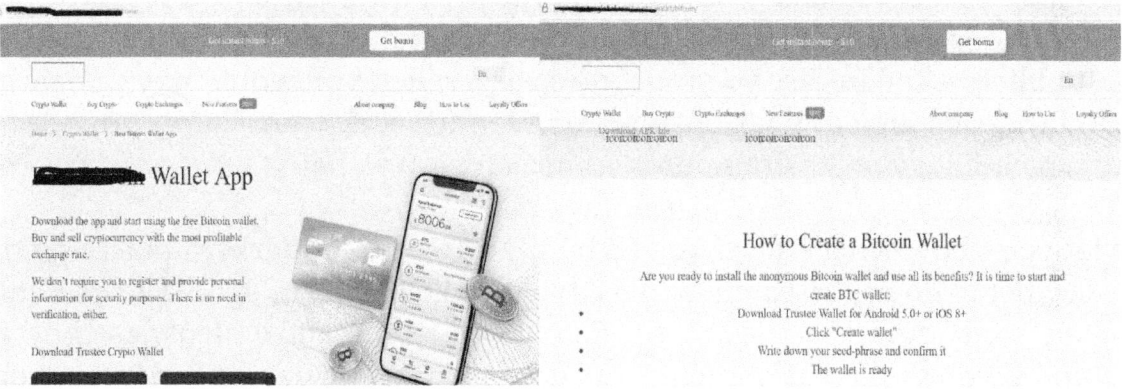

The example above represents a software wallet, therefore all you need to do is download the application of your choice that automatically generates your private key and your Bitcoin address which is derived from the public key through a hashing algorithm.

You can also use a safer hardware Bitcoin wallet. This option requires you to buy a piece of hardware as the only device through which your wallet can be accessed. In both cases, darknet actors like to use wallets with the so called Samourai capabilities, i.e. with automatic generation of a new Bitcoin address after each transaction.

If the price of the „goods" is above usual levels and their nature is extremely sensitive in terms of criminal law, bitcoins are often transferred into XMR. Monero is just another cryptocurrency, but its operation differs significantly from Bitcoin in a way that provides anonymity for all users by default. XMR wallets have special features such as

Stealth Addresses (the same technology as Samourai), Ring Signatures (there are five cryptographic signatures in the wallet, but only one is valid and real), and Ring Confidential Transactions (the amount of the transaction is hidden).

No matter what type of anonymous wallet is used, the holder must keep the private key itself or its so called seed, i.e. a mnemonic of the private key. If he/she loses the private key, the wallet will be inaccessible forever. Additionally, let's be clear about the fact that Bitcoin transactions are always stored on the Bitcoin blockchain and are public and traceable. On the blockchain, each transaction is linked to the corresponding Bitcoin address (which may, however, be easily changed for each transaction in the same wallet, as mentioned above).

Therefore, as a dark market actor, you would most likely chose to undertake two or eventually three steps to sweep your identity and money traces: 1. transfer money from a standard bank account to a legal crypto-exchange in a jurisdiction where you will be saved from undergoing proper KYC and AML procedures, 2. transfer bitcoins into an anonymous wallet, ideally a hardware wallet with Samourai capabilities, 3. exchange BTX for XMR and store your currency in a Monero wallet. And of course, you would always stick to the following practice rules: 1. use the TOR browser for all your transactions in order to make your real IP address untraceable, 2. turn on your VPN for any transactions or logins to illegal darkweb pages, 3. never display your Bitcoin address publicly – and in case you must do so as a seller, you would have a new address generated for each area of your business or even for each transaction provided by the Samourai technology or Stealth Addresses in a Monero wallet.

Just to let you know what pain financed by the BTC crypto-market I had to go through on the darknet to do my research: while the abused children of age 10 years + managed to produce some frozen smiles in the horrific pictures and videos, as they already understand threats and punishments and can, to a certain extent, behave accordingly to avoid them, NONE of the younger children managed to pretend smiling. Some of them were crying, especially babies. I clearly noticed that without even having clicked on any of those mirrors of hell. Unfortunately, there are long video previews that anyone must see and hear even if just research doing that sometimes included doing undercover registration and other necessary steps to trace financial and identity flows. Let me share just a small piece of what I have seen:

And all those extreme darkest acts are paid for using the Bitcoin flows coming from legal crypto-brokers with intentionally insufficient or even missing AML and KYC procedures and cooperating with the darknet Bitcoin wallet industry, often covered, or silently ignored by governments. Not only banks and crypto-exchange providers should implement a KYC and AML policy, but each of us should do likewise, i.e., perform a check of our financial services provider in terms of AML conviction/allegation history and jurisdiction the provider belongs to. Find the links to up-to-date AML blacklist countries below. Countries labeled as high-risk in terms of tax-evasion should be on your own blacklist of financial services providers too, as the financial institutions seeking these jurisdictions attract clients who often have multiple reasons to hide their identity and reduce traceable administration. One of those reasons typically is money-laundering and identity-trace-sweeping with the intention to move to the dark web markets.

AML blacklists:

- EU policy on high-risk third countries | European Commission (europa.eu)
- FATF Blacklists and Greylists: What You Need To Know (complyadvantage.com)
- https://www.knowyourcountry.com/
- Listing of tax havens by the EU (europa.eu)

Other sources of information:

- How Bitcoin Wallets Work | River Financial
- Are Bitcoin Wallets Anonymous? - Coinnounce
- 5 Best Anonymous Bitcoin Wallets [2021 Edition]
- Anonymous Crypto Wallet: Everything You Need to Know | News Blog | Crypterium

Investigating Cryptocurrency and Cybercrimes

By: LaShanda

Cryptocurrency research has generally focused on the transfer of wealth. The involvement of cryptocurrency in large-scale criminal activities is well documented in drug marketplaces or large ransomware campaigns like WannaCry. The main focus has been locating perpetrators' "follow the money" aspects. Technologies have, however, developed since the inception of Bitcoin in 2008. Blockchain technology is now scaling and developing new features to support multiple data and communication protocols across its stack. Law enforcement focus has remained around the prominent cryptocurrencies; however, utilizing innovative contract technology and distributed computing and storage creates a replacement set of problems for investigators and people responding to incidents. There are a variety of cryptocurrency/blockchain assets that will host the information in a very similar nature. A distributed blockchain by its design contains properties that don't seem to be inherent in traditional hosting services. A blockchain is a commonly immutable term that is unstoppable and doesn't have any central authority or body.

Role of the Investigator

The object is to clone the files taken containing Personally Identifiable Information (PII) from a server and host externally. The hosting, therefore, will occur on a distributed blockchain system. A comparison will have to happen to determine if the PII information is legitimate; this may entail a visual comparison of the info. A forensic comparison of the information must be conducted using traditional methods to hash the file contents and examine EXIF data contained within the file. Cyber investigators trying to find hosted material will examine records of web hosting companies to determine the Internet Protocol address (I.P) data for the hosting company and registrar WHOIS information.

- Cyber Investigator / Incident Response - This role will reply to initial reports and records, utilize Open Source Intelligence (OSINT) sources to find evidential information associated with the suspicious address in any given case.

Cryptocurrency Hacktivists Method

Various files with identifiable meta-data are created and hosted on a virtual machine to duplicate an intrusion event. An essential forensic examination is to perform completed to display Modified/Access/Created (MAC) date and times, Meta data, including a geo-data serial number or other EXIF data. The host could be a machine running Windows. Related investigation documents include a picture of a passport used to identify the customer in this scenario and contain PII information. Additionally, to the image are further documents, including XLS and CSV files, containing customer details, including PII data.

Investigation phase

The investigator's job is to search out the details related to the suspicious cryptocurrency address.

1. Find the entities (Website name and top-level domain information, I.P address, Whois, Registration data, e-mail addressing, hosting company (Server hosting), Domain hosting (Name holder), DNS zone transfers, Registrar change history, Ad-sense / analytical tokens – numbers, Robots.txt, Shodan, etc.) relevant to the scam to find information that may reveal true identities of whom is behind the crime.
2. Learn any scam characteristics that could be useful when identifying/investigating future scams or support the investigation of the entities identified or support related investigation.
3. D Document all findings to make a case report supported by facts.

Investigators generally don't rely on expensive commercial tools but perform their investigation using OSINT tools and techniques to follow the case.

Suspicious Address Validation

First, check to see if the suspicious address is a valid address before really diving into the investigation, as shown in figure 1. If multiple addresses are found, a more user-friendly tool shown in figure 2 also helps confirm the address balance.

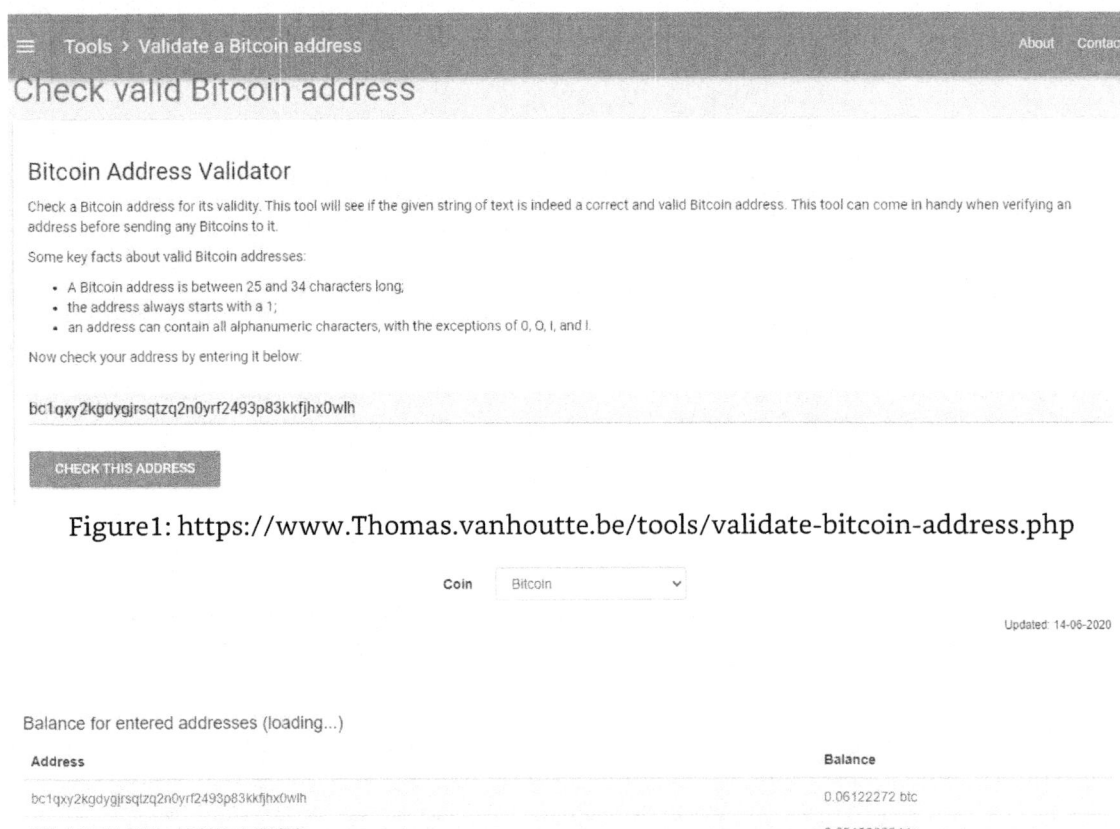

Figure1: https://www.Thomas.vanhoutte.be/tools/validate-bitcoin-address.php

Figure 2: https://www.homebitcoin.com/easybalance/

It would help to recover the dates and amounts of transactions deducted or added to the wallet by putting in the address.

Bitcoin Address Report

We can also use bitcoin whois to find information related to the crime, as shown in figure 3. Using this tool, we can discover balance, address, wallet name, number of transactions, initial and last transactions, website appearance, transaction I.P., etc.

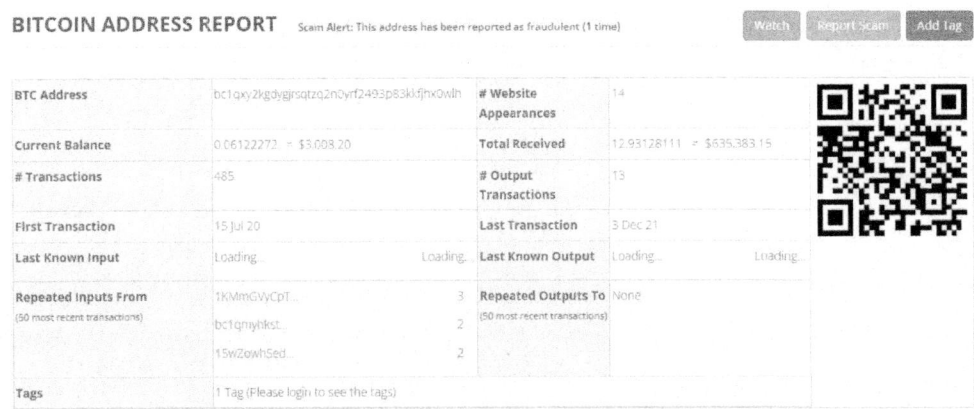

Figure 3: https://www.bitcoinwhoswho.com

Using hashxp.org, we can link transactions together and filter out the common senders and relatable receivers, as shown in figure 4.

Figure 4: https://hashxp.org

Blockchain Explorer

To check the transactions in a raw format, we can use the bitcoin blockchain explorer, as shown in figure 5. We can also check details like the connection to the previous and next transactions within the blockchain.

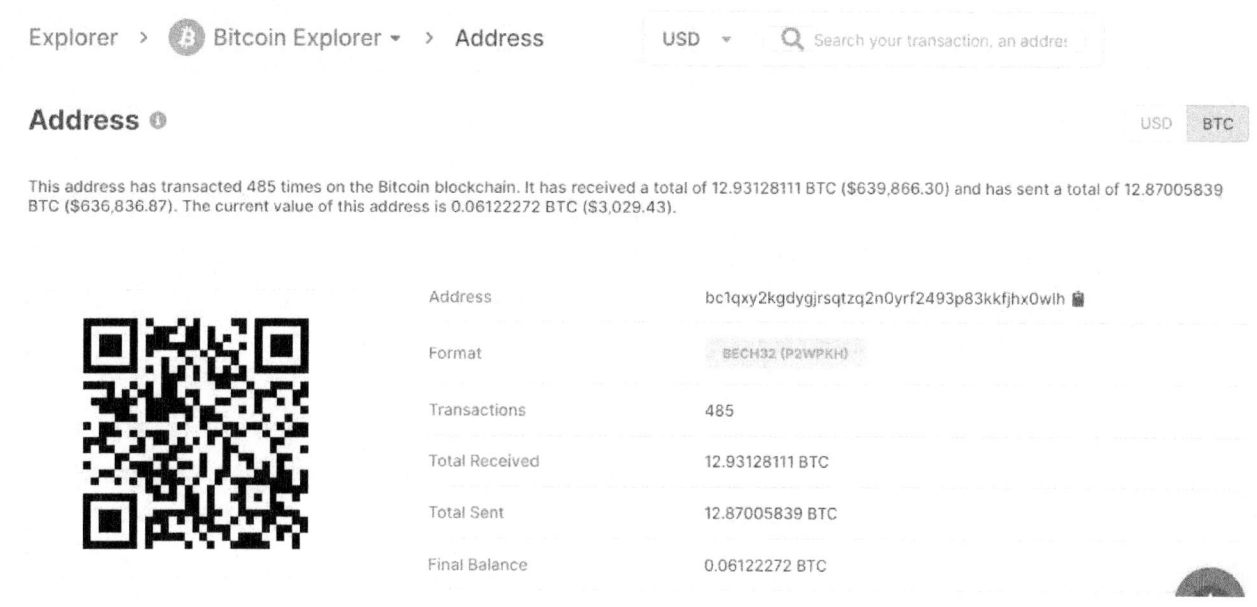

Figure 5: https://www.blockchain.com

Blockchain Domain Naming

The Domain Name Service (DNS) is employed to help with searching the web; it translates a person's readable Uniform Resource Locator (URL) into the relevant Internet Protocol Address (I.P). This directs a question like www.b_a_web_address.com to the basis servers to the Top Level Domain (TLD) and to the domains name server that holds the record of the I.P address example 8.8.8.8. The power to store domain naming information on a blockchain has existed a few times, with services like Namecoin offering various services, including a reputation resolution stored on the blockchain. The criminal use of decentralized DNS services does exist but isn't extensively used [1], [2], [3]. The invention of a recent botnet that was discovered to be cleaning up

90

destructive botnets was observed within the wild using Emercoin's distributed DNS implementation [4]. The (ENS) Ethereum Naming Service provides similar functions to a DNS system and is held and operated over the Ethereum blockchain [5].

Related Domains Identification

Unlike the standard DNS, passive DNS is a real-time system that queries DNS servers and resolvers to translate hostnames into I.P. addresses; passive DNS works the opposite way. There's always a DNS database storing the DNS records, lookup, and stats about everything associated with the domains, servers, and I.P. addresses involved within the everyday DNS communications. This information is saved in a secure database for later analysis, converting the live DNS results into passive DNS data.

Before passive DNS existed, there was no avenue to get the complete historical records of any DNS zone within the world unless you had set your DNS tracking system for your domain names, which the administrator doesn't frequently do. Passive DNS usage is the simplest way to trace name changes over time, recover lost DNS records, relate hostnames with IPs or individuals, catch phishing sites, spoofed domains, and potential network threats. Figure 6 is the example phase of an attack showing the domain change when the attack occurred.

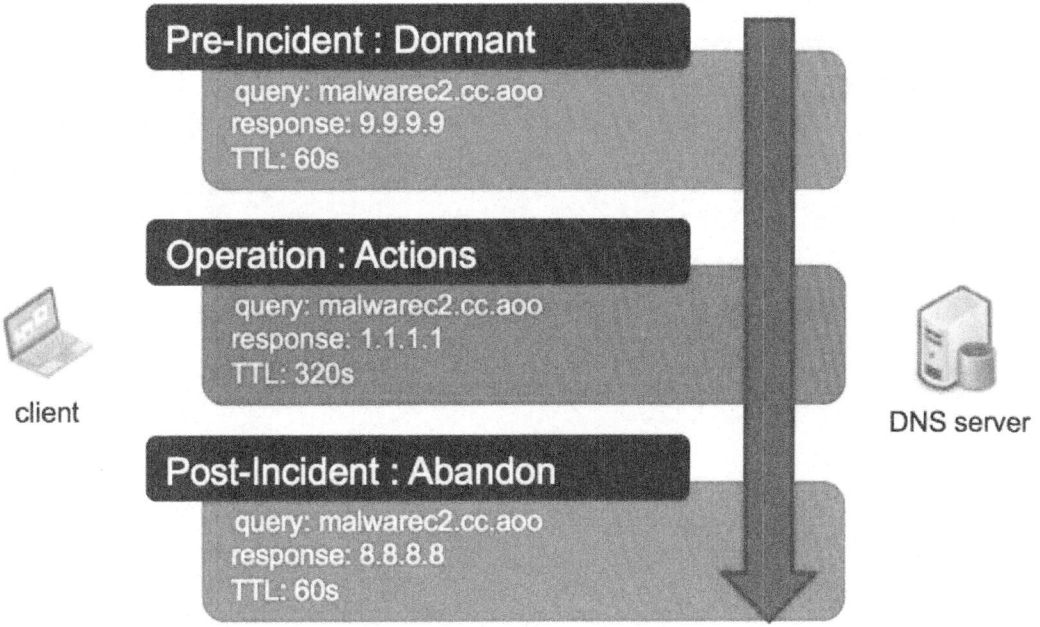

Figure 6: https://securityintelligence.com/wp-content/uploads/2018/11/passivedns-malware.jpg

Related Domains Identifications

We can check all I.P. addresses listed under the last transaction I.P. from the Bitcoin address report by using http://passivedns.nmemonic.no. Some things to note are that the first seen and last seen dates within the address report match the time of the BTC transaction or when the crime was committed.

Now we can check the domains to gather information about who the domain owner is, where it is located, and when it was registered, as shown in figure 7.

```
Registrar Abuse Contact Email:  abuse@porkbun.com
Registrar Abuse Contact Phone: +1.5038508351
Domain Status: clientDeleteProhibited http://icann.org/epp#clientDeleteProhibited
Domain Status: clientTransferProhibited http://icann.org/epp#clientTransferProhibited
Registry Registrant ID:
Registrant Name: Whois Privacy
Registrant Organization: Private by Design, LLC
Registrant Street: 500 Westover Dr #9816
Registrant City: Sanford
Registrant State/Province: NC
Registrant Postal Code: 27330
Registrant Country: US
Registrant Phone: +1.9712666028
Registrant Phone Ext:
Registrant Fax:
Registrant Fax Ext:
Registrant Email:
https://porkbun.com/whois/contact/registrant/bc1qxy2kgdygjrsqtzq2n0yrf2493p83kkfjhx0wlh.com
Registry Admin ID:
Admin Name: Whois Privacy
Admin Organization: Private by Design, LLC
Admin Street: 500 Westover Dr #9816
Admin City: Sanford
Admin State/Province: NC
Admin Postal Code: 27330
Admin Country: US
Admin Phone: +1.9712666028
Admin Phone Ext:
Admin Fax:
Admin Fax Ext:
Admin Email:
https://porkbun.com/whois/contact/admin/bc1qxy2kgdygjrsqtzq2n0yrf2493p83kkfjhx0wlh.com
Registry Tech ID:
Tech Name: Whois Privacy
Tech Organization: Private by Design, LLC
Tech Street: 500 Westover Dr #9816
```

Figure 7: https://whois.domaintools.com/

When using forensics and investigating Dark Net markets, we can use OnionScan, as shown in figure 8. OnionScan is used to gather a list of associated Bitcoin addresses, email addresses, and meta images information. OnionScan searches for cryptocurrency clients, including Bitcoin and Litecoin.

Figure 8: https://fossbytes.com/wp-content/uploads/2016/04/onionscan-tor-1-768x424.jpg

93

Search Engine and Social Media Investigation

Once the domain is identified, it can be searched for more information, as shown in figure 9. The initial subdomain search can be performed on Google, LinkedIn, and on Twitter or Facebook to determine if a person of interest is located.

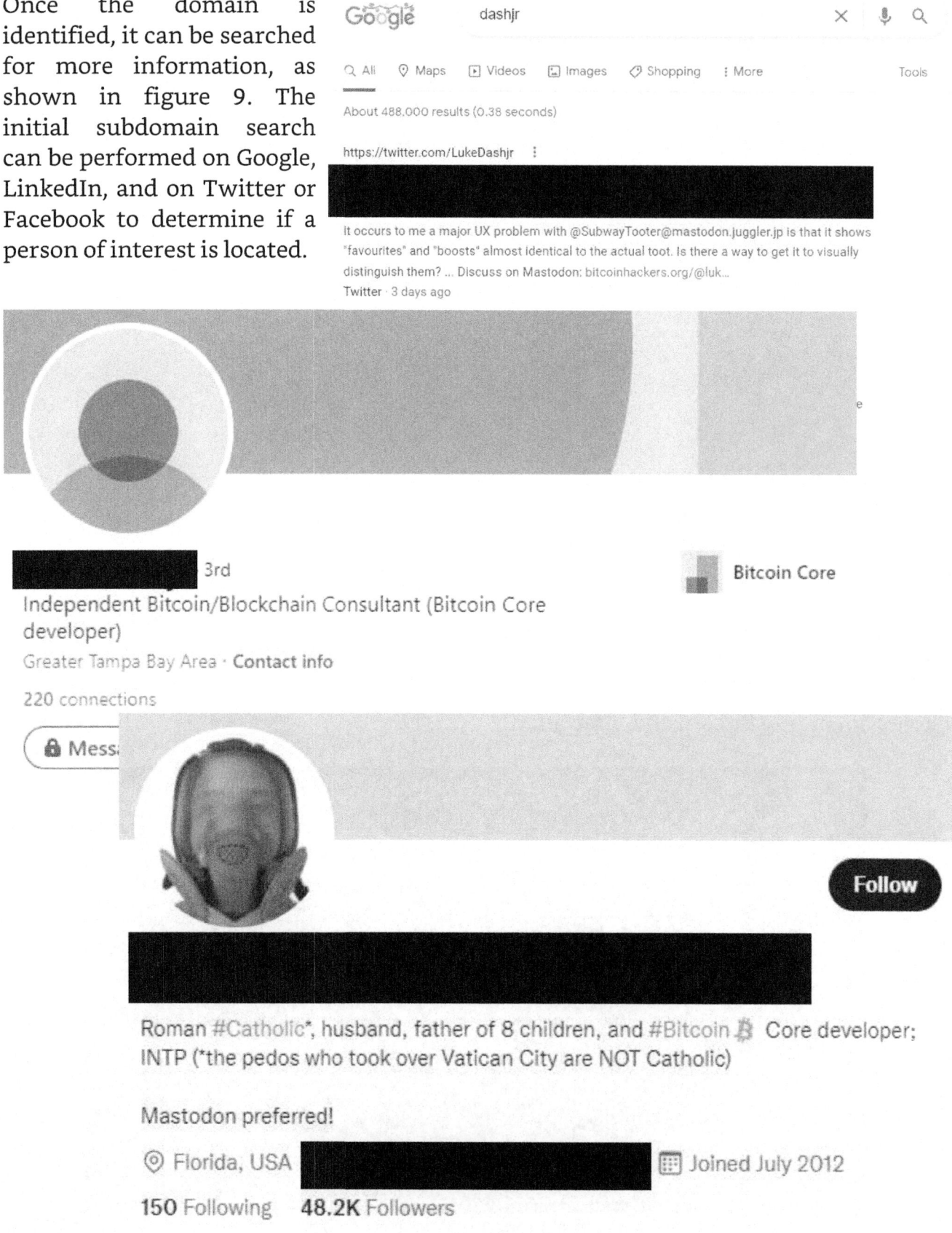

E-Mail Investigation

All the IPs can be checked using the MXToolbox site in the last transaction in the bitcoin address report. It can identify addresses reported to be sending malware. This site can also indicate scam sites relaying mail using servers. SpyTox, as shown in figure 10, can search for names, email addresses, and phone numbers. When additional information is gathered, this tool can be used to find certain background information on the suspect.

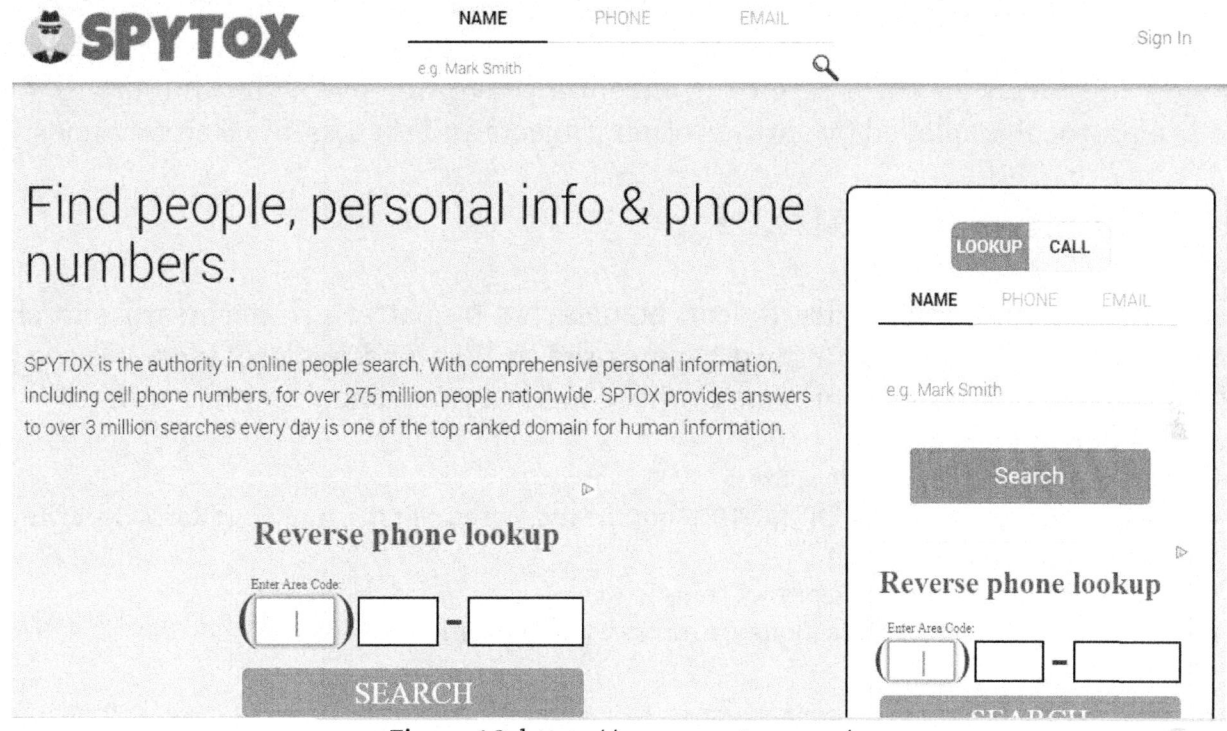

Figure 10: https://www.spytox.com/

Wallet and Exchange Identification

The basic algorithm to determine wallet addresses uses walletexplorer. Using the Oxt.me tool enables us to graph the activity to match the time of the crime and possibly the name of the exchange used in the transaction.

Decentralized Blockchain Storage

Using a coin gateway such as decentralized exchanges are often really hybrid exchanges. Decentralized exchanges have their block explorer, identifying transactions from regular exchanges or private wallets. Decentralized networks are utilized for various cryptocurrency projects to trade tokenized value needed to create Digital money. Blockchain technology itself has evolved behind the scenes. Blockchain technologies' introduction of Smart Contracts allows languages and sections of code to supply complex computational outputs. A variety of blockchain projects consider using a protocol or system to produce blockchain storage using peer-to-peer nodes

95

incentivized to the system. Creating a decentralized storage system solves various computing problems; it creates resilience as files are striped across multiple nodes in an exceedingly system. A decentralized system uses nodes within the control of world users who are incentivized to "mine" or provide a service the same as miners and Bitcoin nodes. Services like Dropbox operate a storage system that enables a cloud storage system; however, the service may be centralized under one organization. Exceedingly decentralized nodes generally hold only partial file fragments, so physical integrity is maintained because the file portion is fragmented and optionally encrypted. There are various decentralized file storage systems, namely, Inter Planetary File System (IPFS) developed by Protocol Labs. This part of the system allows for distributed storage; Filecoin is an extra service to incentivize storage by paying miners to store. IPFS is a protocol employed by various other projects and is cross-blockchain agnostic.

P2P Exchanges Identification

As shown in figure 11, Bisq traffic can be detected by pattern fingerprinting in chain analysis software. A tool like a snort can be used to alert findings provided. We can also see the traffic at Tor exit nodes. This could be made more difficult with CoinJoin.

- Funds go through a multisig address
- All deposits have a 32-byte OP_RETURN output and one output to a multisig address receiving all inputs (minus fees).
- Same-fee taker, deposit, and payout transaction
- Taker fee and deposit transactions are broadcast at the same time.

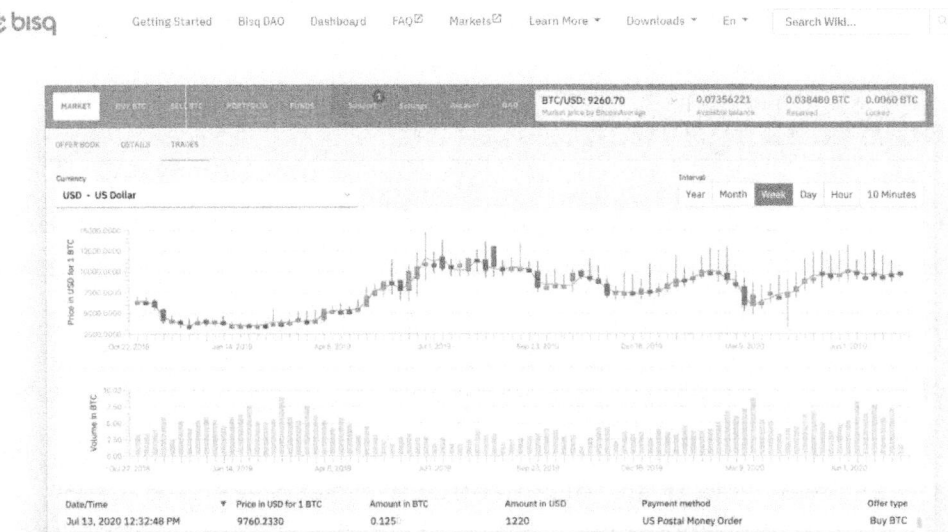

In conclusion, combining chain analysis with passive DNS, alternative coin wallet explorers, and darknet market allows us to gather forensic evidence and different crime relations.

References

- [1] R. Amado, "How Cybercriminals are using Blockchain DNS | Digital Shadows," Digital Shadows_ (Web), 2018. [Online]. Available: https://www.digitalshadows.com/blog-and-research/howcybercriminals-are-using-blockchain-dns-from-the-market-to-thebazar/. [Accessed: 14-Nov-2021].
- [2] "Namecoin," Namecoin (Web), 2019. [Online]. Available: https://namecoin.org/. [Accessed: 16-Nov-2021].
- [3] M. Ali, J. Nelson, R. Shea, and M. J. Freedman, "Blockstack: A Global Naming and Storage System Secured by Blockchains," USENIX Annu. Tech. Conf., pp. 181–194, 2016.
- [4] I. Ilascu, "New Botnet Hides in Blockchain DNS Mist and Removes Cryptominer," Bleeping Computer - Web, 2018. [Online]. Available: https://www.bleepingcomputer.com/news/security/new-botnethides-in-blockchain-dns-mist-and-removes-cryptominer/. [Accessed: 14-Nov-2021].
- [5] N. Johnson, "A developer's guide to ENS concepts – The Ethereum Name Service – Medium," Medium Blogpost Web, 2017. [Online]. Available: https://medium.com/the-ethereum-nameservice/a-developers-guide-to-ens-concepts-7004eea8a073. [Accessed: 25-Jan-2021]

Cool Tool: Karma v2

Karma v2 is a Passive Open Source Intelligence (OSINT) Automated Reconnaissance (framework).

This can be used by Infosec Researchers, Penetration Testers, Bug Hunters to find deep information, more assets, WAF/CDN bypassed IPs, Internal/External Infra, publicly exposed leaks and many more about their target. Shodan Premium API key is required to use this automation.

https://github.com/Dheerajmadhukar/karma_v2nvestigate Windows endpoints that are infected/compromised and offline, on-line, dead, in on-premises, remote, or the cloud, with speed and accuracy.

This is an agentless stand-alone software (which requires no installation) that allows ANYONE to investigate ANY Windows endpoint ANYWHERE the endpoint may be--whether on-premises, in the cloud, offline, "dead" hard drives, with or without an Internet connection

Born of Ashes: The network visualization potential of a CSAM-related cryptocurrencies addresses

By: Carolina Christofoletti

A more user-friendly tool shown in figure 2 also helps confirm the address balance if multiple addresses are found. I recently talked with some LEA friends about cases where cryptocurrencies appeared associated with Child Sexual Abuse Material (CSAM) crimes. "Have you ever seen something like that?" I asked. If you want to read the current findings of the financial scenario related to CSA and CSE crimes in a Research Report, ICMEC has actual results on the amount of those mechanics. They told me yes.

> *"And did you solve it through the crypto addresses"?*
> *"No."*
> *"But was it solved"?*
> *"Yes, but through other means."*
> *"Would a cryptocurrency analysis tool have helped you and how much"?*

When we think about cryptocurrencies involved in CSAM crimes, we have at least two people we would, at least considering talking to: Banks, that should be trained to identify CSAM patterns in their transitions monitors once those patterns were identified, and Law Enforcement Agencies, that must be able to deal with speedily, sometimes in a scenario of missed data.

For researchers, whose function would have been to set the methodology to compile this data, the question is many times that of a "retrospective nature." Unfortunately, we have to start from the end. In the end, he asks if those addresses were found together with CSAM images. Those cases tend to be identified during the investigation.

I do not like the word 'teaser' in this context, but we are talking about a "dog whistle," as you will. For example, criminals could be announcing it only textually or with legal material (such as a neutral victim picture) in CSAM forums where everybody understands this "neutral image means." With all the live-streaming complexities to compile this data haven't already come to the table and are known about after the fact.

How this live-streaming appears in criminal forums is a further point of research and whose data probably do not exist at present due to the collection methodology of those compilations. I want to explore the information where it exists. This includes cryptocurrencies addresses found on CSAM forums or websites.

What would we find if we started looking for patterns over financial transitions that originate on Child Sexual Abuse Material (CSAM) forums? What would we find if we started to compile things like Bitcoin addresses that appear as payment instructions on illegal forums where CSAM streaming is advertised? No idea.

The problem with crypto paid crimes, as a whole, is that often those cryptocurrency wallets are never found. This is especially with cases where intelligence is disseminated somewhere on the other side of the ocean.

Courts and criminal investigators usually see only a tiny picture fragment of something that belongs to a significant picture context. If we don't see that bigger picture, we are only prosecuting some crimes and potentially missing some victims.

With all the complexities of a CSAM criminal procedure, criminals trust that law enforcement agencies are not prepared to deal with live-streaming (a fake assumption). There is no intelligence track involving it. My claim is that this now needs to be created.

In the live-streaming case, we shall count on the hypothesis that CSAM streaming viewers negotiate, possibly, directly with the streamer. Still, we should also count on the possibility of things being more "criminally organized" than one would initially think. And that is something we only see if we have something, like interrelated financial transactions, to compare. To allow this as legal evidence (retrospective evidence), judges will need to know how the Prosecution Office came to this conclusion. Mapping it, so, matters.

What if one came to the finding that the very same Bitcoin address found previously in a seized CSAM forum "recomposes" itself in another illegal forum of the same nature? What value are those addresses for Open-Source Investigators that might have led to a successful prosecution?

The missing points are found somewhere else based on the original reference. The problems with those crypto-related cases are, more than an investigative one, a logical one. To investigate anything, one needs to have this "anything" to investigate. And having "anything to work with" involves keeping a diligent track of the probable cause or the data most of the time.

The problem with cryptocurrencies is not anonymity anymore but intelligence. Before banks, international transactions were impossible. When banks arrived, transactions were traceable with your personal documents. When cryptocurrency came, the "global financial market" needed, more than ever, integrated intelligence to solve the "no-legal-authority-to-request-anything" problem.

The best chance is to have the crypto coin address abuse notice and start to investigate and monitor the transaction ledger.

Chain Analysis is a company dedicated to Bitcoin analysis and has been partnering with the Internet Watch Foundation in the UK since 2016. One of their goals is to analyze Bitcoin addresses related to Child Sexual Abuse Material on the Dark Web. Even though we must recognize the impact potential of such a partnership, I miss the global monitor on this behalf.

www.chainalysis.com

Internet Watch Foundation, a CSAM hotline based in the UK, provides a possibility of partnership. This would give an investigative edge with the ability to receive information about Cryptocurrencies addresses that were linked with Child Sexual Abuse Material. For obvious reasons (the same as the Open-Source Investigators), those databases are closed by Membership Requirements. Forensic Tools aiming at the CSAM detection domain should, as such, think about the benefits of having the IWF Virtual Currency Alerts in their working database.

www.iwf.org.uk

More about the Virtual Currency CSAM alert. This initiative would be a great asset to be used beyond the UK. In my opinion, the possibility of Law Enforcement Agencies getting involved and adding new tips to it adds a great value. While "following the money" tips in a Child Sexual Abuse Imagery investigation, the Italian police seized 14,000 Bitcoin wallets worth around €1m (£800,000) in 2015. That is $813,218,000.00 as of the end of 2021. Think of how much this could have helped other similar cases.

We need CSAM intelligence to be global. The CSAM related cryptocurrency addresses hardly ever come to the discussion table of the Courts. With that said, those same addresses can be found in CSAM forums, and maybe, its monitoring would be a crucial tip to find out where the next crime stays or, translating it, how things are interconnected inside the criminal world. Where and how, after all, all those CSAM cryptocurrencies cross.

This data needs to be crossed in individual criminal investigations and inside the network of similar data. Identifying authorship is essential but identifying networks and how they communicate with each other also.

For Investigators, maybe we could add some further questions of interest: Are CSAM live-streaming after all commercial in nature? If so, are crypto coins involved in those transactions? If so, how permanent are those crypto coin addresses? Is that the case that those addresses receive, during a specific time, a considerable number of transitions, and then it suddenly stops? Are those transactions identifiable through any pattern? If we needed to supply streaming forensics with a "where to look" data based on those transactions, could we do it anyhow? Are those payments "access ransoms" never paid in advance? How do payments and streaming data come, after all, together?

Questions to think about…

Navigating the Dark Web

Now that you have an idea of what is on the Dark web let's walk through how to navigate. We are going to focus on the popular tool Tor Browser. Before we use it, though, we need to create a baseline of our Internet or Surface Web presence. Keep in mind; these hidden services can change or disappear without notice.

Verify your external IP address

1. Open a regular internet browser.
2. Type *ipinfo.io* into the address bar and press enter.
3. Write down the IP: "???.???.???.???" address.
   a. This is your external Internet address that everyone sees.
4. Connect to Tor using TorVPN.
5. Type *ipinfo.io* into the address bar and press enter.
6. Compare the results

AHMIA.FI Dark Web Search Engine

Surface Web location: *ahmia.fi*
Dark Web: *juhanurmihxlp77nkq76byazcldy2hlmovfu2epvl5ankdibsot4csyd.onion*

We want to go to a search engine that focuses on Tor Hidden Services. These hidden services are just like regular services on the surface web, but they are "hidden" on the Tor network. This means that you can only access them through a Tor gateway.

1. Type *ahmia.fi* into the address bar and press the Enter key.

You should now see the AHMIA search engine. At this time, it looks like this:

This search engine spiders or crawls through Tor websites added to its database and allowed you to do some basic searches.

Dark Market Search

To start, we will look for the term "dark market" and press Search. Below is the result as of when this instruction was written. Remember, the hidden service websites constantly change, and the examples covered may no longer be available. Most of these websites may also require an account to be created to get beyond the front page. This means you will most likely need a covert email address and possibly a bitcoin wallet.

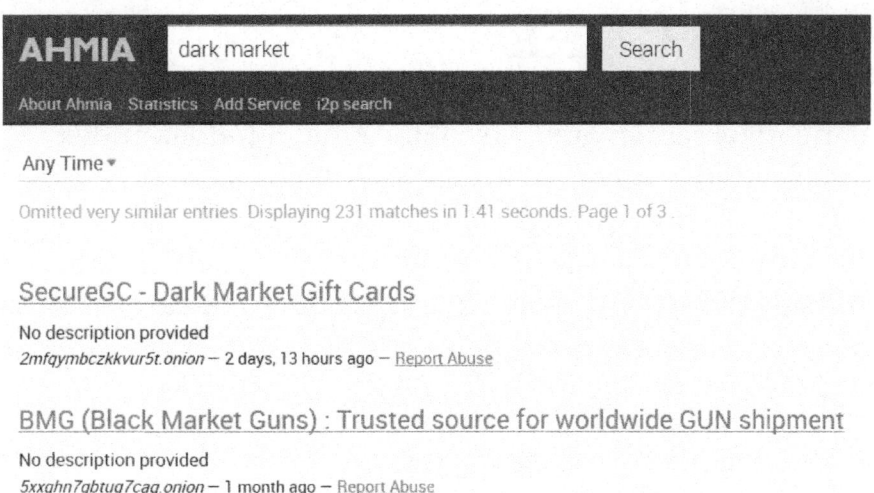

Notice the address
"**bmgunsyop5qa34nzrayd6shsovsukwbbscyo2hbu3ri7b2ghw6sjgrad.onion**" is going to
"**BMG (Black Market Guns).**"

1. Click on the "BMG (Black Market Guns)" link.
2. Verify that you are forwarded to "*5xxqhn7qbtug7cag.onion.*"

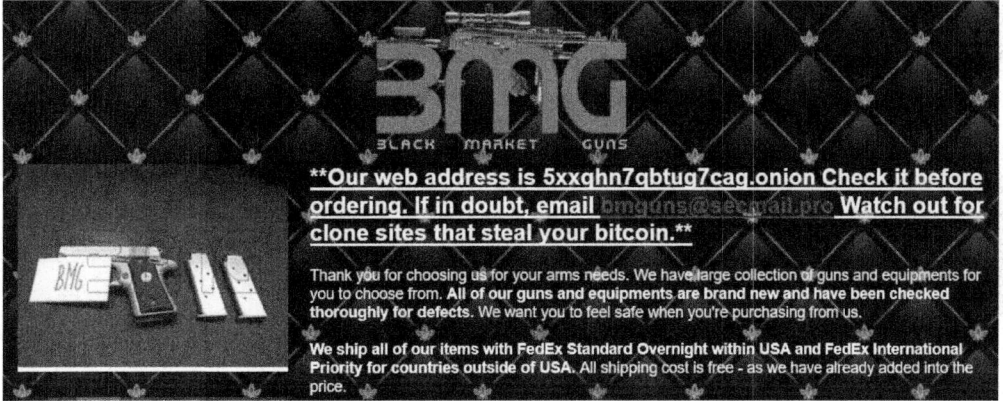

Let's go back to ahmia.fi and repeat the process. This time let's search for "drugs dark market."

After searching, a few interesting sites came up, including:

> TorShops | Create your own .onion store - buy and sell drugs, guns,
> counterfeits, fake ids, fake passports for bitcoin
>
> TorShops - buy and sell drugs, guns, counterfeits, fake ids, fake passports for bitcoin - great silk road alternative -
> get your .onion store today
> *mgibojrlzdfoajbn.onion* — 1 week, 2 days ago — Report Abuse

You can see that many of the items in this area can contain harmful content. However, AHMIA does try to minimize access to these, and if they see child pornography will add it to a blacklist. This list is located at ahmia.fi/blacklist.

AHMIA Unrestricted search

This is a more dangerous search area, but AHMIA has a hidden index of all the links they have searchable. This address is ahmia.fi/address and is not filtered. Most sites will not have a description. It is extremely easy to stumble across sites that contain illegal content outside the scope of your investigation, so be careful.

1. Type "*ahmia.fi/address*" into the address bar and Press the Enter key.
2. Press the CTRL key and F at the same time to break up a search box.
3. Type in the word "Drugs" and Press the Enter key

The site drugsxxx....onion was found and shows this:

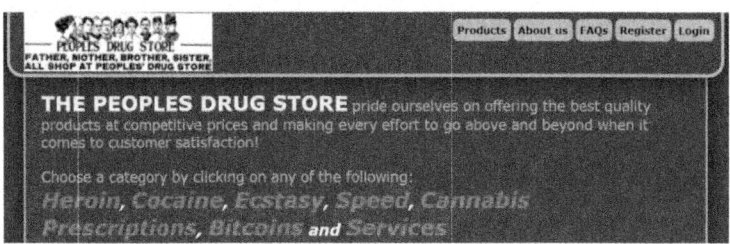

Torch Search Engine

Torch is a Tor search engine that has a similar index to AHMIA and seems to have replaced the GRAMS search engine. This tools indexes many of the dark markets and other hidden services.

Current link: 5psvjgcvmlrg52xckfawq3ggadcjchy5lkyunczbc65ydq7lt6umrgad.onion

1. Type the address into the address bar and Press the Enter key.
2. Type "credit cards" into the search field.
3. Document your findings.

1. Cloned credit cards with PIN code -TRUSTED VENDOR- - Wall Street [7.178%]
   ... Register Board index General Cloned credit cards with PIN code -TRUSTED VENDOR- ... Wed Apr 16, 2014 11:14 am Cloned credit cards with PIN code -TRUSTED VENDOR- ... Hi there, I'm selling cloned credit cards with PIN code, ready for using ...
   - http://z2hjrn7uhwisw5jm5.onion/viewtopic... - 32652 bytes [text/html] - Fri, 02 Nov 2018, 18:20:24 GMT
     [Cached copy]

2. Cloned credit cards with PIN code -TRUSTED VENDOR- - Page 58 - Wall Street [7.185%]
   ... Register Board index General Cloned credit cards with PIN code -TRUSTED VENDOR- ... Wed Aug 31, 2016 4:29 pm Re: Cloned credit cards with PIN code -TRUSTED VENDOR- ...
   - http://z2hjrn7uhwisw5jm5.onion/viewtopic... - 31682 bytes [text/html] - Thu, 01 Nov 2018, 08:39:51 GMT
     [Cached copy]

3. Valhalla [0.331%]
   ... DEAL , ALL THESE TUTORIALS: -Amazon credit guide. - How I Get $180-$240 per Month ... Amazon Gift Certs -Free Amazon Gift Cards -Double Dip, Triple Dip, Double Dip + ...
   - http://valhallaxmn3fydu.onion/products/1... - 6937 bytes [text/html] - Sun, 28 Oct 2018, 15:35:20 GMT
     [Cached copy]

Further down the page, there was a link to Dark Markets including Valhalla and DeepMart.

DuckDuckGo Dark Web

This is the default search engine provided with the **Tor Browser** is DuckDuckGo. If you go to the .onion site, it should index websites for the regular web and the Dark Web. Unfortunately, this site is a lot more censored than AHMIA.fi

Current link: duckduckgogg42xjoc72x3sjasowoarfbgcmvfimaftt6twagswzczad.onion

1. Type the link into the address bar and Press the Enter key.
2. Try searching for "The Hidden Wiki"

Dark Web Email Services

If you need to set up an email account to get access to any of these sites, here are some Dark Web email services that you can us for account validation while keeping yourself separate from the Surface Web.

TorBox – Web based email you can only access through Tor

Current link: torbox36ijlcevujx7mjb4oiusvwgvmue7jfn2cvutwa6kl6to3uyqad.onion

Here is a list of other good Tor resources:

- The Hidden Wiki: lqiahcviyl5srgewpr4q3phxgupyaxqk2iabzz3e2zcqu3sm7irhkwyd.onion
- TorLinks: tlink2vs7rwo7pmnvzcfbjjxmt777ixnnah4k54rreeu6ntafmtvsrqd.onion
- Dark Fallen: darkfailenbsdla5mal2mxn2uz66od5vtzd5qozslagrfzachha3f3id.onion
- Privacy Tools Pastebin: privacy2zbidut4m4jyj3ksdqidzkw3uoip2vhvhbvwxbqux5xy5obyd.onion
- DarkTor Pastebin: darktorhvabc652txfc575oendhykqcllb7bh7jhhsjduocdlyzdbmqd.onion
- TempMail: csmailsbb4arfihowfmrpotsceq6pe66t43q2els2nib2qdoj745j5ad.onion
- DepwebTempMail: deepweb4wt3m4dhutpxpe7d7wxdftfdf4hhag4sizgon6th5lcefloid.onion

Creating a Tor Hidden Service

By Jeremy Martin

Press "Tor allows clients and relays to offer onion services. That is, you can offer a web server, SSH server, etc., without revealing your IP address to its users. Because you don't use any public address, you can run an onion service from behind your firewall." – Torproject.org

Whether you need to create a honeypot for intelligence collection or a method for secure and anonymous communications on the Tor Dark Web, a Hidden Service is a great way to accomplish those goals. There are some key things to understand before you get started.

1. Tor is a network. Almost anything you can run on the Surface Web, Clearnet, or the Internet; you can run as a Hidden Service. This means web, email, file transfer, video streaming, and other servers.
2. You need to install the server you want to run as a Hidden Service before you can access the service through Tor.
3. You must understand how to set up and administer that service, and it must be accessible on 127.0.0.1. You will be able to test this before you move forward. This includes understanding HTML/PHP type code if you build a web server.
4. You must be connected to Tor for the service to be accessible within Tor.
5. You will only access this service within Tor if you secure it properly. The .onion domains only work within the Tor network.

We will walk through the steps for creating a Tor .onion service web page using Apache. This will allow us to build any website you would make on the Internet.

The first thing to do is update the software repository list with "apt." This tool will require elevated privileges, so we must use "sudo." Then we will use the "apt" program to install the Apache webserver.

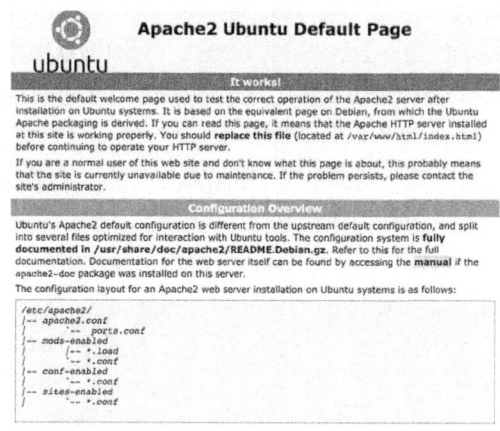

```
sudo apt update
sudo apt install apache2 -y
```

... When done ...

```
google-chrome 127.0.0.1
```

To edit the web page, you can use an Editor

```
sudo gedit /var/www/html/index.html
```

```
google-chrome 127.0.0.1
```

Now it's time to practice some good old Tor fu... We are going to edit the Tor config file torrc. This is located at /etc/tor/torrc. Using gedit will open the file into an easy to modify text Editor. You must open the file as root or use sudo.

```
sudo gedit /etc/tor/torrc
```

Once the file is open, about halfway down, you should see the following:

```
#HiddenServiceDir /var/lib/tor/hidden_service/
#HiddenServicePort 80 127.0.0.1:80
```

Remove the "#" comment tags. You should now see this:

```
HiddenServiceDir /var/lib/tor/hidden_service/
HiddenServicePort 80 127.0.0.1:80
```

Save the file and type this:

```
sudo service tor restart
```

It would be best if you had a fresh new .onion site name that you can find by typing:

```
sudo cat /var/lib/tor/hidden_service/hostname
```

This may take a few minutes to propagate through the Tor network, but you should be able to access this new .onion address through the Tor Browser or by turning on the CSI TorVPN and going to the site through Chrome. Now, you can do whatever you want with your new . Onion Hidden Service that is accessible to anyone on the Tor network.

Spiderfoot

Running Spiderfoot locally on 127.0.0.1will secure your instance from others by only being accessible from the CSI system. What if you want to share your access securely with other Investigators? There are several options, and we will focus on the Tor Hidden Service option. The process is the same as above.

Run the Spiderfoot application from the Social Media section within the CSI Case Management application. Verify it is running by opening a Chrome browser and pointing it to 127.0.0.1:5441. You should see a Spiderfoot login screen.

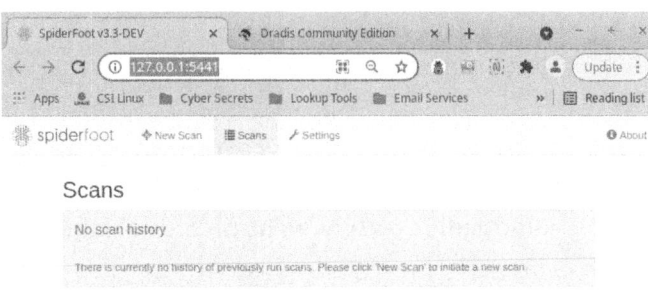

```
sudo gedit /etc/tor/torrc
```

Once the file is open, about halfway down, you should see the following:

```
#HiddenServiceDir /var/lib/tor/hidden_service/
#HiddenServicePort 80 127.0.0.1:80
```

Add a line to the HiddenService Port section.

```
HiddenServiceDir /var/lib/tor/hidden_service/
HiddenServicePort 5441 127.0.0.1:5441
```

Note: I am not using "80 127.0.0.1:5441" because this will make it a little more challenging to find. Security by Obscurity does have its place.

Save the file and type this:

Now when you connect to the CSI TorVPN, you should be able to open up a Chrome Browser and access Spiderfoot using ?????.onion:5441 along with anyone else you want to share the new link with. Make sure to remember to add the ":5441".

If you can't access the .onion website, go back into a terminal window and type:

```
sudo service tor restart
```

For other services like Dradis, rinse and repeat. Just change the torrc to reflect the port listening locally on the system.

Building a Honeypot

You can copy a prebuilt web page or *capture ("mirrored") into the Apache web folder* at /var/www/html. We will create a quick honeypot site by finding a target .onion service we want to mimic as a honeypot.

Create a case using the Case Management System and remember the <CaseName>. I am going to reference the CaseName as Case001. I will use the version 3 domain bmguns7xglvmnlnz5nd543dczp3fnsfd6jecwpjomvhov4dn4ikxmqyd.onion as an example.

Note: Remember that sites within Tor generally do not last as long as those on the surface web. This specific site may no longer be available, so pick one that is.

Then open a terminal window and type:

```
cd ~/Cases/Case001/Export
httrack 7pm3fdcn564ftiw6g5qgrcd6g5gvbemgrnisxhdzw2kvxlhsbjeuohyd.onion
```

When HTTrack is finished, you will see the new folder ~/Cases/Case001/Export/ 7pm3fdcn564ftiw6g5qgrcd6g5gvbemgrnisxhdzw2kvxlhsbjeuohyd.*onion inside* this file is a copy of the site I just cloned. Copy the contents of this folder to the Apache folder.

```
sudo su

cd /user/csi/Cases/Case001/Export/

cp -a    7pm3fdcn564ftiw6g5qgrcd6g5gvbemgrnisxhdzw2kvxlhsbjeuohyd.onion
         /var/www/html
```

Overwrite files.

... To verify ...

```
google-chrome 127.0.0.1
```

If everything worked out, you should see the web page you cloned.

Alter the webpage code as needed. You can add a database to capture user input or do anything any other web page could do. This does take a little bit of web design or coding knowledge. Once complete, follow the steps to create the Hidden Service. Verify the site is accessible with the new .onion address. You just created your honeypot...

Did You Know?!

What is a Honeypot?

A Honeypot is a machine developed to mimic typical targets from cyber actors. This system can detect and/or divert cyberattacks from a genuine machine.

Two Different Types of Honeypots

Production Honeypot
- Most common honeypot, used to collect intelligence about cyberattacks within the network. Businesses uses production honeypots to reveal undiscovered vulnerabilities.
- However, more intelligence can be gathered using research honeypots.

Research Honeypot
- Research honeypots focuses more on the specific methods and tactics cyber actor's use.
- The difference between research honeypots and production honeypots is that research honeypots consist of falsified data to replace actual sensitive and valuable information.

Attributes of Honeypots

Low-interaction Honeypot
Uses few resources to collect basic information about the cyber actor. Easy to develop and maintain. However, it is unlikely to lure the attention of a cyber actor.

High-interaction Honeypot
Intended to grab the attention of cyber actors for extended period of time. It gives analyst a better understanding of techniques used and possibly their identities. High-interaction honeypots typically come with a honeywall or the security around the honeypot to successfully monitor the point of entry and exit.

Lo Cole

What are the odds of catching a catfish... About 279,359 to 1

By Justin Casey

SOCMINT / Dark Web Case Study: Catfish

Let's take a gander at how luck, the OSINT Mindset, and a little physical surveillance helped to unmask a malicious catfish!

Background: I was contacted by a client whose family member recently passed away; it had come to their attention that some malicious person had created a fake Instagram account using the name of the recently deceased individual. This catfish not only cloned the name but had been uploading images from *a late Person of Interest's* Instagram page and writing some horrible captions. The original real Instagram account was private, which means that whoever was behind the *catfishing* profile was following the *actual original* page as it was copying images that *were* only ever posted on the real account; however, the *actual* account had thousands of followers, which meant that it could be *any one* of them.

So, to start, I was sent a screenshot of the *catfishing* profile, and based on this, I took the username and began to deploy some of the usual SOCMINT tools for Instagram data sources such as OSINTGRAM and INSTAGRAMOSINT (These can be found via GitHub or already preprogrammed into CSILINUX VM from CSILINUX.COM).

Unfortunately, this time around, neither tool successfully grabbed anything other than the UID, which meant I had to try a different approach, so with limited options, I decided to try the old original favorite of "Forgotten Password" to see what I could stumble across...

The Process

Go to Instagram login page

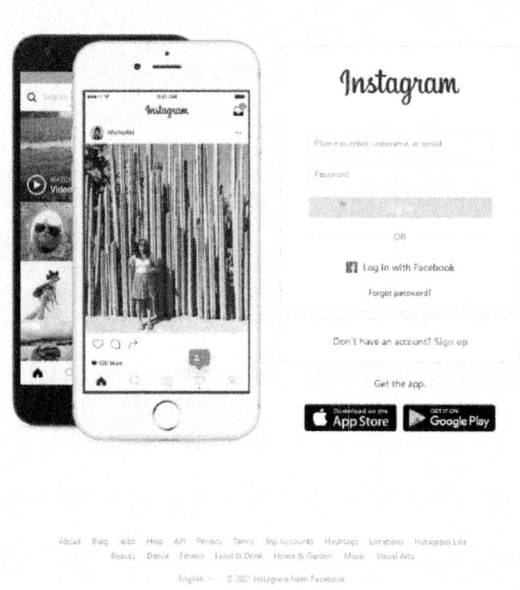

Click the '**Forgot Password**' option

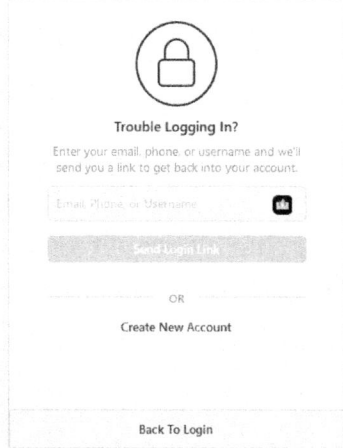

In this case, we did not have a phone number or email address, so input the target username instead.

Once I hit the send login link button, *it displayed a censored phone number that* might not seem like much as it only *shows* the last two digits of the phone number used to set up this fake malicious account.

OK, now this is where the OSINT mindset begins to come into play as for most people, they would hit a brick wall and say that the last *two* digits of a phone number *are* useless to us; however, based on our known/unknown framework I knew that the deceased person was born and lived in Tallaght, Dublin, Ireland but how can this information help us?

Using the FB dataset obtained by a dark web source, I had access to over 535 million phone numbers and FB *UIDs. As* it is categorized via country and includes phone numbers, this means we could try *to* work out how many of the 1.9 million Irish phone numbers *end* in '19' (The last two digits of the number used to set up the catfish account). Knowing this dataset is over *two* years old, I was aware not all data is still current and accurate but had no other avenues to *pursue.*

First off, I opened the Irish .txt file from the FB dataset into notepad++ as this has advanced search methods rather than the standard notepad...
Next, open the search options by hitting CTRL+F, then *type* in '19' into the search bar and hit 'Find.'

113

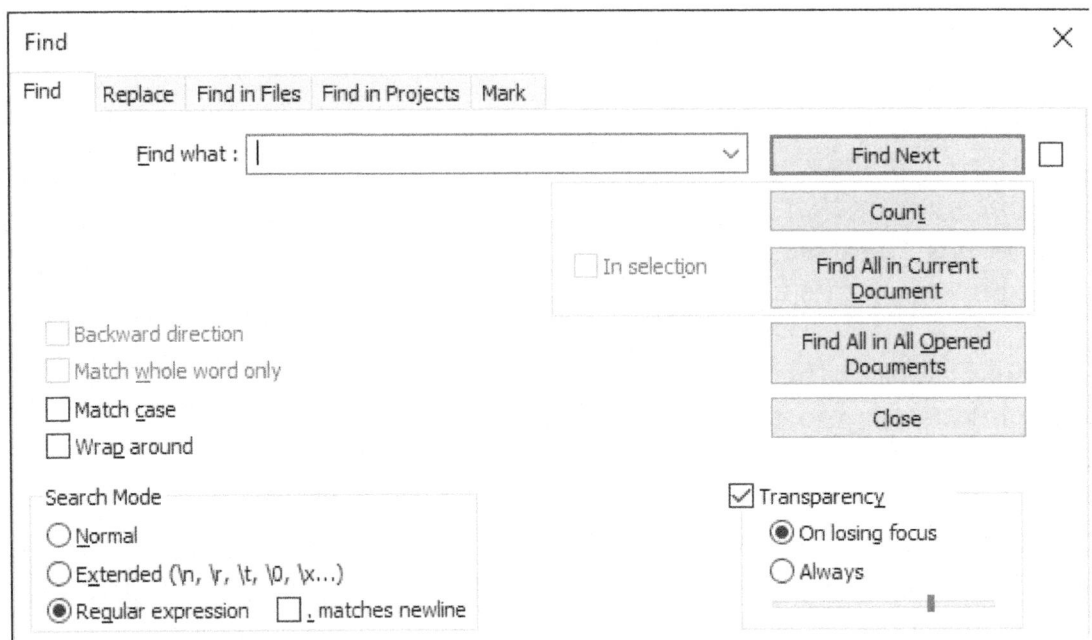

- *Search query: '19'*
- *Number of hits = 279,359*

Ok, maybe this is still way too many to assess individually but let's continue....as the data is separated using a *semicolon* and the digits are the last two digits, it means that it will have a *semicolon* after the two numbers so we can alter our query to include the *semicolon.*

- *Search query: '19:'*
- *Number of hits = 28,157*

We are getting there but still way too many to assess!

When we are searching for something, we can use what is known as a 'wildcard.' *This* is when we do not know the full context. *For* example, in this scenario, we only have the last *two* digits and do not know the whole phone number, but from the data set, we can see that each phone number includes the country code prefix of 353, so we know it must start with 353 (Country code) and end in 19 (Last two digits), but we don't know any of the other *seven* digits in-between, so instead we can add the wildcard which is '.*' in notepad++

- *Search query: "353.*19:"*
- *Number of hits: 26,024*

It might still seem very high but ruling out over 2,000 suspects is a lot!

Now we are going to narrow our search based on location. *As* mentioned before, *the deceased spent their whole life in Tallaght, Dublin, and his family was sure that somebody local* held a grudge...

- *Search query: "353.*19:.*Tallaght"*
- *Number of hits: 175*

Now we are getting somewhere, but as I went down through the list, I could see that some did not live in Tallaght but instead, as their occupation was listed, it included things like "Tallaght hospital" stating that they worked in the hospital and not actually that they lived in Tallaght. *Hence,* I went through the list and removed any that did not live in Tallaght, which now brought the list down to just 79 potential suspects!

From here, I began to *cross-reference* each account on the list to try *to identify* any ties to the deceased; *after* about 3 hours of this, it turned out that only 1 of the names on the list followed the deceased's Instagram page, this information was then passed onto the family of the deceased who said that they knew the suspect and was aware of a past dispute between them and the deceased.

However, as OSINT analysts/Investigators, this is not a valid verification as just because the number ended with the same last two digits and because they had access to the deceased private Instagram account from where the pictures *were* cloned does not mean that they were the same person who made the account, so this didn't sit well with me as I prefer a solid resolution to a case, so I had a plan.......

After *discussing* with the client, we deployed physical surveillance on the lead suspect. *Once* we had control of the target, we then resent the login link via the Instagram forget password option, which sent a text message to the *suspect's* phone, which was evident as they took out their phone from their pocket each of the *three* times, we had the login link sent throughout an hour. BINGO!!!

When confronted by a family member of the deceased, they admitted to what they had done and made an apology.

This was certainly not a typical case by any means, nor was it a particularly easy one; however, thankfully, on this occasion, luck was on our side, and the OSINT mindset helped!

I am sharing this to push across the fact that OSINT is a mindset, a way of thinking, and not just about relying on tools. In this case, it was far from just OSINT as OSINT should remain passive; *this* case required some additional methods that are not always suited depending on the task at hand along with physical covert surveillance but most of all, a lot of LUCK!!!

Facebook OSINT Investigation

By: Mirjana Ivanic

Facebook is the largest social media platform. According to Facebook's most recent investor's report, is currently has 2.895 billion monthly active users. The number of Facebook's daily active users stands at 1.908 billion people, meaning 65,9% of the total monthly users log in on a mobile device or desktop each day (Statista). Huge source of all kinds of intel one can find online and legally about someone. This is a valuable resource of information which are best starting point to other social media platforms for different types of researchers, Investigators, journalists, detectives, law enforcement agencies, analysts, and hackers.

Collecting information about target and searching techniques

The aim of OSINT investigation is to collect as much as possible information about target we investigate: the target's full name, including their first name, middle name, or initial and last name, names of any known family members, friends, colleagues, associates, roommates, teammates, age, current address (full address or at least city-state), phone number, target's employer, schools attended, targets hometown (city and state), birth date, targets activity, frequency of posting, lack of activity, sleeping patterns, video clips, live streaming, attended events, what target like and dislike, places visited, check -ins . To harvest that intel, we will need to check targets Facebook posts on daily bases, comments, pages liked, followers, images, friends' information, relationships, groups target belongs, marketplace activities, any other sensitive info and use different tools and techniques.

In OSINT research we need to stay anonymous, as what you visit, influences your online profile and you should be aware that your real profile can finish as recommendation for targets contact connection on FB. Don't forget that you are leaving digital traces online with every single click. Level of anonymity depends on who/what you are "hiding" from. Do we need to hide from other FB users or from FB itself, do we need passive or active OSINT investigation, do we need to befriend with target or just track activities? In any case FB sock puppet account is needed before starting any activity, to protect ourselves and the case. Preservation of evidence can be very hard and sometimes impossible If target founds out that it is tracked. Evidence can be destroyed, keep that in mind!

Building FB sock puppet account (an alternative online identity used for purposes of deception) can be very daunting task, and every day it's getting harder and harder as FB frequently updating code to lock and reveal fake accounts. Services want more information. Things change quickly. Profile should present real person, starting with as little info that is necessary to keep profile live. Advice is that profile should represent group type you like to get it. Facebook look at no friends/too many friends as suspicious, but it is possible to create multiple FB profiles and connect them together as friends although behind all of them is only one person. Best method it to use "burner phone, new sim card, and public wife, as Facebook will notice if you are using VPN.

Target activities can be captured very easy as many people don't follow security tips and reveal their intel publicly. They place comments, friends list, tag people on pictures, post their thoughts, tag visited places and events. On the other hand, some think that they are safe if not putting anything important or personal on FB profile, but truth is that it is enough to have private FB profile and the hacker will assume that they have also Instagram and Twitter too. On the basis of that assumption one can get all intel from 3 social media accounts, get a lot of data and pivot from them and find even more. Just one background photo on Instagram pictures can reveal location with reverse image searching.

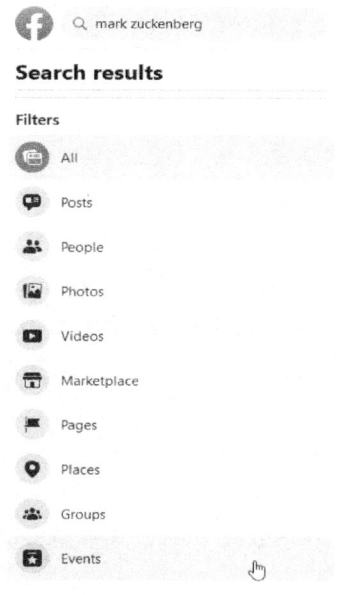

Basic search via search bar

Usually, we started searching with typing name of the target and that can be name, surname or both. After typing name, search results will give us advanced searching options, possibility to filter them and we will get 11 search categories in the menu on the left.

On this way we can search for target by categories (URLs added)

Posts – look for your friends posts or those mentioning your friends

www.facebook.com/search/posts/?q=mark%20zuckerberg

People – find people based on location, education, or workplace. Type the name of the city as keyword in the search field, click on people, then add city once more, not as keyword but as location and add company,on this way you can find people who are working for a small company, in a small town, if your keyword is the town itself. Or can also search for people working in some company by using name of the company as keyword or you can also search for residents of a town at random, without knowing a specific name.It is possible also to search for profession, in combination with employer although some of the results are not that privacy friendly.

www.facebook.com/search/people?q=mark%20zuckerberg

Photos – search for photos by type, location, year, or even person (the poster)

www.facebook.com/search/photos?q=mark%20zuckerberg

Videos – look for videos by the date, location, or whether it's an FB live

www.facebook.com/search/videos?q=mark%20zuckerberg

Marketplace - this category allows you to search for products that are available on Facebook's market. Not all users can access this option, depending on the marketplace's availability in your country

www.facebook.com/marketplace/ineligible/?query=

Pages - you can use various filters to narrow down specific pages. For example, you can search for products or business pages and stores from which you can purchase products and services.

www.facebook.com/search/pages?q=mark%20zuckerberg

Places – here you can look for places like restaurants, clubs, takeout places, and more. You also get a map of your location for more convenient searching.

www.facebook.com/search/places?q=mark%20zuckerberg

Groups – narrow down groups by location, private or public status, and your membership status.

www.facebook.com/search/groups?q=mark%20zuckerberg

Events – choose if you're looking for an online or physical event. Set the location, set how many days in the future you'd like to search, and define what kind of event you're looking for. Finally, you can select if you're looking for a family-friendly event and if it's popular with your friends.

www.facebook.com/search/events?q=mark%20zuckerberg

Advanced search and how to find FB User ID number (FBID)

In early 2013 Facebook offered advanced semantic search called Graph Search. Facebook users could now type in their queries in the search box to return accurate results based on their questions/phrases and combined words. This feature is removed in 2019. Users are still able to utilize Graph search, but they need to build their graph search manually. After Facebook removed direct support for Graph Search, they improved search functionality and added more filters.

Following URLs work only when you are logged to your FB account. Language setting should be in English US. It is not necessary to be friend with your target. For example, you can find mutual friends of two profiles if your targets friends list is hidden. On that way you can form targets friends list regarding mutual friends two persons search query.

Mutual friends, userID1 and userID2

facebook.com/browse/mutual_friends/?uid=USERID1&node=USERID2

Friends in common, posts and photos in common, and any other linking data, such as hometowns, schools, etc.

facebook.com/browse/mutual_friends/?uid=USERID1&node=USERID2

Pages liked by person

www.facebook.com/browse/fanned_pages/?id=USERID

More unique Graph URL you can find on acebook Matrix link, plessas.net/facebookmatrix
A Facebook ID (AKA FBID) is a unique numeric identifier that every FB user/page/group/event has. Sometimes the user ID will be displayed on the user's profiles URL, after "id" or the user's name. If not on the user profile, it can be found

when you right click on FB page and select View Source, click CTRL+F and search for the form User_id. Number that is found is FB ID number (FBID). Other id numbers:

- **User pages: userID**
- **Business pages: pageID**
- **Event pages: eventID displayed in the URL**
- **Groups: groupID**
- **Location ID Things-to-do-in (first number after this line)**

In some cases, the group or user page ID will be in the original URL, but "place" is always in URL.

Data",[],{"ACCOUNT_ID":"10000   "USER ID":"10000   "NAME":   "SHORT_NAME":

More about formulas for searching Facebook, fb Directory links, native and advanced techniques/tools can be found on Facebook Matrix, plessas.net/facebookmatrix

Third party tools which are based on Graph Search that are working now, but keep in mind that FB frequently changes policies and tools can go offline.

- Who posted that? www.whopostedwhat.com/
- Facebook Graph Searcher intelx.io/
- Graph.tips graph.tips/beta/
- LookupID lookup-id.com/
- Sowdust sowdust.github.io/fb-search

Graph search and JSON, code 64

If you perform Facebook search based on category, you will have filters on the left sidebar. There is option to create custom filters, but they are not keyword searches, nor you can use ID numbers if you know them. They will suggest your certain number of search results and you must choose one of their suggestions, which limits you to find right one. Some results won't show up in suggestions unless you are friends or friends of friends. With this kind of methodology, we can create new combinations and discover new searches, and to do that we are using format JSON and then converting (encoding) it in base 64 code in order to use it in Facebook URL.

Base URL that we always use

facebook.com/search/top/?q=people&epa=FILTERS&filters=

Categories to choose from:

- top/ Search for top content
- posts/ Search for public posts
- people/ Search for people
- photos/ Search for photos
- videos/ Search for videos
- pages/ Search for pages
- places/ Search for places

1. Perform keyword search in basic search box
2. On the Facebook search results page, choose category of search, posts, people, photos…
3. Choose filter, any filter as the goal is to get the Facebook URL to include the =FILTERS&filters=language

After this point in the URL, you will notice a string of letters and numbers, where base64 code begins.

Delete the current base64 code so the URL ends with =FILTERS&filters=, identify ID numbers that you need to search (placeid, personid, pageid, groupid and identify JSON formulas you intend to use.

JSON formulas:

People who have indicated they live in a certain place on Facebook

{"city":"{\"name\":\"users_location\",\"args\":\"PLACEID\"}"}

People who have identified that they attend(ed) a certain educational facility

{"school":"{\"name\":\"users_school\",\"args\":\"PAGEID\"}"}

People who have identified that they work for a certain employer on Facebook

{"employer":"{\"name\":\"users_employer\",\"args\":\"PAGEID\"}"}

A list of the user's friends (ready to be combined with other filters). Results will have open friendslists only. Results page will not have an indication of filter used.

{"friends":"{\"name\":\"users_friends_of_people\",\"args\":\"USERID\"}"}

Posts, videos, or photos (choose via search tab) from a group

{"rp_group":"{\"name\":\"group_posts\",\"args\":\"GROUPID\"}"}

Posts, videos, or photos (choose via search tab) a user or page has posted

{"rp_author":"{\"name\":\"author\",\"args\":\"PAGEID\"}"}

Posts, videos, or photos (choose via search tab) tagged to a location

{"rp_location":"{\"name\":\"location\",\"args\":\"PLACEID\"}"}

Recent

{"rp_chrono_sort":"{\"name\":\"chronosort\",\"args\":\"\"}"}

Posts, videos, or photos (choose via search tab) on an exact date

{"rp_creation_time":"{\"name\":\"creation_time\",\"args\":\"{\\\"start_year\\\":\\\"2019\\\",\\\"start_month\\\":\\\"2019-8\\\",\\\"end_year\\\":\\\"2019\\\",\\\"end_month\\\":\\\"2019-9\\\",\\\"start_day\\\":\\\"2019-1-10\\\",\\\"end_day\\\":\\\"2019-09-01\\\"}\"}"}

Facebook Live

{"videos_source":"{\"name\":\"videos_live\",\"args\":\"\"}"}

Verified Pages

{"verified":"{\"name\":\"pages_verified\",\"args\":\"\"}"}

Combination search (note the one set of outer braces are surrounding the whole query and there is a comma in between parts of the query where the outer braces from individual searches met): People who have identified that they attend(ed) a certain educational facility and who have identified that they work(ed) for a certain employer on Facebook

{"school":"{\"name\":\"users_school\",\"args\":\"PAGEID\"}","employer":"{\"name\":\"users_employer\",\"args\":\"PAGEID\"}"}

Copy JSON formula into a base64 coding tool (basecode64.org) and CyberChef (gchq.github.io/CyberChef)

Copy the base64 results and return to Facebook

eyJycF9jaHJvbm9fc29ydCI6IntcIm5hbWVcIjpcImNocm9ub3NvcnRcIixcImFyZ3NcIjpcIlwifSJ9

Paste base64 results immediately after =FILTERS&filters= and press Enter.

facebook.com/search/posts?q=baseball&epa=FILTERS&filters=eyJycF9jaHJvbm9fc29ydCI6IntcI
m5hbWVcIjpcImNocm9ub3NvcnRcIixcImFyZ3NcIjpcIlwifSJ9

You should have results of your search choices.
More about JSON and base64 code, translator tools and variables to use, you can find on Osintcurio.us link
 osintcurio.us/2019/08/22/the-new-facebook-graph-search-part-1/

Keep in mind that these searches can be blocked by making full use of Facebook privacy options.

Facebook Google Dorks

Another way to search target on FB is by using google dorks. Here are some examples:

- site:facebook.com inurl:safetycheck inurl:(identifyingkeyword)
- site:facebook.com inurl:(first name) inurl:(last name)
- site:facebook.com/places/Things-to-do-in (city name)
- site:facebook.com/pages/(non-city place name) region -inurl:region
- site:facebook.com "medium geo area" (non-city place name) "keyword"
- site:facebook.com inurl:ref=page_internal get all the content or entities that match these keywords and are linked to a page

Working FB Directories:

Places

- www.facebook.com/places
- www.facebook.com/Directory/places/

Pages

www.facebook.com/Directory/pages

CSI Linux and Facebook information gathering tool

Facebook information gathering tool (FBI) is part of CSI linux. From this tool we can get sensitive data about home, date of birth, occupation, telephone number, and email address. In order to start using it, you should have FB user account and password, which you can get using some sort of social engineering techiques.

First we will generate access token using "token" command. Then you will need to enter targets name and password and hit "Enter". It will create an access token and save it as a log file. To view the token use "cat_token" command. This token information can be used in many types of attack vectors, so store it in the right place.

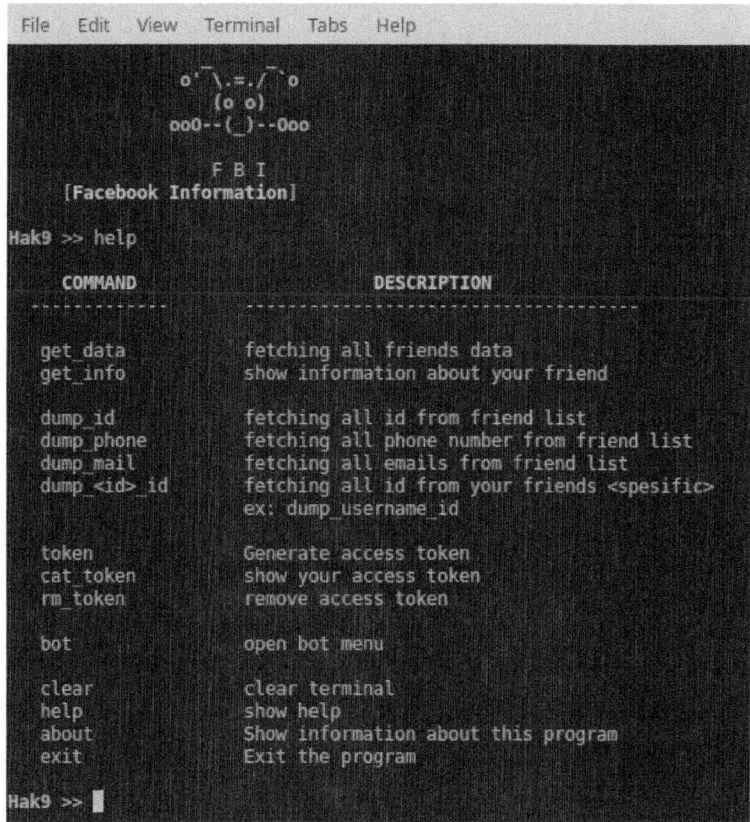

If you want to know all available information about the target and his friends, use "get_data". To get all phone numbers of targets friends user command "dump_phone". This toll will fetch all phone numbers from the friends list and save them to "fbi./output" Directory as text file.

With this tool you can:

Fetching all friend's data
Show information about your friend
Fetching all id from friend list
Fetching all phone number from friend list
Fetching all email from friend list

Feature "bot" will open bot menu which will give you options to mess up with target profile: auto reactions, auto comment, auto poke, accept all friend requests, delete all posts in your timeline, delete all friends, stop following all friends, delete all photo albums.

Most times you will need to be logged in FB account in order to use some tools (CSI Linux – FBI Facebook Information Gathering Tool) so don't get locked by FB and get burned your personal account.

Private profile, fake profile...

Private profile -it happens that when you open profile, you see couple of likes and maybe 1-2 photos. Nothing else in about section, and maybe one or two posts.

First check URL and if you have ID number, then you can get rough idea when profile is created. If you have username, then you can search for ID number and again find out when profile is created.

Check profile picture and run reverse image check to see if there is same picture elsewhere online.

Click on any button that you can. Sometimes you can see in friends list people that following this profile. You can check about section, check-ins.

In friends search box you can enter targets personal name, surname, to identify old account and members of family. If there is no friends list, you can check comment, as those are comments from friends.

There is also little magnifying glass on FB profile, which will give you opportunity to search for all public information related to this specific profile. You can type person's name, surname, nickname, or anything that can be related to this profile, happy birthday, dinner...If you don't see magnifying glass icon, extract the users ID number, and place it in this url and replace keyword with the keyword of your choice:

facebook.com/profile/ID/search/?q=KEYWORD

Search family members, go their account where their pictures are attached, association to other persons photo, comments. Search for friends that have open friends lists. Also searching for mutual friends.

Fake profile – Usually serves to spread fake news, spams and to track victims to give personal sensitive information, for money begging, romance scams, text message scams, for impostor-ism (to impersonate public figures, politicians and celebrities are usually victims), etc.

They usually don't have many pictures or there are no pictures at all (one profile picture is on profile for couple years, or profile picture is of some celebrity, you can use google image search for verification), no photo album

Profile is new (one of the reasons why it may become important to know when a particular Facebook profile or page was created as fake profiles are usually newly created and then soon removed or blocked by Facebook)

Bio information on the account seems weird, (or there is not much information, there is nothing in about section, usually you can see only one attractive women or man)
Many foreign friends, no local people
Different names in URL and profile
There is no history, many links to websites with ads or low personal engagement rate, generic comments, it doesn't message, person don't reply to anyone, has lots of likes, blank wall.

Click on more button to see if there are activities like check ins, music, films, etc.

Fake accounts can appear in form of multiple accounts which often occur due to loss of password or when accounts are being violated. Many users in that circumstances decide to create new account instead to resolve security issue. You can see also accounts with different names of same person, changing names and gender also makes account suspicious as no one can create another account with the same name.

In order to find phone number of targets, you can use recovering techniques, but this method is a less advisable as target will know that someone want to gain access to its account. www.facebook.com/login/identify?ctx=recover

Facebook evidence and forensics

Document all steps and information that you collected. Collection, preservation, and authentication of FB evidence can be foundation for admittance in a court. Keep in mind that evidence should be identical to original and collected in a forensically sound manner. FB and other social media entities are protected from disclosing information by the Stored Communication Act and are not subject to civil subpoena for content not will they respond to criminal subpoena unless they originate from a law enforcement agency,  this can be handicap unless you have approval from owner account to ask FB for data. Facebook Information for Law Enforcement Agencies, you can find on this link, www.facebook.com/safety/groups/law/guidelines

One of the essential Facebook OSINT tools is Maltego. Maltego can easily help you correlate and find links between individuals, organizations, geolocations, addresses, emails, and phone numbers. You can collect people, images and create chain associations between friends in order to get larger picture.

For online evidence collection great application is Hunch.ly, which automatically tracks the URL, timestamps, and hashes every page you visit during an investigation. Hunch.ly Evidence Guide you can find on,
 www.hunch.ly/resources/Hunchly%20Evidence%20Guide.pdf

Facebook footprints can be found in volatile memory (RAM), browser cache file, virtual machine image files, virtual machine snapshot files, iPhone file system dump, Android phone file system dump. Some of the tools which can be used in Facebook forensics are|:

Internet Evidence Analytical Tools

1. Internet Evidence Finder – data recovery tool that searches hard drive or files for Internet related artifacts. www.forensicfocus.com/reviews/internet-evidence-finder-ief/
2. Facebook JPG Finder – searches selected folder for possible Facebook JPG images
3. CacheBack – forensic Net analysis tool specializing in browser cache, history and chat discovery for forensic investigations.

Memory Analytical Tools

1. Bootable Linux – for making forensic images
    a. CAINE
    b. CSI Linux
    c. Deft
    d. Sift
2. Win32dd- toolkit for memory dump conversion and acquisition on Windows
3. FTK Imager – computer forensics and image acquisition software solution

Mobile Device Forensics Tools

1. Axiom Forensics
2. Celebrite – Mobile Forensics
3. Oxygen Forensics Suite -advanced mobile forensics software
4. XRY – mobile device forensic system

In order to authenticate and verify Facebook postings we need sources of evidence. Two excellent sources of information are: directly from Facebook via consent to release private information and via consent when the owner of the profile gives consent for the profile to be accessed for the purpose of collecting information from the profile. Here is one example of how consent should look like:

In order to authenticate and verify Facebook postings we need sources of evidence. Two excellent sources of information are: directly from Facebook via consent to release private information and via consent when the owner of the profile gives consent for the profile to be accessed for the purpose of collecting information from the profile. Here is one example of how consent should look like:

Consent to Release Private Facebook Information

I, [LEGAL NAME], am an account holder with Facebook, Inc. My profile user ID is [UID, ALIAS] and my login email address is [USER LOGIN EMAIL]

Please do not include your password, I do hereby voluntarily authorize Facebook to release the reasonably available data as check marked below, from my Facebook account profile for the period of [date range]

I hereby indemnify Facebook, Inc. against all claims for damages, compensation, and/or costs in respect to damage or loss to a third party caused by, or arising out of, or being incidental to release of my data.

My date should be released to***:
[CONTACT NAME, PHONE NUMBER, FAX NUMBER, ADDRESS AND EMAIL ADDRESS]
*** please note that user data will be sent to the user or the user's legal representative]

Please release the following data:
[Check all the boxes that you are requesting]

Profile information
- recent logs (recent means the past 2-3 days from process data
- status updates
- notes
- mini-feed
- shares
- wall-posts
- friends list
- groups
- events
- videos
- applications
- Facebook message inbox (received messages)
- Facebook message outbox (sent messages)
- photos and user's comments (all photos available will be sent if this box checked)

Afiants Name (User please print) _____
Affiants Signature _____
Date _____
Notary public/Individual Duly Authorized to Administer Oath
[THIS CONSENT MUST BE NOTARIZED. See attached]

When you have access to the profile, you can use Download Archive function on their Facebook account settings page to download everything in the profile.

 to Second way of getting FB evidence data is from computer or device that is in control of the person posting to Facebook's. Preserve everything you can. Facebook will retain all of the information and content for 90 days from deletion in order to give the user time to change their mind.

1. Use preservation letters is one of the best options to prevent loss of evidence.
2. Preserve all devices, get forensics copy of HDD
3. Use forensics Experts

IP address information can be obtained from internet history on the hard drive or device, the IP address assigned to computer, as well as potentially from email or Facebook chat histories that may be resident on the storage media of the computer for device. It is not possible to authenticate print out of fb page sit provides no external method for authentication.

Conclusion

Undoubtedly Facebook is the most popular social network and that makes it excellent target for all kinds of OSINT investigations. With various OSINT tools and techniques presented in this research, we can analyze and prevent individuals but also organization from exposing sensitive data online and protect against attacks.

References:

[1] Photo by Rinson Chory on Unsplash
[2] Facebook forencisc finalized, Kelvin Wong, captain@vxrl.org, Security Researcher, Anthony C. T. Lai, darkfloyd@vxrl.org, Security Researcher, Jason C. K. Yeung, taku@vxrl.org, Security Researcher, W. L. Lee, leng@vxrl.org, Security Researcher, P. H. Chan, sweeper@vxrl.org
Link: www.fbiic.gov/public/2011/jul/Facebook_Forensics-Finalized.pdf
[3] Getting Facebook into Evidence – A Technical Perspective, by Larry E. Daniel
[4] Osintcurio.us Facebook Tips osintcurio.us/2020/04/02/facebook-tips/
Facebook Tips #2, osintcurio.us/2020/04/02/facebook-tips
What to do when a Facebook profile is private, osintcurio.us/2020/10/19/what-to- do-when-a-facebook-profile-is-private/
Facebook Graph Search – part 1, osintcurio.us/2019/08/22/the-new-facebook-graph-search-part-1
The new Facebook Graph Search – part 2, osintcurio.us/2019/08/22/the-new-facebook-graph-search-part-2
[5] Open Source Intelligence Techniques, Michael Bazzell, inteltechniques.com/book1.html
[6] Facebook Matrix, plessas.net/facebookmatrix
[7] Facebook information gathering tool, medium.com/geekculture/facebook-information-gathering-tool-f3dd34cbcf13

©https://www.hunch.ly/

Hunchly

By: Khadija Naz

"Hunchly is a web capture tool designed specifically for online investigations. Hunchly quietly runs in your web browser and automatically collects, documents, and annotates every website you visit." [einvestigator.com]

Why Hunchly?

Online research is used in almost every private investigation case. Typically, the research process begins with you turning on your computer, opening a web browser, and typing search keywords into one of the big search engines like Google or Bing. After that, you go over the search results page and begin browsing other websites and extracting data, taking screenshots etc. All of this can take a lot of time. Here the Hunch.ly works.

Hunch.ly is best in:

- Fast documentation
- Fast reporting
- Create audit trail for online investigation.
- Safe storage
- Robust search

Hence Hunchly saves you time during your research and investigation process. When you tie the information with tools like Maltego, you can add a lot of value to your investigations.

Download

Get Hunch.ly from   https://www.hunch.ly/downloads

©https://www.hunch.ly/

At this time, Hunchly only supports the Chrome browser, so you have to use Chrome to capture your online evidence with Hunchly. Then you will need to install the Hunchly browser extension. After this is installed, install the application. The link above has a great walkthrough on this process.

Hunchly Walkthrough

Capturing Page

1. Start hunchly Desktop by searching

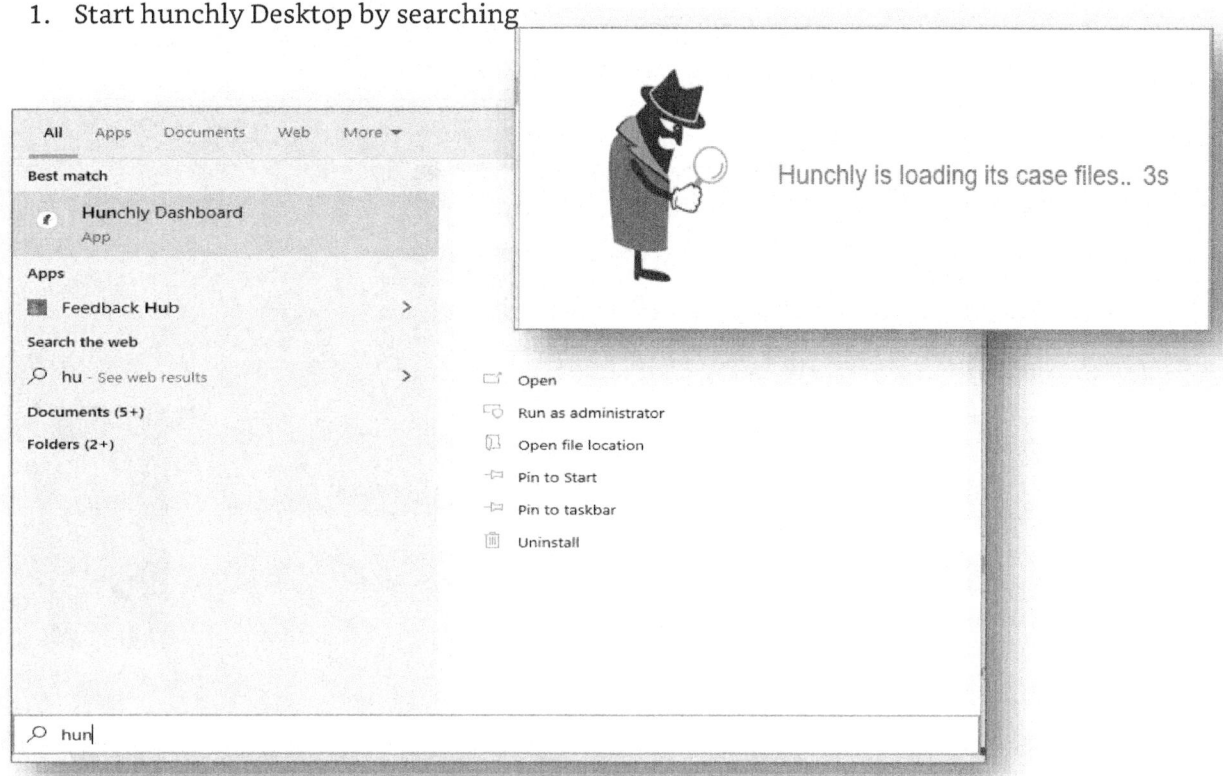

Add new case

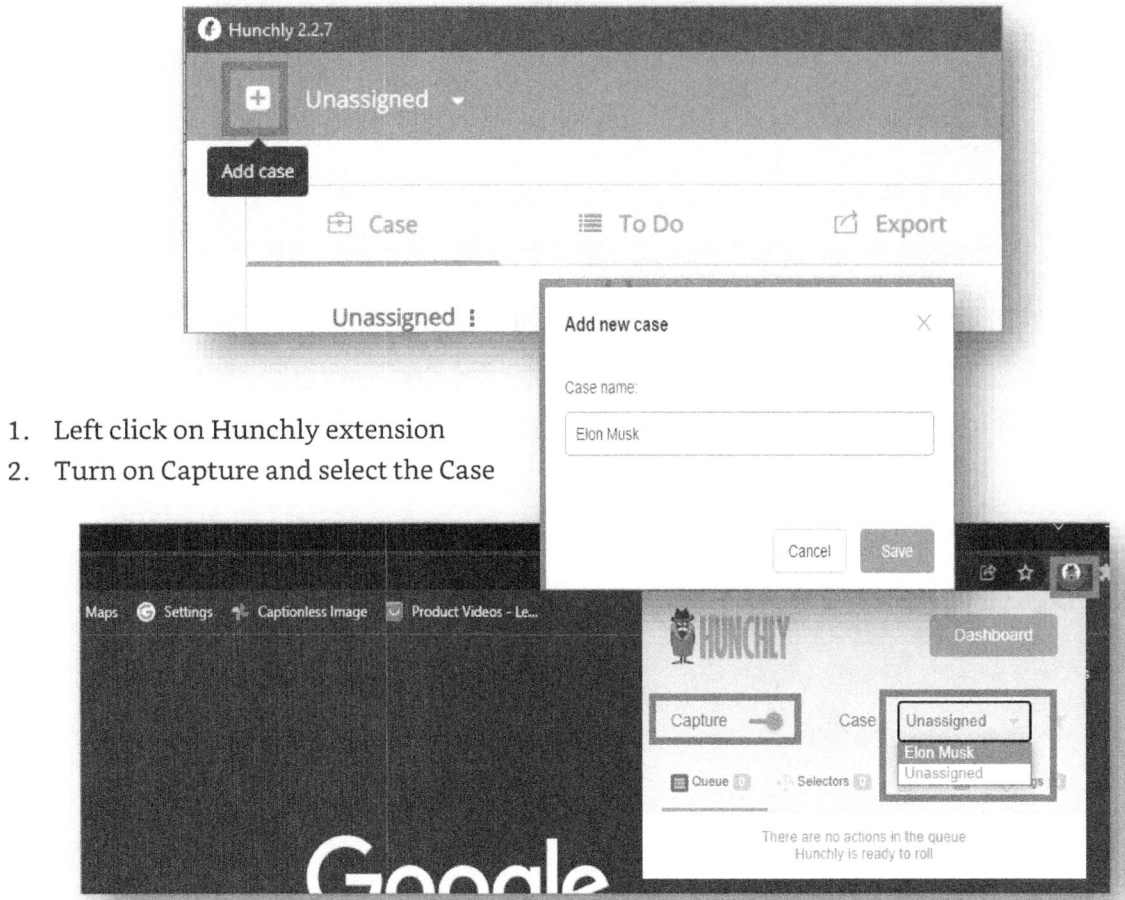

1. Left click on Hunchly extension
2. Turn on Capture and select the Case

3. Now start your searching.

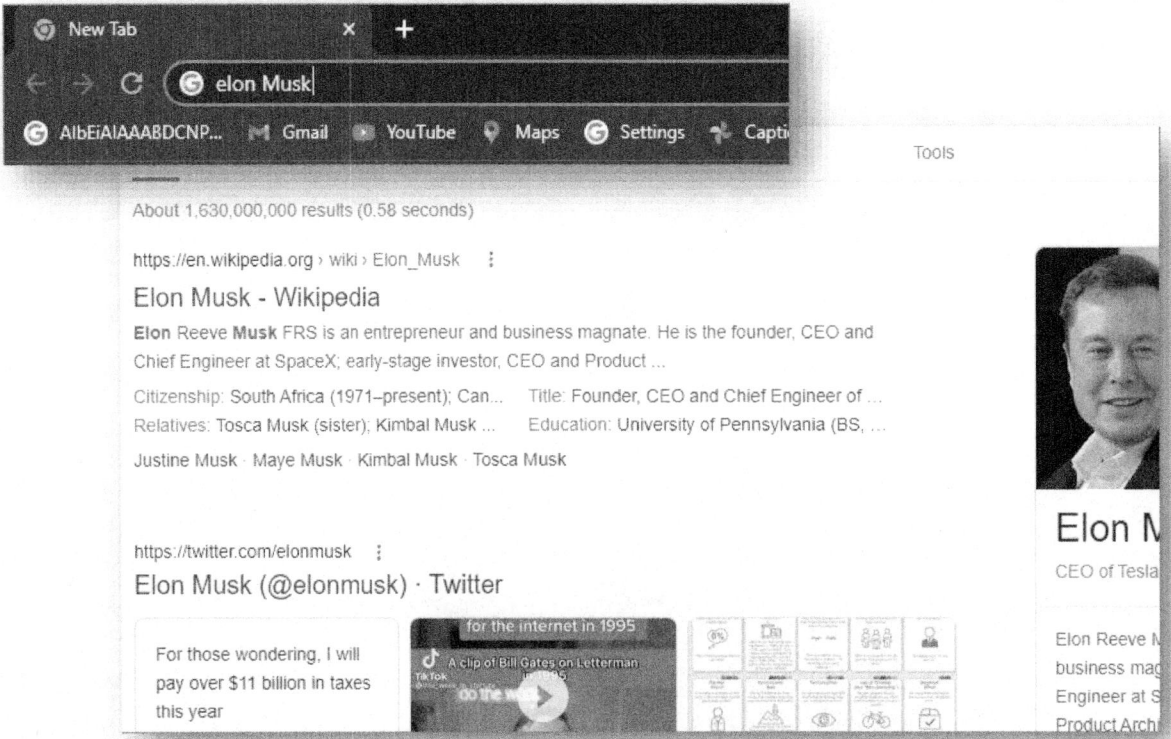

4. All the pages that you have visited will be saved in history of selected Case.

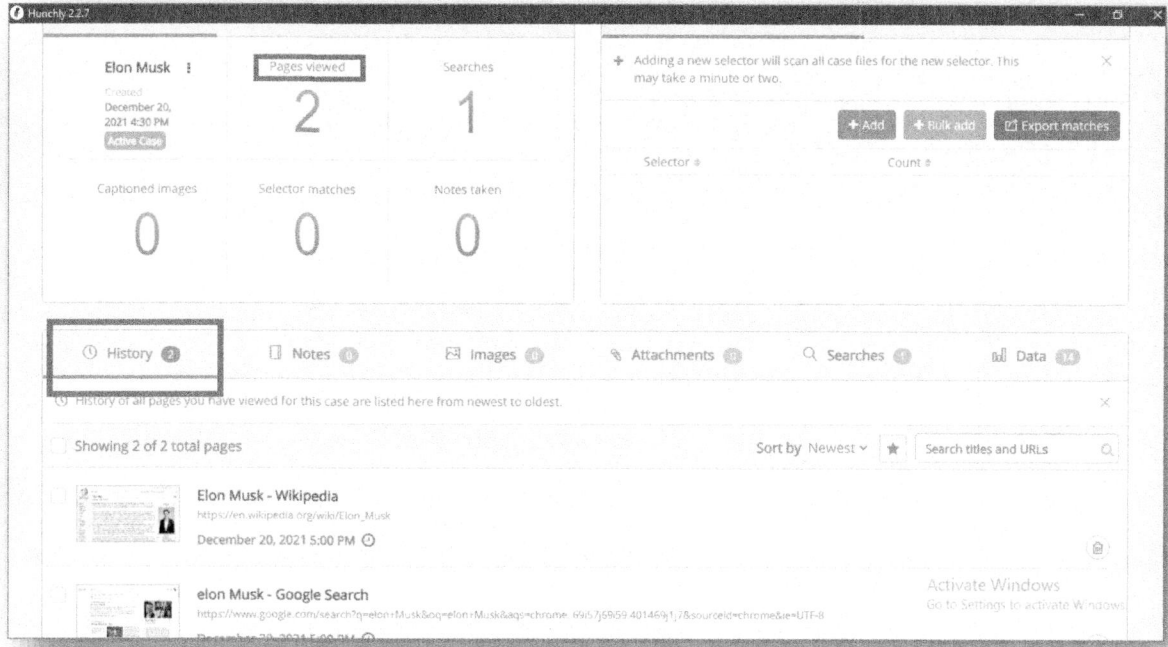

OR

5. Without turning on Capture on hunchly extension,
6. Right click on page
7. Select Hunchly>Capture

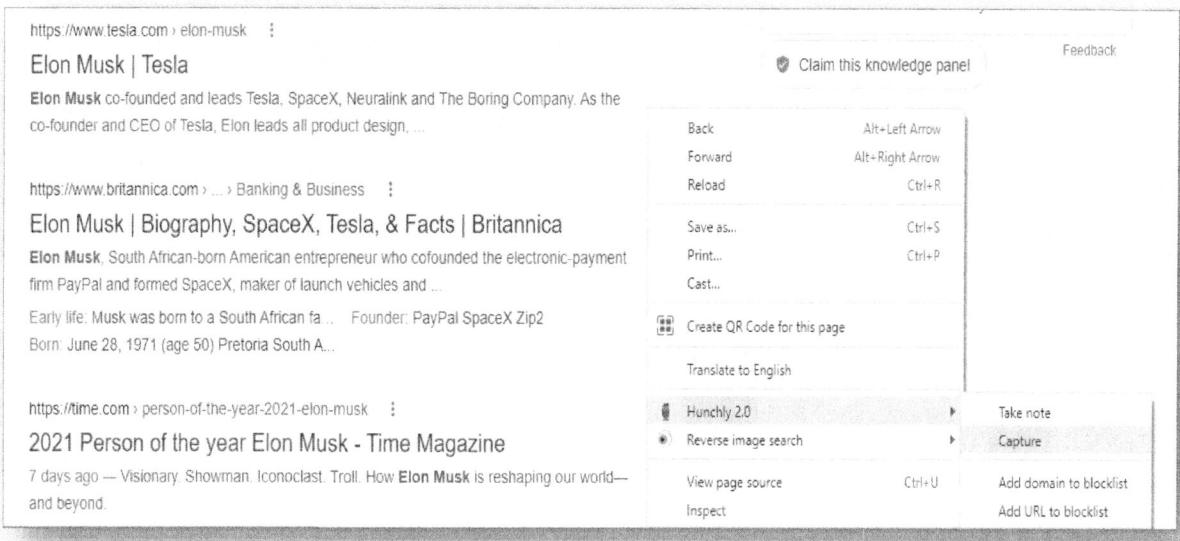

Taking Notes

1. Right Click on webpage
2. Select Hunchly > Take note

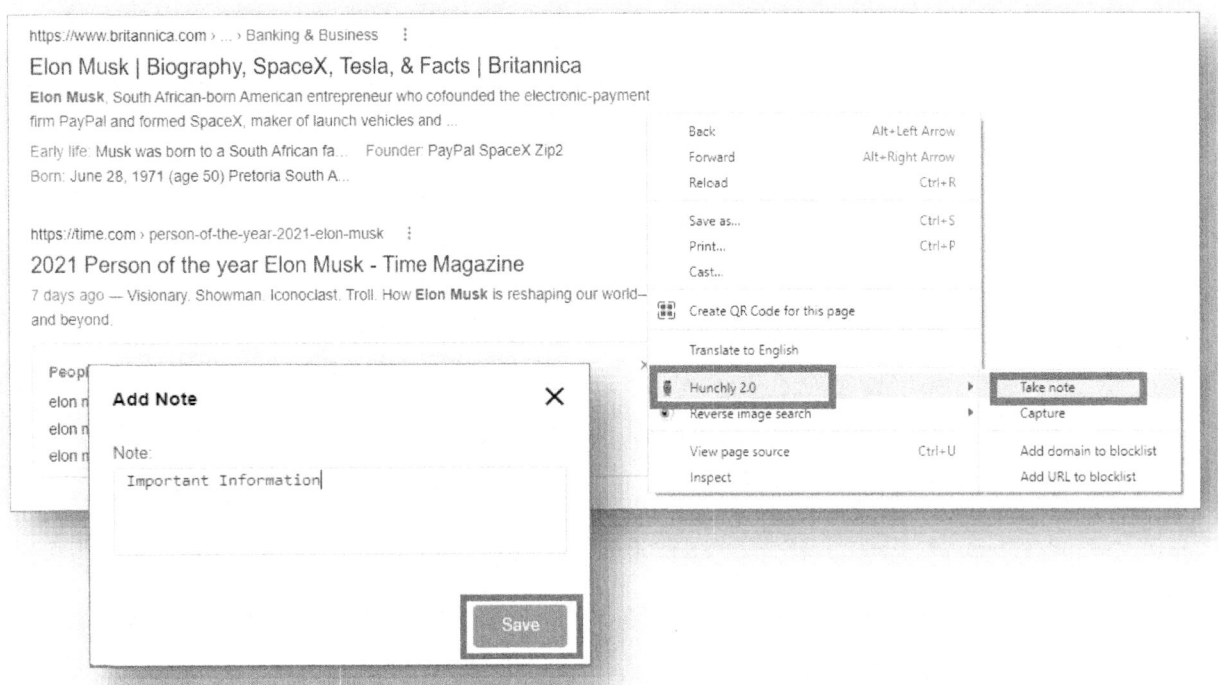

OR

3. Open the Hunchly Extension
4. Left click Notes
5. Enter your notes
6. Left click Save Note

Verify the notes were added

7. Left click Dashboard

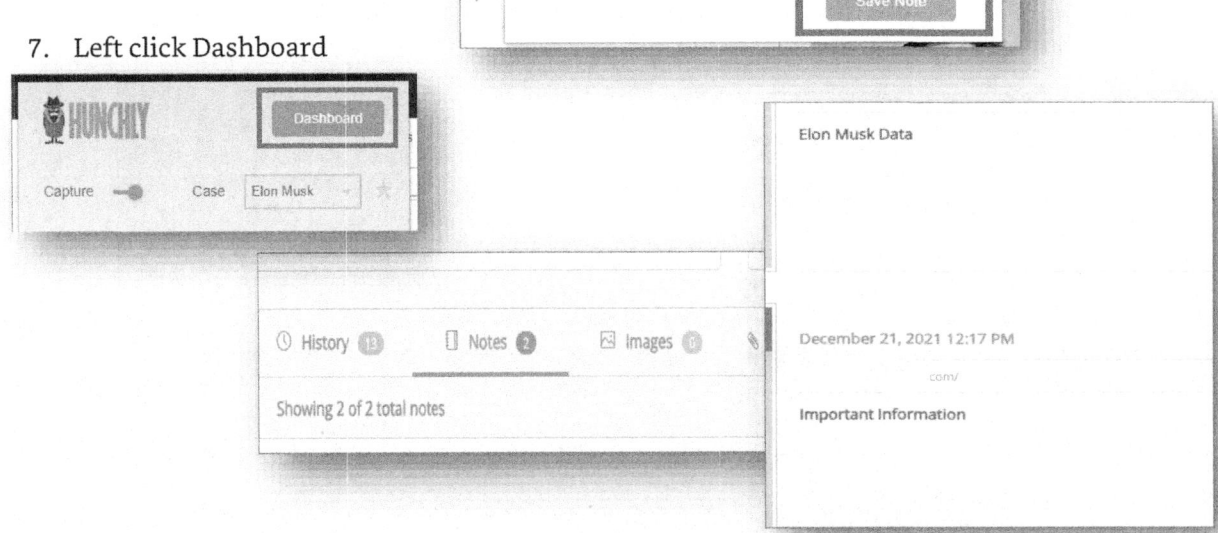

Report Builder:

1. Open Hunchly Desktop
2. Left Click on **Export**
3. Left Click on Open Report Builder
4. Now Drag and Drop the required element from Left pan to right pan

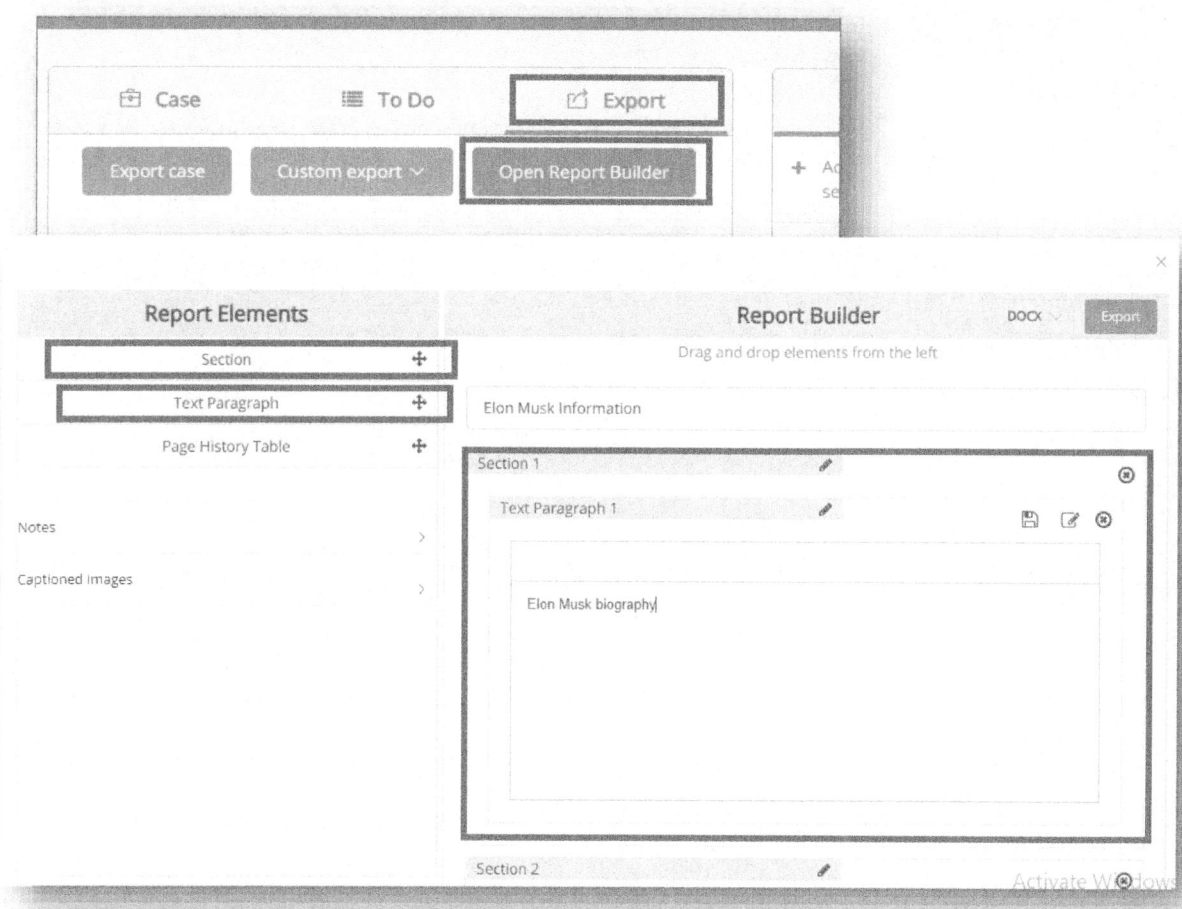

5. After that drag and drop Notes and images in report and "Export" the report

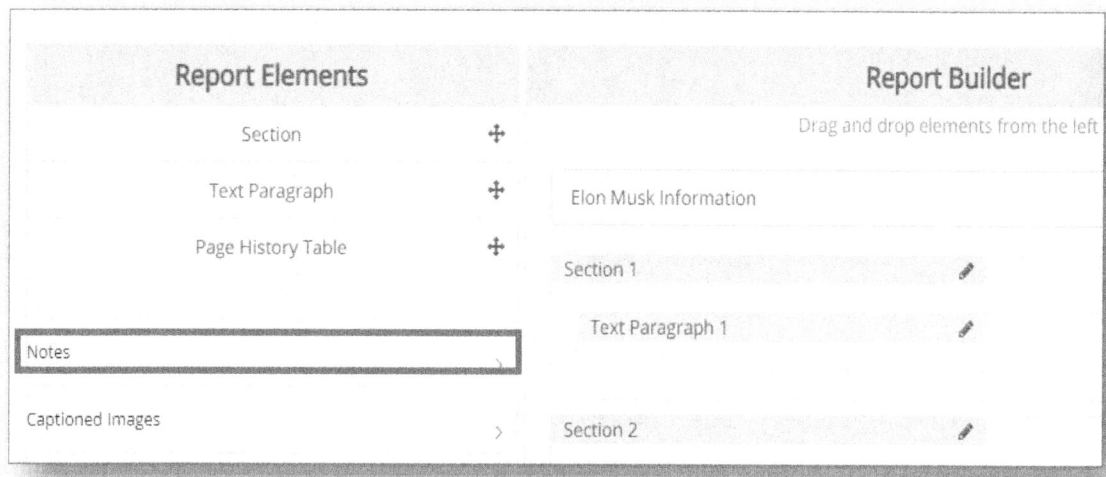

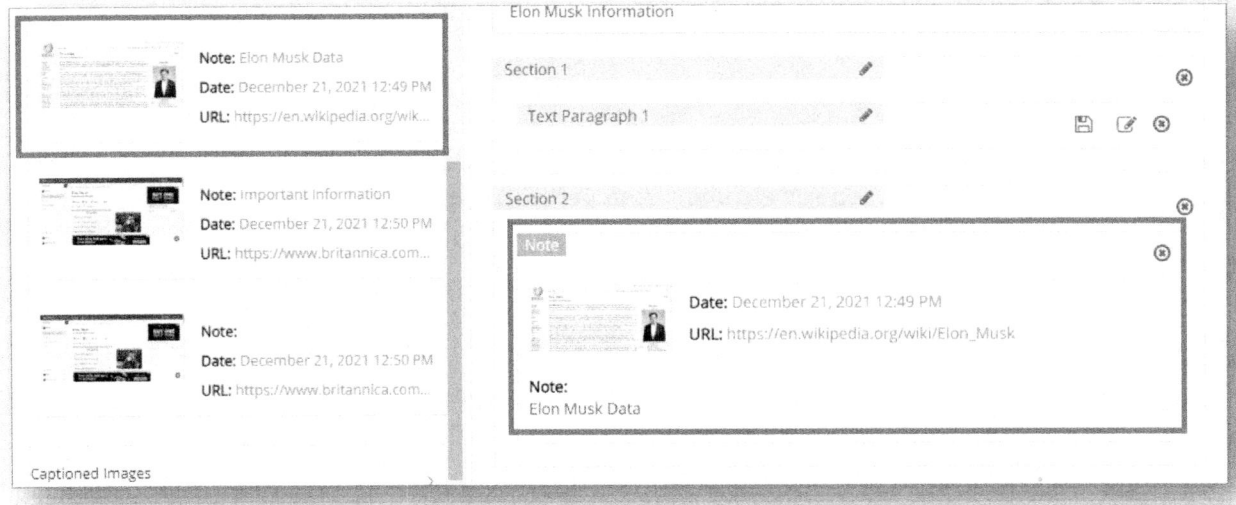

6. Pick the file type you want to export to
7. Left click "Export"

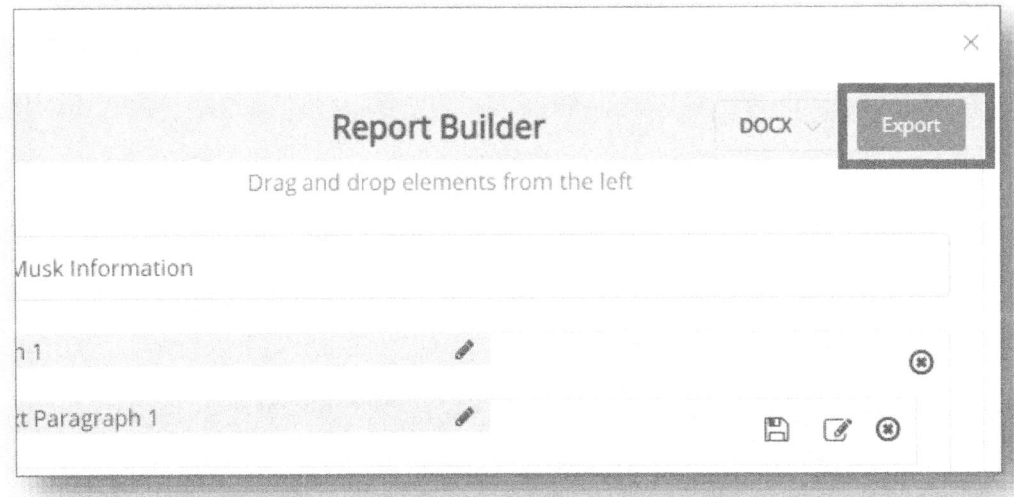

Reference

[1] https://www.hunch.ly/

Twitter Investigations/OSINT

By: Luna Winchester

It is likely that during an investigation, there will undoubtably come a time when you will stumble upon information needed in a Twitter account. At a first glance one would say that finding deleted information on a scrubbed account would be a fool's errand. What they would be discounting would be the tools in your arsenal available to you as what is posted online is very rarely permanently destroyed. Here we will talk about a few of these in our toolbox as well as in general OSINT tools.

Aware Online – Twitter Search Tools

Aware Online provides a wide array of options at your fingertips including Twitter. This starts out with your run of the mill search tips and tricks. For example, one of the ways that you can optimize your search is to enter in the Name/Username into the Search for a user selection and hit check. This will run through the information through search engines as well as analyzing Twitter for any matches).

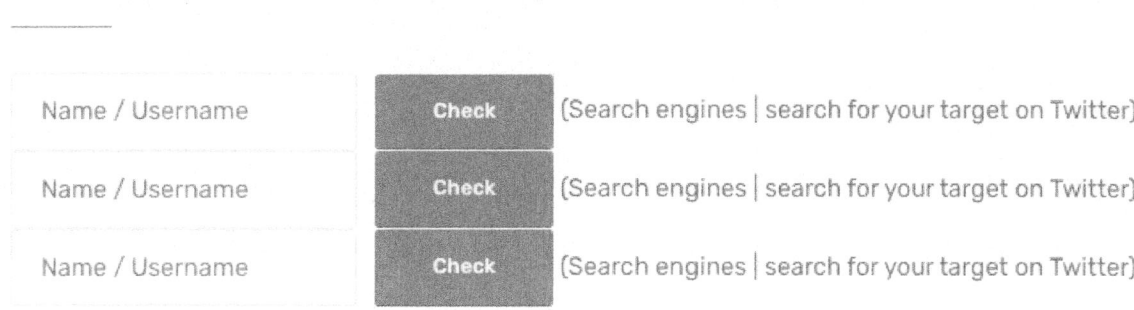

The second avenue is to run it through Search for a user on Twitter (combinations) as this gives you the chance to select the Name/Username and a keyword to narrow in on closer matches.

Search for a user on Twitter (combinations)

Name / Username	Keyword	Check	(Combined search)
Name / Username	Keyword	Check	(Combined search)

The third part is the analysis which does a deeper dive overall. It offers a three-part analysis which gives you all of the information from the users/your target's messages. Secondly, it provides the information from messages that are sent to the user/your target. And lastly you can receive all of the information from all messages where the user/your target is referenced in all messages.

Analyze an account on Twitter

Name / Username	Check	(All messages from your target)
Name / Username	Check	(All messages addressed to your target)
Name / Username	Check	(All messages in which your target is mentioned)

This next portion is straight forward as the search options are for various selections such as language, keywords, hashtags, exact expressions, and so forth.

The next selection is very similar to past sections except that where others were for all information, this acts as a filter for specific information or excluding certain information.

Search for posts on Twitter

Keyword(s)	Check	(Search for all these words)
Exact expression	Check	(Search for an exact expression)
Hashtag (#)	Check	(Search for this hashtag (#))
Keyword(s)	Check	(Search for words written in Dutch)
Keyword(s)	Check	(Search for words written in English)
Keyword(s)	Check	(Search for words written in French)
Keyword(s)	Check	(Search for words written in German)
Keyword(s)	Check	(Search for words written in Spanish)
Keyword(s)	Check	(Search for words written in Polish)
Keyword(s)	Check	(Search for words written in Russian)
Keyword(s)	Check	(Search for words written in Arabic)

Search for posts on Twitter (combinations)

Keyword(s)	–Keyword	Check	(Exclude)
Hashtag (#)	–Keyword	Check	(Exclude)

This option is unique in that if you know where you are seeking, or a general area, this is where you can dig for some information. Where this area differs is that there an option to search by latitude and longitude and not just by city, state, zip code/postal code.

Search for messages from a specific location

Longitude (LAT)	Width –free (LON)	Check	(1000 meters from location)
Longitude (LAT)	Width –free (LON)	Check	(100 meters from location)
Longitude (LAT)	Width –free (LON)	Check	(10 meters from location)
Longitude (LAT)	Width –free (LON)	Check	(1 meters from location)

The last portion for Twitter specific searching falls under messages. If you know the time frames, this will allow you to input that data in and run it.

Search for messages posted on a specific date / between dates

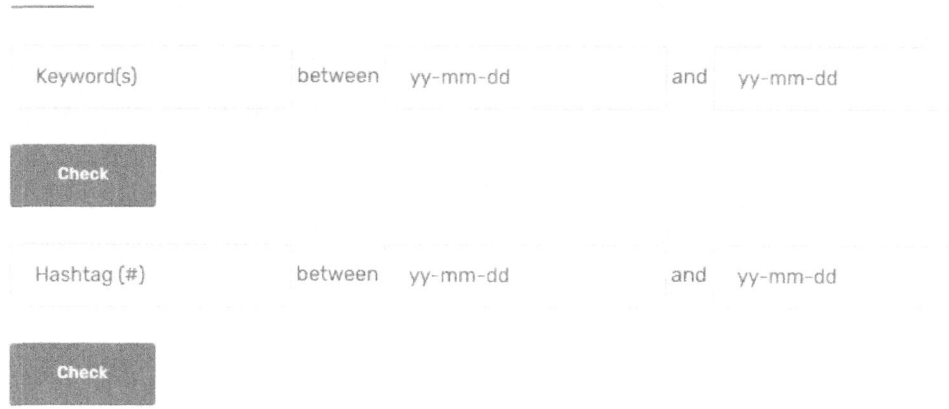

The only caveat with using this site is that it will redirect you to a third-party site for any results.

Internet Archive Wayback Machine

This site is one of the most creative and unique sites I have had the opportunity to visit. I also truly feel that it reinforces my statement earlier that what is submitted to the internet is very often difficult to remove. Sites like this are built with the intent to preserve data. In our situation as investigators, we leverage the information available to us. Sites like this make it easier to be able to dig into long forgotten tweets, messages, profiles, and information that others have forgotten about, lost access to, or attempted to destroy.

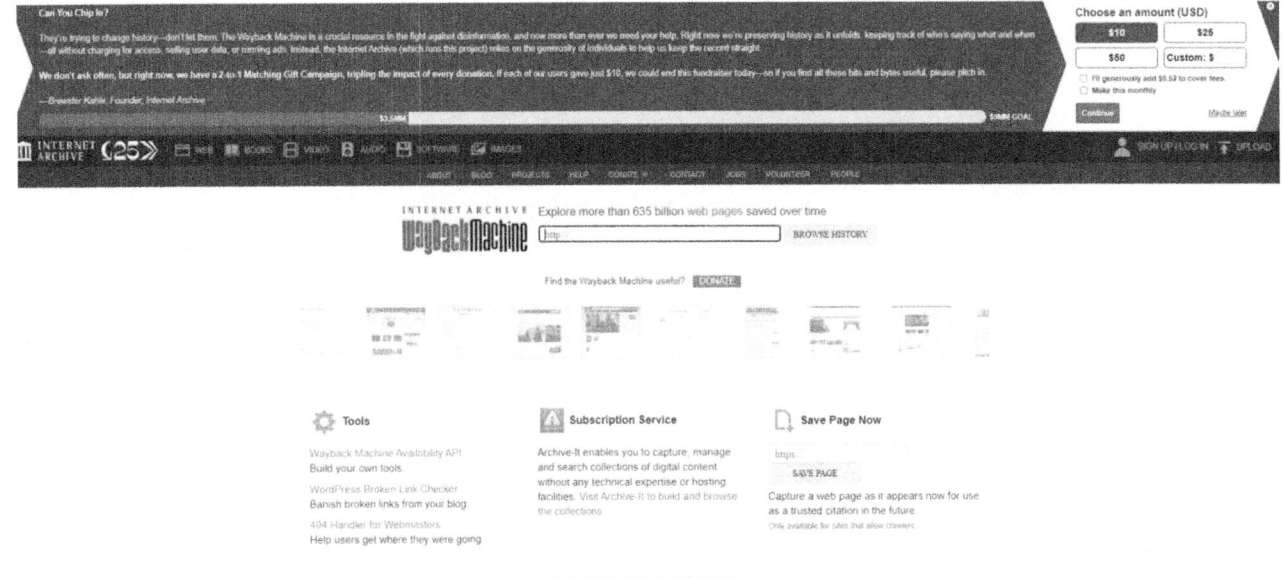

The way that you utilize this search function is simply to input the address of the page that you are searching for. Say that you do know the name of the person whom you are researching. You would plug in their username in the search bar and press enter and any pages that they have had under that name will populate.

Final words

We have only reviewed a small handful of tools that are available to investigators today. This is in no way to say that these are the only methods of searching for users who have attempted to bury their posts. I have referenced additional resources that I have worked with in my pursuits of targets and data needed to be obtained. The sky is truly the limit as we are continued to be forced with turning to out of the box solutions. We owe many of these due to out of the box thinking. And we will continue to create alternatives and refine what we use now as time goes on.

References

[1] *Twitter*. OSINT Essentials. (n.d.). Retrieved December 6, 2021, from https://www.osintessentials.com/twitter.

[2] *OSINT Tools*. OSINT Techniques. (n.d.). Retrieved December 6, 2021, from https://www.osinttechniques.com/osint-tools.html.

[3] Agarwal, A. (2020, June 10). *The best twitter search tricks*. Digital Inspiration. Retrieved December 6, 2021, from https://www.labnol.org/internet/twitter-search-tricks/13693/.

[4] *Twitter search tool – twitter investigations*. Aware Online Academy. (2019, August 5). Retrieved December 6, 2021, https://www.aware-online.com/en/osint-tools/twitter-search-tool/.

[5] *Internet Archive Wayback Machine*. Internet archive: Wayback Machine. (n.d.). Retrieved December 6, 2021, from **https://archive.org/web/**.

[6] *Search for a user on Twitter*. (n.d.). Aware Online. photograph. Retrieved December 6, 2021, from https://www.aware-online.com/en/osint-tools/twitter-search-tool/.

[7] *Search for a user on Twitter (combinations)*. (n.d.). Aware Online. photograph. Retrieved December 6, 2021, from https://www.aware-online.com/en/osint-tools/twitter-search-tool/.

[8] *Analyzing an account on Twitter*. (n.d.). Aware Online. photograph. Retrieved December 6, 2021, from https://www.aware-online.com/en/osint-tools/twitter-search-tool/.

[9] *Search for posts on Twitter*. (n.d.). Aware Online. photograph. Retrieved December 6, 2021, from https://www.aware-online.com/en/osint-tools/twitter-search-tool/.

[10] *Search for messages on Twitter (combinations)*. (n.d.). Aware Online. photograph. Retrieved December 6, 2021, from https://www.aware-online.com/en/osint-tools/twitter-search-tool/.

[11] *Search for messages from a specific location*. (n.d.). Aware Online. photograph. Retrieved December 6, 2021, from https://www.aware-online.com/en/osint-tools/twitter-search-tool/.

[12] *Search for posts posted at a specific date/between dates*. (n.d.). Aware Online. photograph. Retrieved December 6, 2021, from https://www.aware-online.com/en/osint-tools/twitter-search-tool/.

OSINT With Google GAIA Numbers

By: Jerry Hartsell

The purpose of this article is to briefly explain what a GAIA Number is, how to find it, and how you can use it while conducting OSINT investigations to find a person's location, reviews, calendar, etc. It is also ideal for the average user of the internet who may not be aware of the extent of information you may make available for anyone to see. The idea behind this article was inspired by an OSINT challenge titled "ID Exposed", hosted on one of my favorite platforms: HackTheBox.

Sure, there are tons of tools and scripts that do this, one of my favorites being Ghunt, but I'm a firm believer in the importance and benefit of knowing how to do things manually. So, let's get started.

What is a GAIA Number?

First off, some of you are probably asking, "What is a GAIA Number and how does it relate to me and my privacy?!" Well, GAIA stands for "Google Accounts and ID Administration" and is a 21-digit unique user identifier Google assigns to each account associated with a Google domain (email@gmail.com), or any other e-mail address from another domain that has been configured by a G-Suite administrator.

Through the course of this article, you'll see what it has to do with you and your privacy. More on that later

Before we jump in to finding the GAIA number, we'll pretend we're conducting some OSINT on some individual(s). Since the GAIA is associated with Gmail or G-Suite, we first need to verify that our target has an account! So, let's do that first!

Verifying an account

Let's say you have a list of usernames which you're seeking to find as much information as you can about the owners of the accounts. For demonstration purposes, let's suppose you have the following usernames:

- Obviouslyfakeaccount
- Superfakeaccount123
- Forafakepurposeonly123

To verify an account, go to Google's login page:

Now you will enter one of the usernames you are researching to verify whether it is a real account:

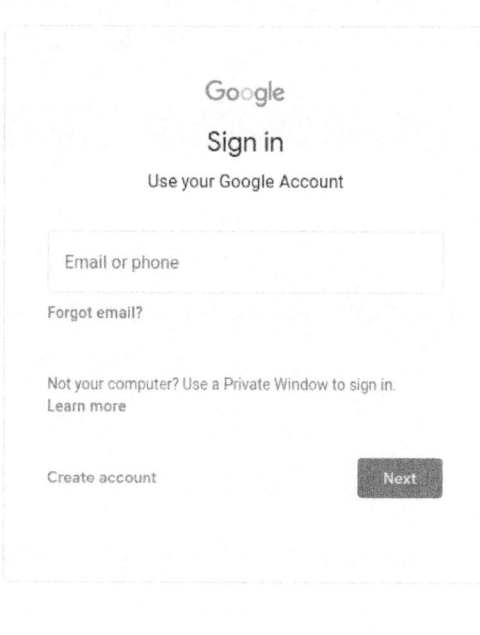

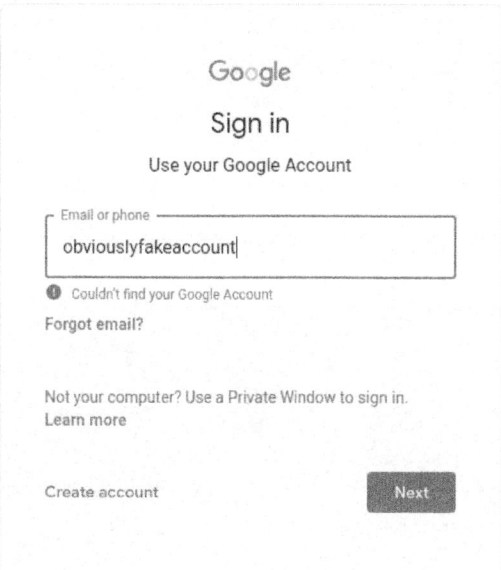

Note: If an account does not exist, Google will let you know that it could not find the account

So, what happens when we hit next? Well, success will come in the form of a new form:

Note: Do NOT attempt to enter the password unless it is your own personal account!

As you can see, if the account exists, Google will redirect you to a new form and request a password. This verification process can also be done via the command line as well.

To verify via command line, simply enter the following curl command:

```
curl -v mail.google.com/mail/gxlu?email=user@gmail.com
```

So, in our case, it would look like this:

```
csi@csi:~$ curl -v https://mail.google.com/mail/gxlu?email=forafakepurposeonly123@gmail.com
```

This command will supply you with a lot of information in the output, but how can you tell if it is an account of not? Well, let's look. We only need to focus on the bottom section of the output.

When we curl:

> curl -v mail.google.com/mail/gxlu?email=obviouslyfakeaccount@gmail.com

We receive the following output:

Note: Keep in mind that "obviouslyfakeaccount" was NOT found to be an existing account

```
> GET /mail/gxlu?email=obviouslyfakeaccount@gmail.com HTTP/2
> Host: mail.google.com
> user-agent: curl/7.68.0
> accept: */*
>
* TLSv1.3 (IN), TLS handshake, Newsession Ticket (4):
* TLSv1.3 (IN), TLS handshake, Newsession Ticket (4):
* old SSL session ID is stale, removing
* Connection state changed (MAX_CONCURRENT_STREAMS == 30)!
< HTTP/2 204
< cache-control: no-cache, no-store, max-age=0, must-revalidate
< pragma: no-cache
< expires: Mon, 01 Jan 1990 00:00:00 GMT
< date: Mon, 22 Nov 2021 00:16:11 GMT
< server: GSE
< alt-svc: clear
```

Now when we curl:

> curl -v mail.google.com/mail/gxlu?email=forafakepurposeonly123@gmail.com

We receive the following output:

```
> GET /mail/gxlu?email=forafakepurposeonly123@gmail.com HTTP/2
> Host: mail.google.com
> user-agent: curl/7.68.0
> accept: */*
>
* TLSv1.3 (IN), TLS handshake, Newsession Ticket (4):
* TLSv1.3 (IN), TLS handshake, Newsession Ticket (4):
* old SSL session ID is stale, removing
* Connection state changed (MAX_CONCURRENT_STREAMS == 30)!
< HTTP/2 204
< cache-control: no-cache, no-store, max-age=0, must-revalidate
< pragma: no-cache
< expires: Mon, 01 Jan 1990 00:00:00 GMT
< date: Mon, 29 Nov 2021 22:59:57 GMT
< server: GSE
< set-cookie: COMPASS=gmail=CooBAAlriVeHXAovojYItFFlVDYuxnlA8EbT1ehg
wX1pnjnNfQt9s5iwph2OSDgqw_2Oqh_iBW6I7kqGWnK9V_KH5xMKG52sVZEKLTlY0GGp
H8peGE_g0u21YLKl6VMD9NasDbc1MmitbaG5ol4emgJ3poLASdrPsuK43xIj_4PsUIoL
T; path=/mail; Secure; HttpOnly
< alt-svc: clear
<
* Connection #0 to host mail.google.com left intact
```

As you can see, when the account is an actual Google account, the curl command will output a "set-cookie" parameter. So, there you have it.

Forafakepurposeonly123@gmail.com is a real account. Now we can find the GAIA Number!

Finding GAIA Numbers

So, you have a valid Google account. Maybe you are interested in seeing if that account has checked in to any locations of interest. How would you do that? Well first, you need to find the *Google Accounts and ID Administration* number, which we'll refer to as GAIA. Follow the steps below and you'll be able to locate the GAIA number in no time.

Finding GAIA in Google Hangouts

1. Add the google account to your own google contacts. If you don't have a google account, make a fake one, even if it is for this one time use to learn a new trick.
2. Creating a contact is easy. Simply go to your Google Contacts page, click "Create contact" and enter the   appropriate information:

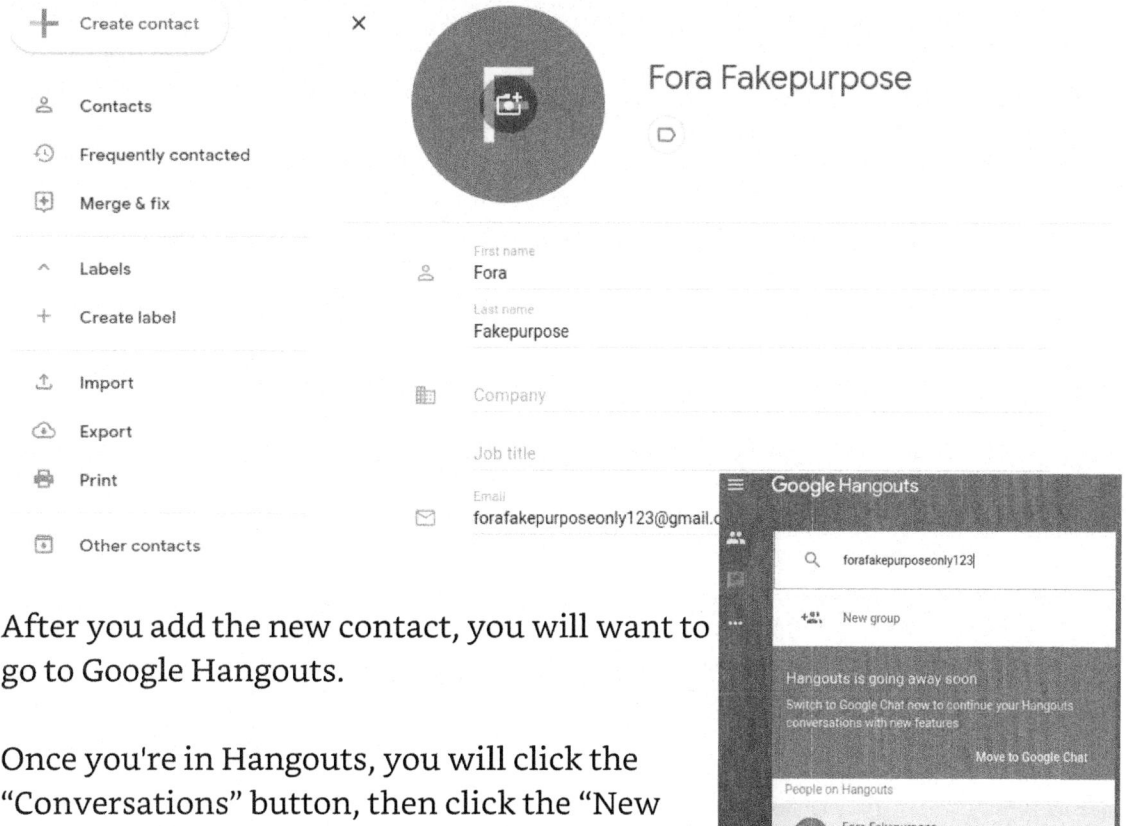

3. After you add the new contact, you will want to go to Google Hangouts.

   Once you're in Hangouts, you will click the "Conversations" button, then click the "New conversation" button and enter in your new contact that you just created.

4. Now right click on email address and choose "Inspect". Alternatively, you can hold CTRL+SHIFT+C and that will open the Developer Tools as well.
5. In the Dev Tools Inspector, you will want to find the "oid" as seen below:

```
▼<div class="xjI6Lb">
  ▼<ul class="tj">
    ▼<li class="eh XcEgrf fp pu hy" hovercard-oid="111524361474613883186" hovercard-email="forafakepurposeonly123@gmail.com"
      oid="111524361474613883186" draggable="true"> event  flex
      ▶<div class="yYPPEY pJ">…</div>
      ▼<div class="Jv"> flex
        ::before
        ▼<div class="Kv"> flex
          <div id=":i8.ti" class="qmDVub cj DNdEBb">Fora Fakepurpose</div>
          <div class="ElsTJc Rj">forafakepurposeonly123@gmail.com</div>
        </div>
      </div>
```

In our case, the OID is: **111524361474613883186**. This is the GAIA number that belongs to that account.

I would like to add that if you followed me thus far, you would have noticed Google's information alert in Hangouts stating that Hangouts will be going away soon, encouraging you to try "Chats" instead. The same principles can be applied to Chats as well.

Finding GAIA in Google Chats

1. Go to Google Chats and then click "Find a chat"

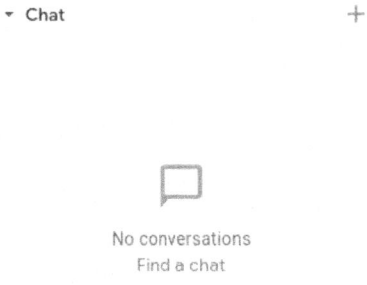

2. Search for your new contact to start a chat with.

3. Just like before, in Hangouts, you will right-click the e-mail address and choose "Inspect"

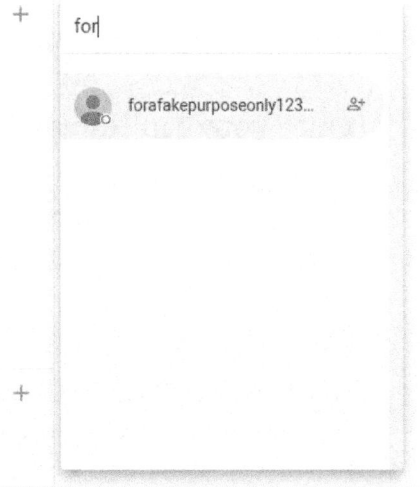

Note: This is a lot trickier than Hangouts, but the same information is still available, it's just displayed differently.

Within the <body> there will be a particular <div> layer that contains an <iframe>. Inside the <body> of that iframe will be another <div> layer that contains a "jsdata" parameter which will show the GAIA number.

There you have it. The same GAIA number from Hangouts but hidden in the source of the new Chats service. Granted, it is more difficult to find via Chats, but Hangouts will be gone soon, so Chats will be your only option out of those 2 eventually. To make it a little easier to find, you could always search for "jsdata" and cycle through the results until you come across what appears to be the correct GAIA number.

I find those 2 methods a little easier on the eyes, however, you can still find the GAIA number in Google Contacts as well. I saved this method for last because in my opinion, it is the most difficult to find.

Finding GAIA in Google Contacts

1. Create a new contact as we previously did in "Finding GAIA in Google Hangouts" section. If your contact already exists, simply bring up the contact as if you were going to edit it.
2. Also as in the previous sections, right-click the email address and click "Inspect"
3. In the inspect window, you will search for whatever name you gave your contact. In this example, I will search for "Fora Fakepurpose" since that is the name I designated to my contact.

You will notice in one of the <script nonce=""> sections, there will be a block of data that matches our search query. In this block of data, you will find the GAIA, however, it does not carry the "oid", "jsdata" or any other easily recognizable parameter that we found in the other methods previously explained. From what I found though, the number is shown twice in that block of data, and I underlined each instance so you can get a better idea of how/where to look.

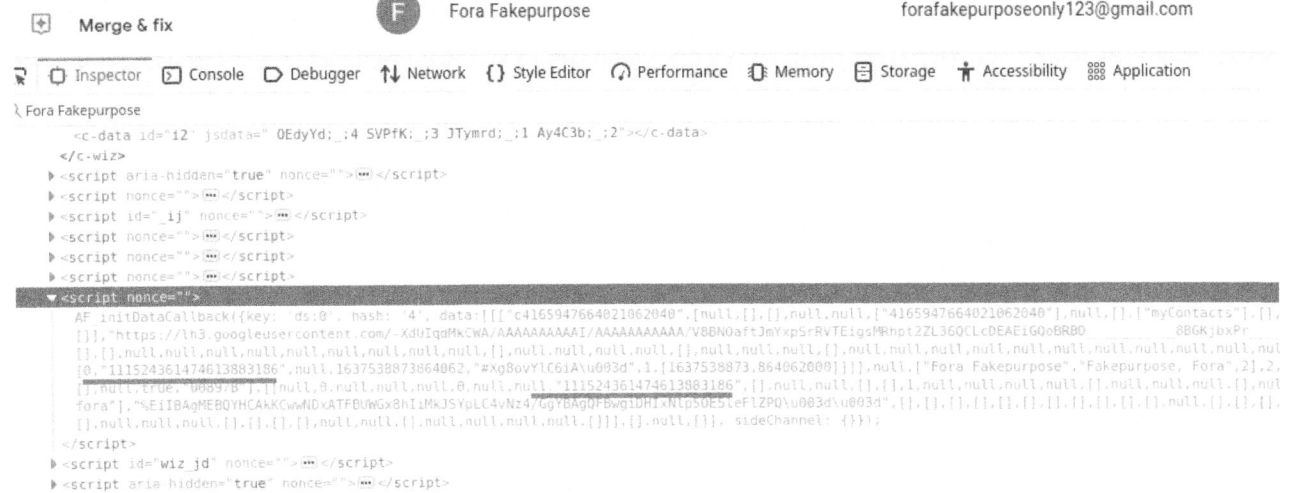

As you can see, 3 different ways to obtain the unique GAIA #. There may be more ways, but I will leave them for you to find on your own if you're interested.

Moving forward, now that we successfully found your user's GAIA number, what can we do with it? Maybe we can find locations/check-ins, reviews, etc.? That sounds fun, right? Let's see how it's done.

Finding locations, reviews, etc.

Now that you have verified an account exists and found its associated GAIA number, we can have a little bit of fun. Say you're investigating a person but you're not quite sure of any of the places they visit. Well, we can take that GAIA # and potentially discover any reviews they may have left an establishment, or checked in to, if they decided to leave a review and otherwise allow their account information to be seen publicly. Yes, these following 'tricks' will only truly work if the user has their privacy settings set to allow their information to be seen publicly. Otherwise, you'll unfortunately hit a dead end.

Anyway, we have a valid user, we have a GAIA #, so let's just see what we can find.

1. Go to the following URL: google.com/maps/contrib/<GAIA #>
    In our case, we would visit the URL:

    google.com/maps/contrib/111524361474613883186

If the user has checked in, added a review, or posted photos with their account, it will show here. As seen below, Fora Fakepurpose posted a review to a Chicago restaurant:

I only visited one place for the sake of this assignment, but you can imagine how much data you might be able to find on certain people who take advantage of Google's check-in/reviews/etc.

You can also note, on the previous photo it shows "1 contribution >". Had Fora reviewed multiple establishments, you would be able to click on the contributions to view them all.

Finding Calendars with GAIA

Yes, we can even find a user's calendar with their email. The same rule applies though. The user must have their calendar set to public! Otherwise, random strangers such as yourself won't be able to view them. However, I've found that in some work settings, such as office spaces, companies will sometimes keep a lot of things public to make it easier for all the departments to communicate and retrieve information. So that is something to keep in mind.

To reiterate, finding a user's calendar is by far the easiest thing to do out of what we discussed thus far. It only requires 2 things.

- A valid user account
- Calendar(s) set to Public

I went ahead and set up Fora Fakepurposes' calendar to public with a couple events placed in November and December of 2021 for example purposes.

All you need to do is visit the following URL:

calendar.google.com/calendar/u/0/embed?src=ADD-GMAIL-ADDRESS-HERE

In our case, you can browse to:

calendar.google.com/calendar/u/0/embed?src=forafakepurposeonly123@gmail.com

So... How does all of this actually work?

In short, Google has TONS of APIs (Application Programming Interfaces) which allow communication with Google Services and their integration to other services. Unfortunately, I'm not a programmer or any kind of developer, so I can't really explain too much about APIs except that I know they're responsible for allowing us to extract user data.

Google even has a web page where you can play around with some of their APIs.

To keep in scope of this article, I'll share one page with you, but I encourage you to navigate the page and play around.

If you go to: developers.google.com/people/api/rest/v1/people/get

You will be greeted with Google's People API, which you can test out on your own. The page itself has tons of information and explains things better than I could, but it is pretty simple to use. I'll show an example below

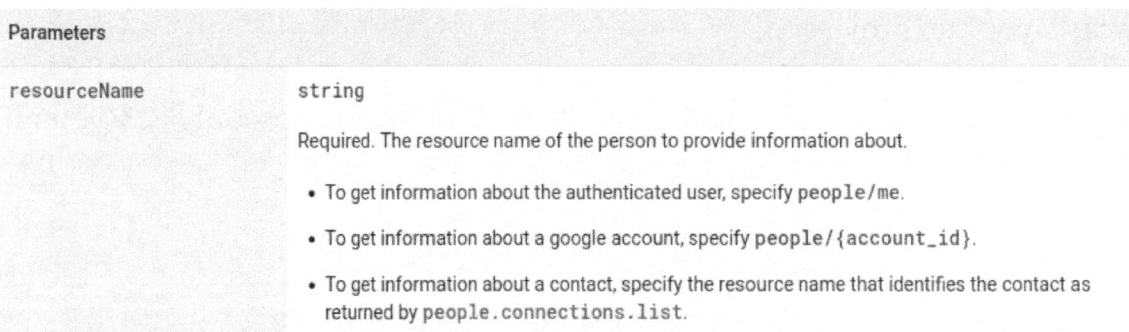

At the top of the page, you can see the basic syntax of how this will work.

We see the 2nd bullet point; we must set the resourceName to "people/{account_id}"

As explained previously, the account ID is the GAIA number. So, we'll use the same one we've been using.

The next input will be "personFields". Again, the web page has a detailed list of values to enter here, such as but not limited to addresses, events, locations, photos, relations, etc.

Note: Keep in mind majority, if not all these things must be *set to Public in order for them to be seen by prying eyes**

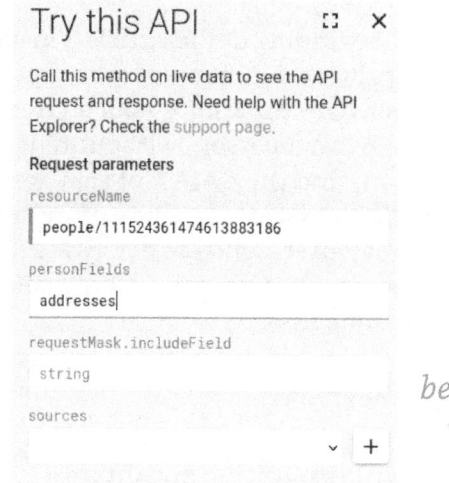

With that said, let's try addresses.

Everything else can stay default, so go ahead and click the Execute button.

```
200 OK                                          ✕

  {
    "resourceName": "people/1115243614746138831
    "etag": "%EgUBEC43QBoEAQIFByIMcjE2Wnk4TmV4W
    "addresses": [
      {
        "metadata": {
          "primary": true,
          "source": {
            "type": "PROFILE",
            "id": "1115243614746613883186"
          }
        },
        "formattedValue": "123 fake street",
        "type": "home",
        "formattedType": "Home"
      }
    ]
```

As you can see, since we called the resourceName of
"people/1115243614746613883186" with the personFields value set to "addresses" -the
"formattedValue" in the json output shows the address of the user!

The downside to this, a user can obviously enter any address they wish when they create their account. However, it could still be useful information depending on the target.

Final Words...

In the beginning of this article, I mentioned that you might be asking what a GAIA has to do with you and your privacy. I'm hoping by now you can see exactly what I was meaning to convey in that regard. You saw how an innocent e-mail address is more than enough to virtually find out everything you need to know about a person, without relying on tools or programming. You now know how to verify a Google account, find the GAIA # of that account, and if the user doesn't really care about their privacy, you will be able to extract all kinds of information. This is great for OSINT Investigators, but not so great for everyday users who are not aware. So, if anything, regardless of who you may be; an OSINT Investigator or just an average person browsing the web, I hope you enjoyed the article, and I hope you learned something new.

Until next time.

Links of inspiration and interest

- HackTheBox Challenge-   app.hackthebox.com/challenges/id-exposed
- ID Exposed Writeup   -   samanthactf.medium.com/hack-the-box-id-exposed-60a6034c4c19
- Ghunt   -   github.com/mxrch/ghunt
- Google APIs Explorer -   developers.google.com/apis-explorer/

Cool Tool: Karma v2

Karma v2 is a Passive Open Source Intelligence (OSINT) Automated Reconnaissance (framework).

This can be used by Infosec Researchers, Penetration Testers, Bug Hunters to find deep information, more assets, WAF/CDN bypassed IPs, Internal/External Infra, publicly exposed leaks and many more about their target. Shodan Premium API key is required to use this automation.

https://github.com/Dheerajmadhukar/karma_v2nvestigate Windows endpoints that are infected/compromised and offline, on-line, dead, in on-premises, remote, or the cloud, with speed and accuracy.

This is an agentless stand-alone software (which requires no installation) that allows ANYONE to investigate ANY Windows endpoint ANYWHERE the endpoint may be--whether on-premises, in the cloud, offline, "dead" hard drives, with or without an Internet connection

https://www.netsecurity.com/threatresponder-forensics/

Maltego

By: Khadija Naz

"Maltego is software used for open-source intelligence and forensics, developed by Paterva from Pretoria, South Africa. Maltego focuses on providing a library of transforms for discovery of data from open sources, and visualizing that information in a graph format, suitable for link analysis and data mining." [wikipedia.org]

Features

Maltego supports the creation of custom entities, permitting it to express any sort of data in addition to the software's basic entity types. Maltego's basic features are:

- Mine: Collect data from different sources with ease.
- Merge: All data is automatically linked and combined into a single graph.
- Map: Investigate your data's links visually.

Maltego is available on CSI Linux and Parrot, else you can also download it from https://www.maltego.com/downloads/

How to use Maltego

In this we will demonstrate how Investigator use Maltego to find information of a person, any domain or website.

Person Reconnaissance

Maltego help us to find different information about person like its email address, its information shared on social media, phone number and friends etc. So, let's start it.

1. Start Maltego.

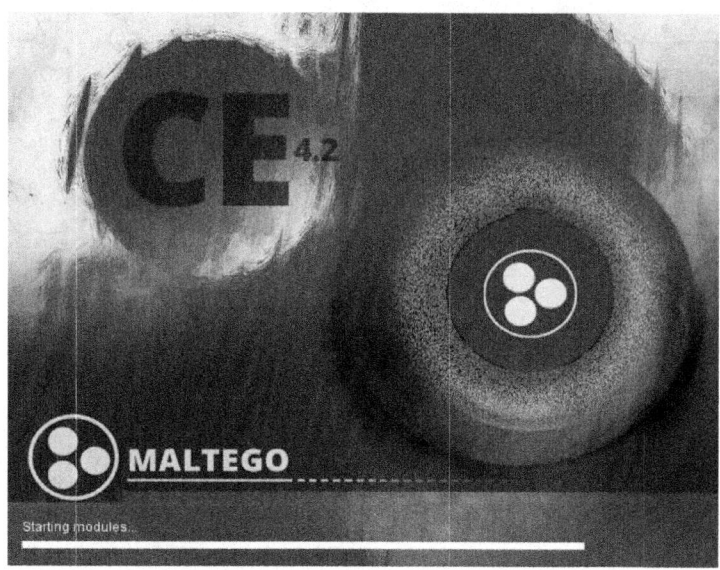

2. Create a new graph

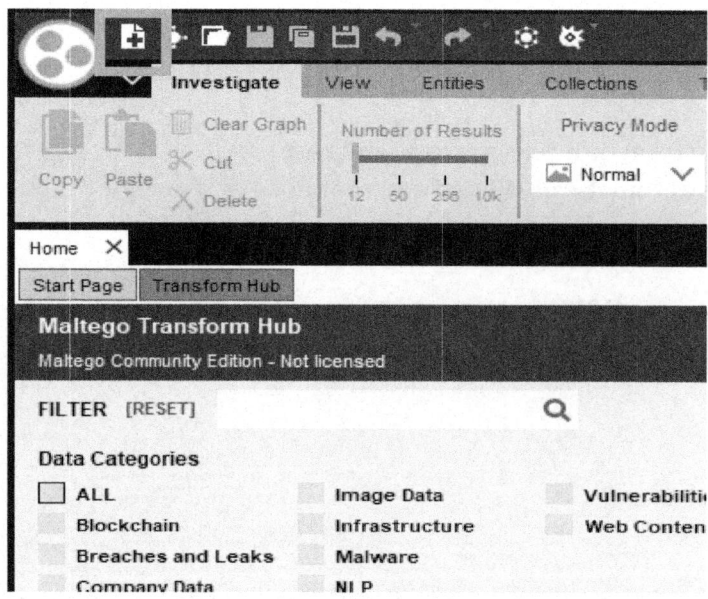

3. Now select person entity from Entity Platte and drag it to graph.

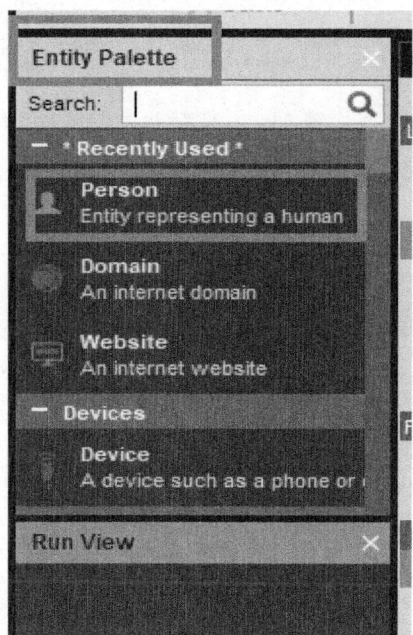

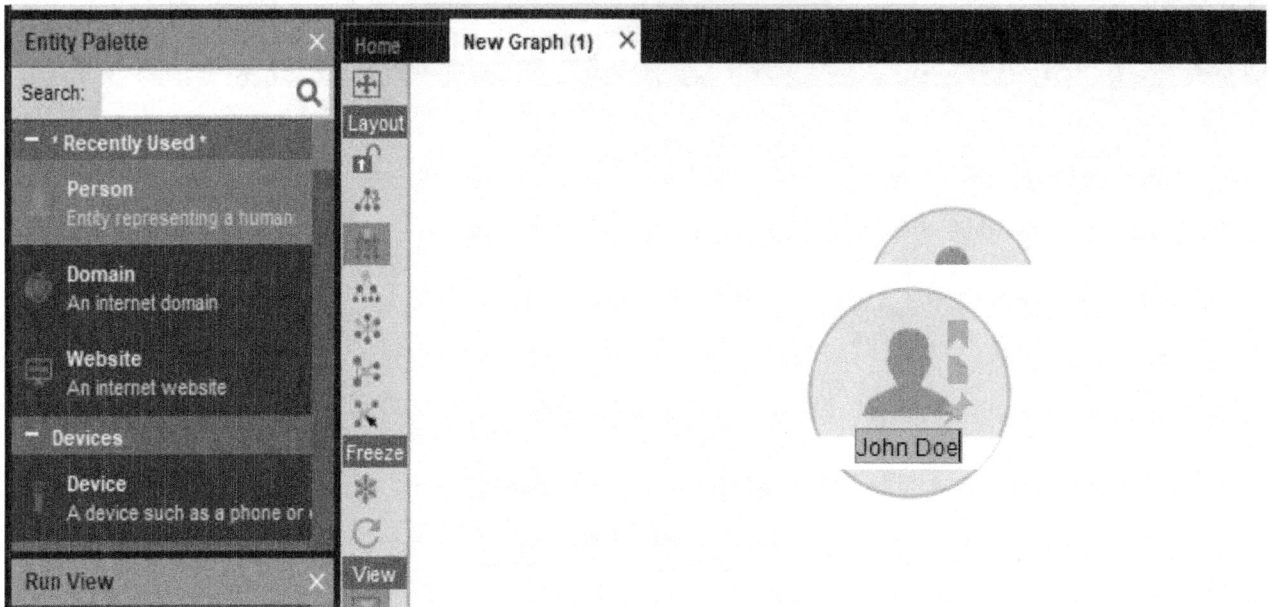

4. Double click on the name of person entity and write the name whose information we want to get.

We will search for information on Elon Musk.

5. Right click on the entity and select option relevant to person information.

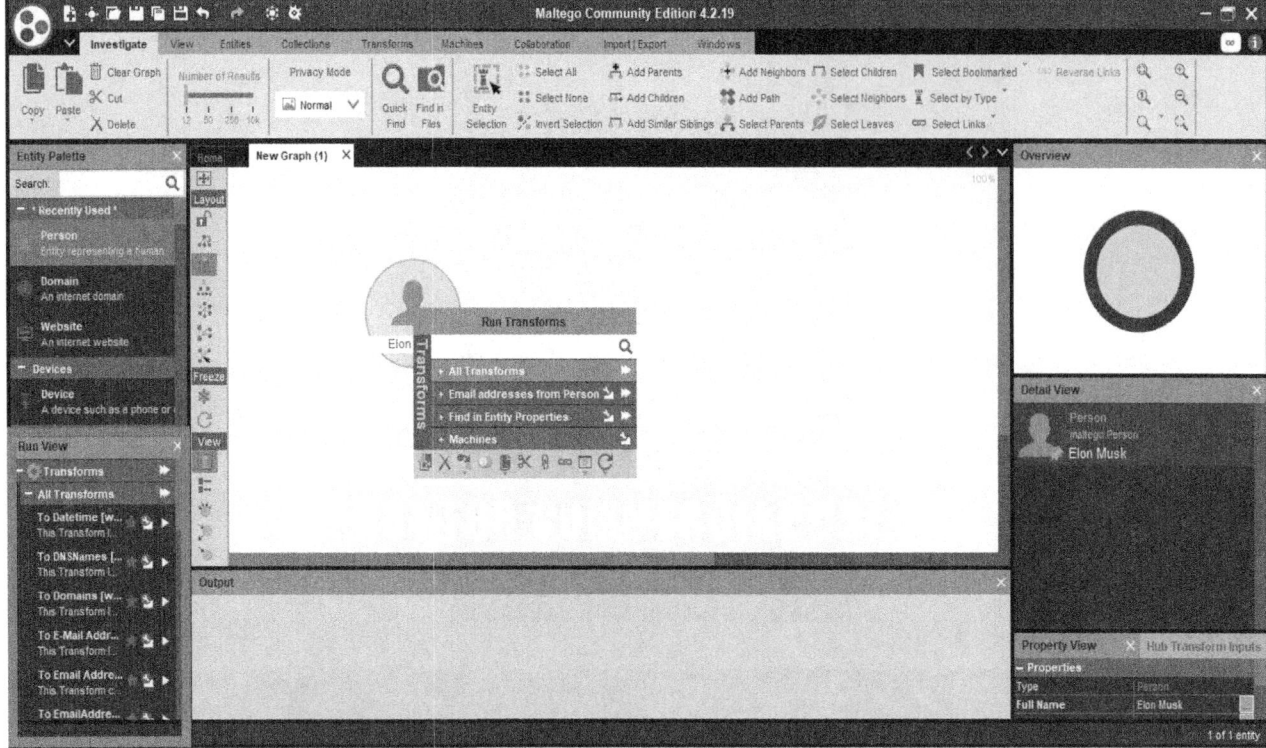

6. Now find email addresses of a person and left click on

7. Two options will be shown, we can select any relevant option

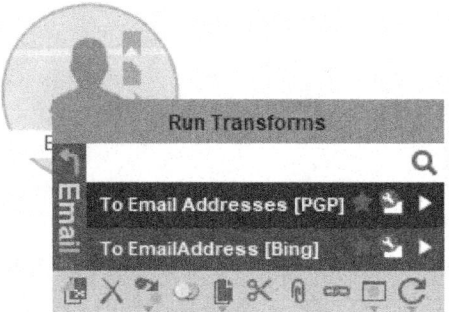

Or we can also run all option in email category by run button.

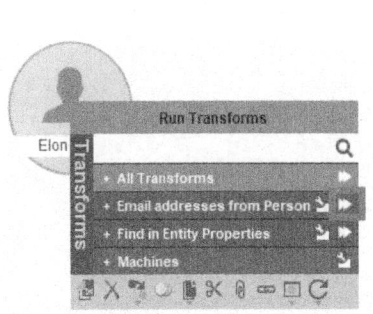

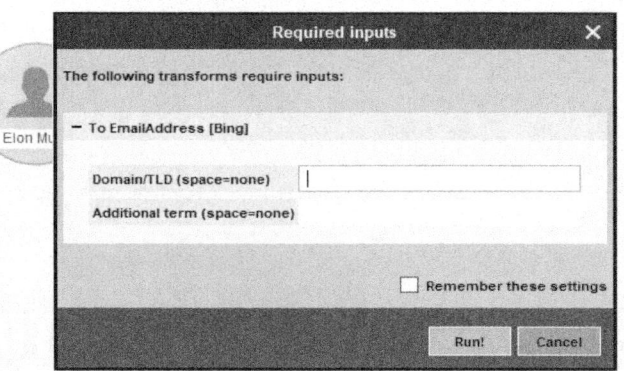

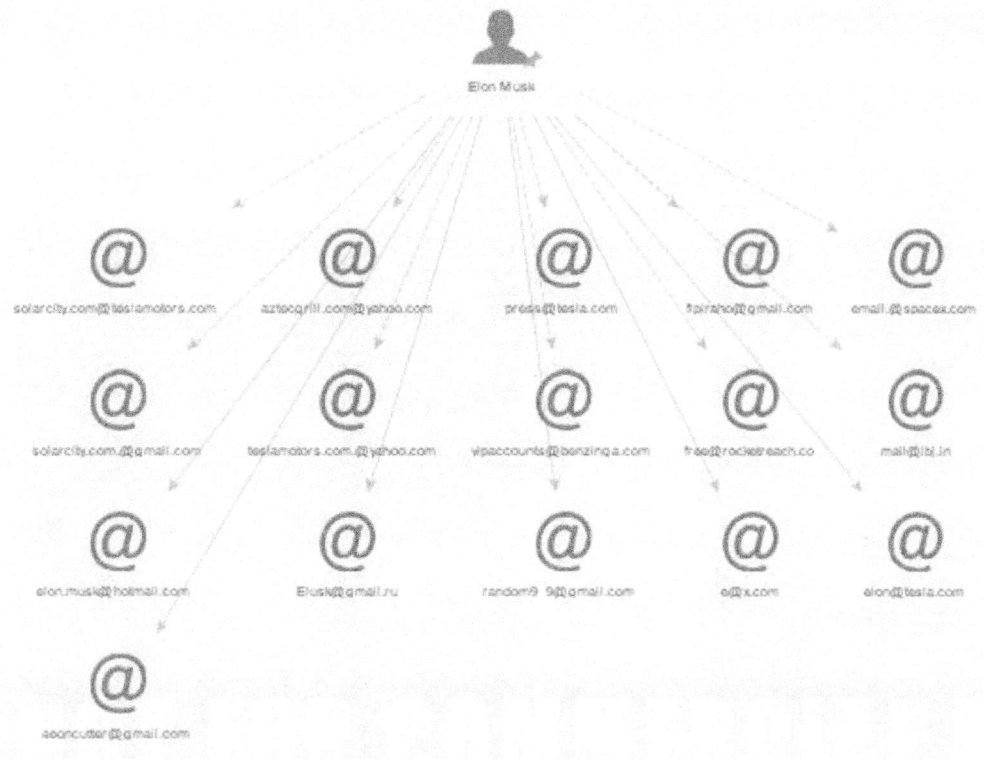

Maltego also have an option to check that the email is valid and exist or not.

1. Right click on any email entity and select email address

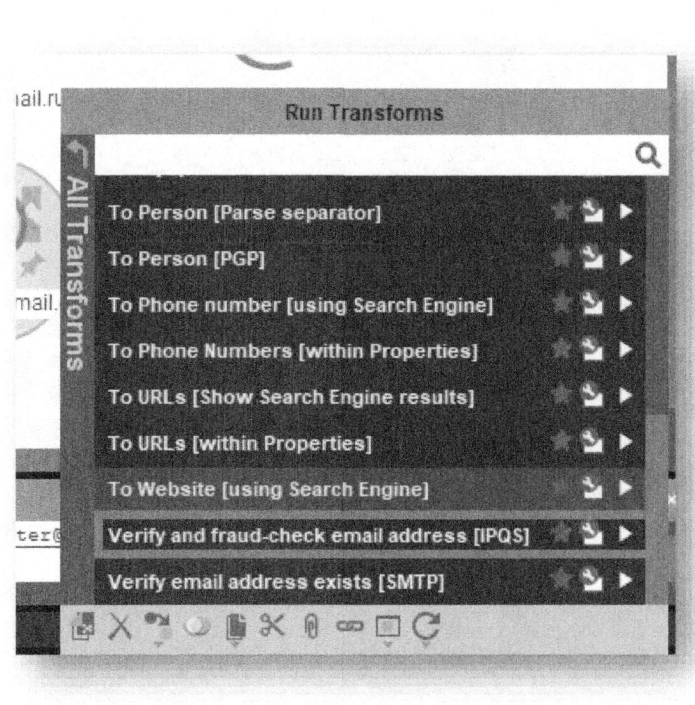

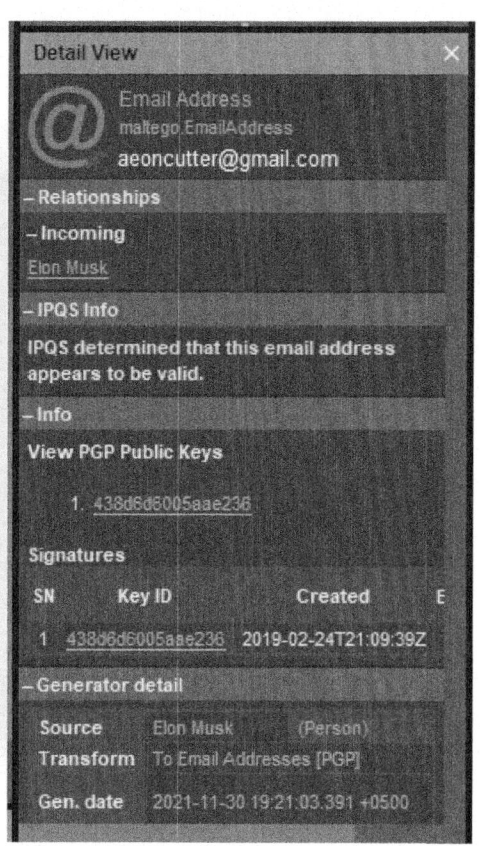

Similarly, we can find phone number of a person.

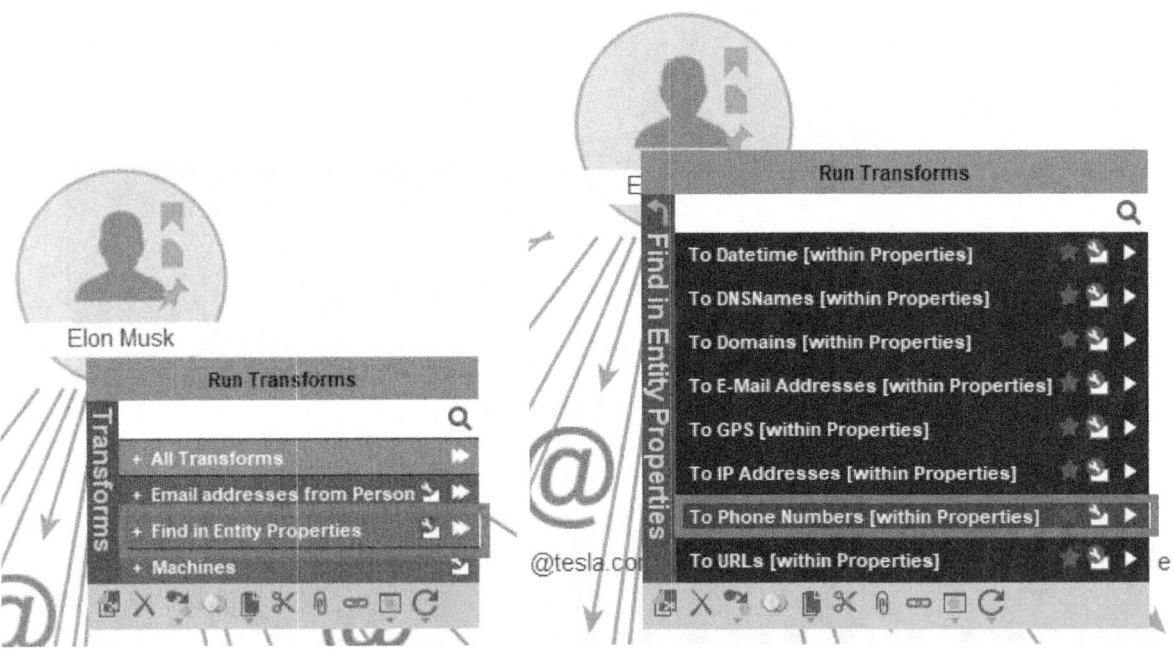

We can also run all transformation which extract phone number of a person from different websites of data sources.

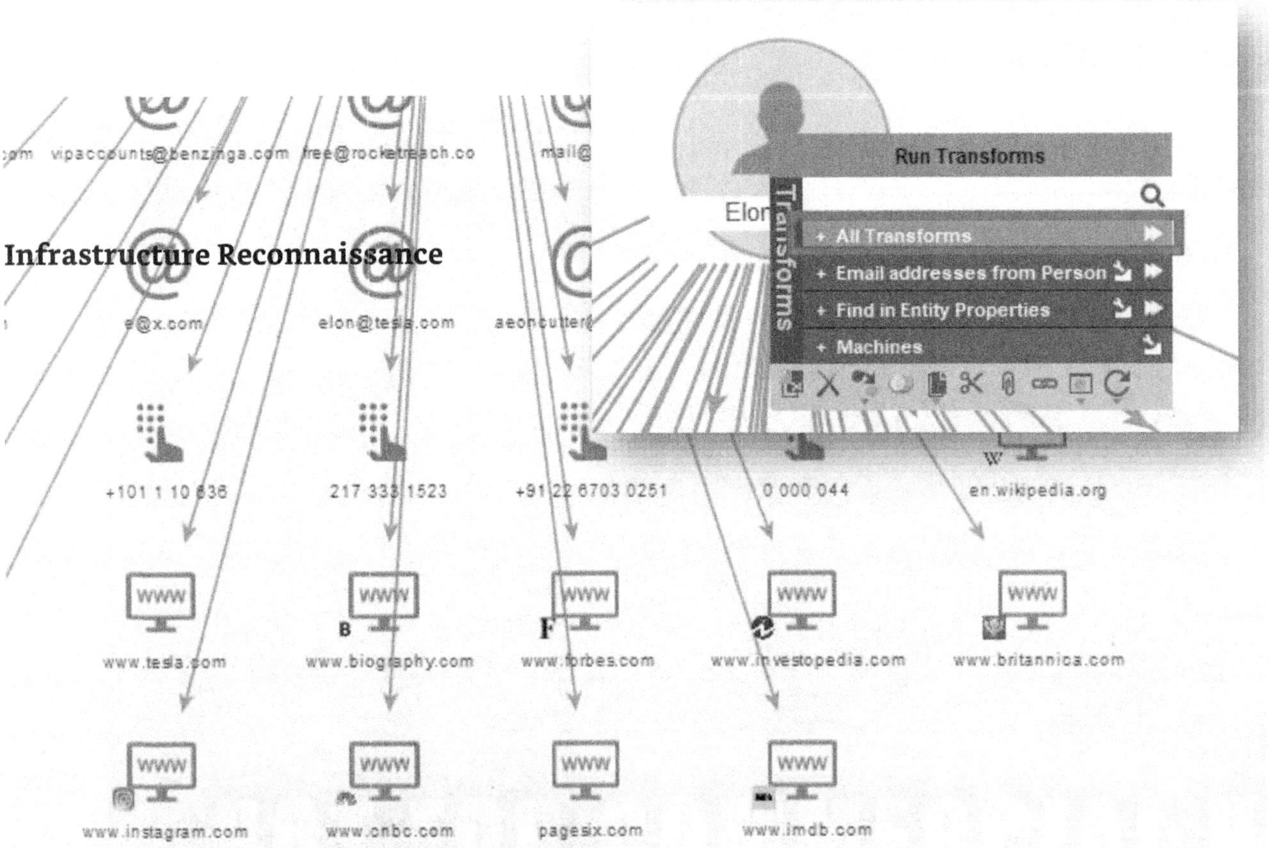

Infrastructure Reconnaissance

Maltego helps to gather information about infrastructure like domain and websites information. Now we will gather Domain information. We select and drag domain entity from entity palette to graph, and right click on the entity and we will choose relevant option.

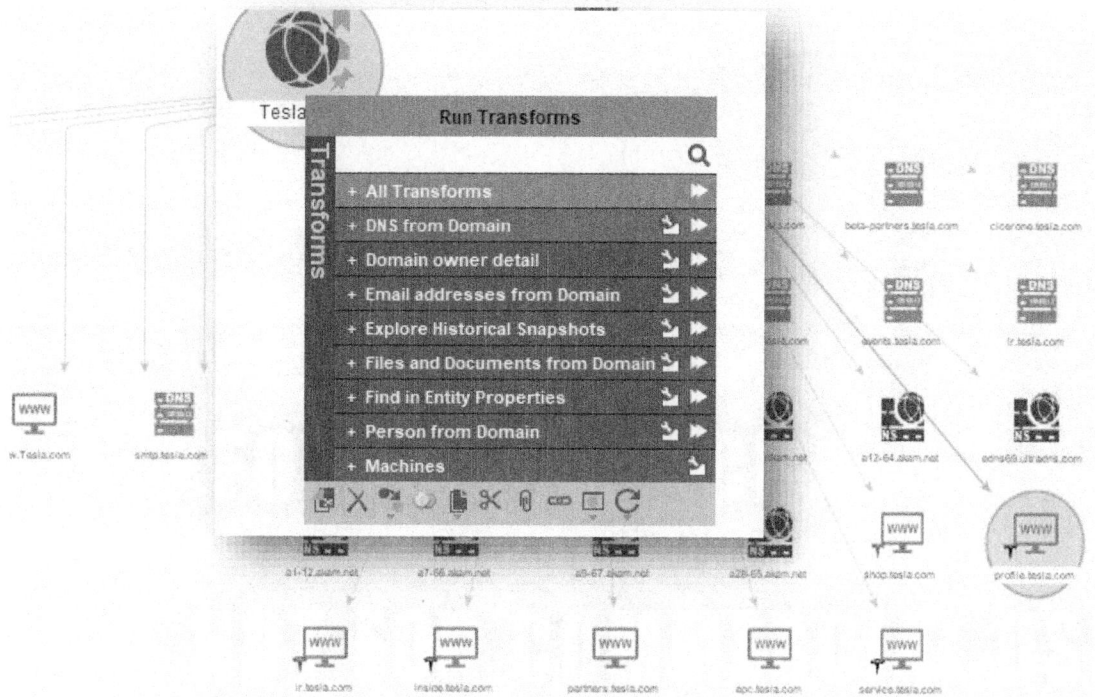

Keep going down the list

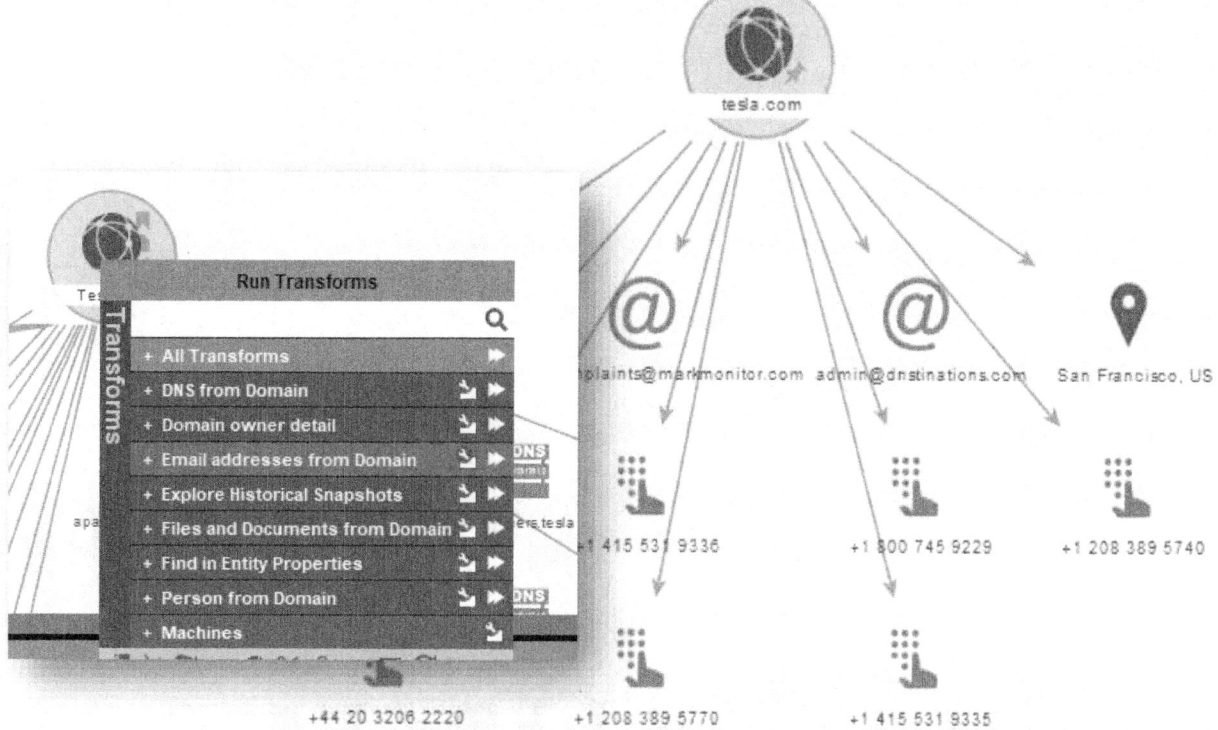

Let's look for users at Tesla, that have a PGP key, commonly used with emails.

1. Right click on the Tesla.com icon

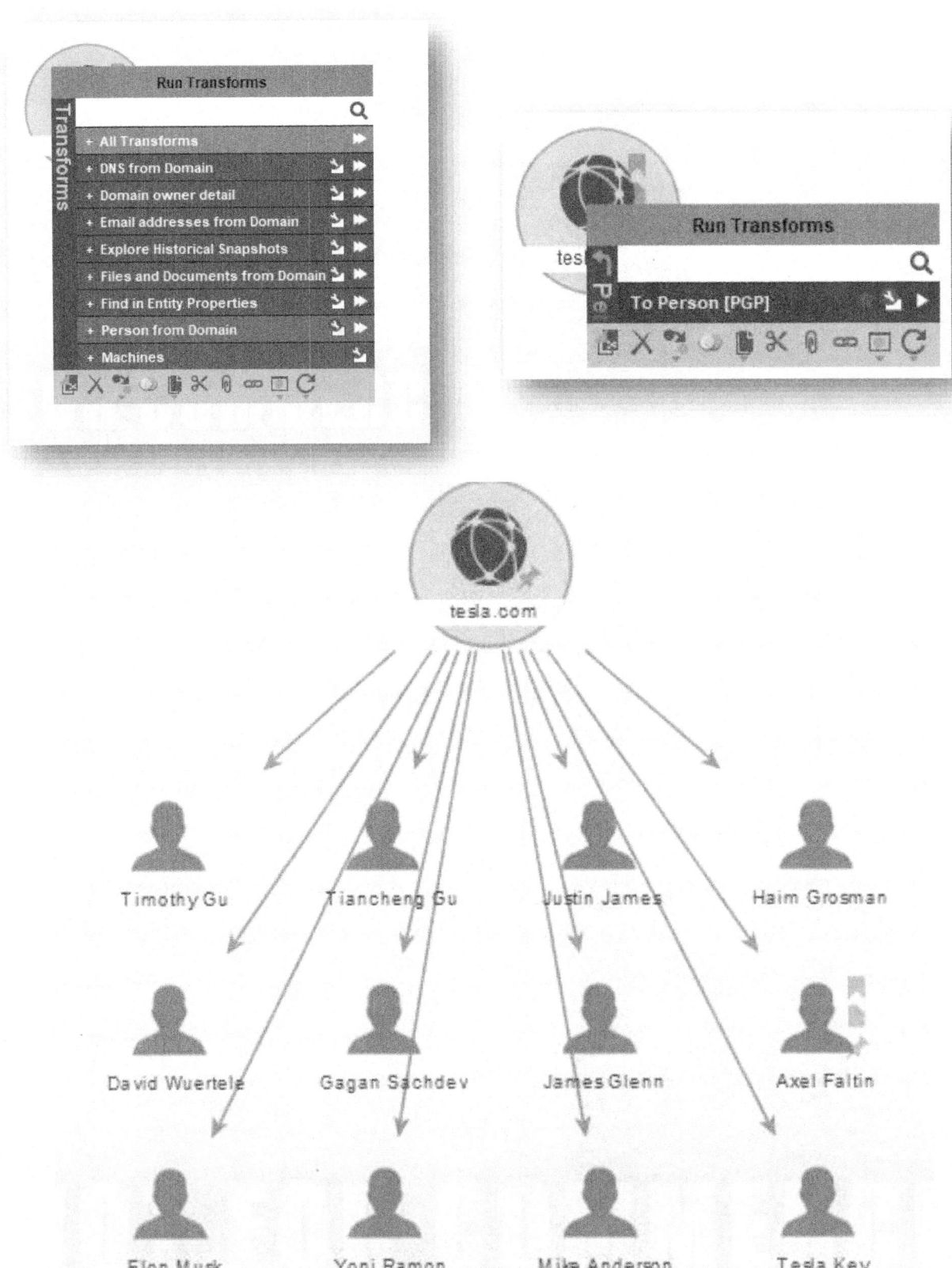

Generating Report

Maltego has a feature to generate report in different format like xml, image, or table.

Let's generate a report

1. Left click Import Export
2. Left click on "Generate Report"

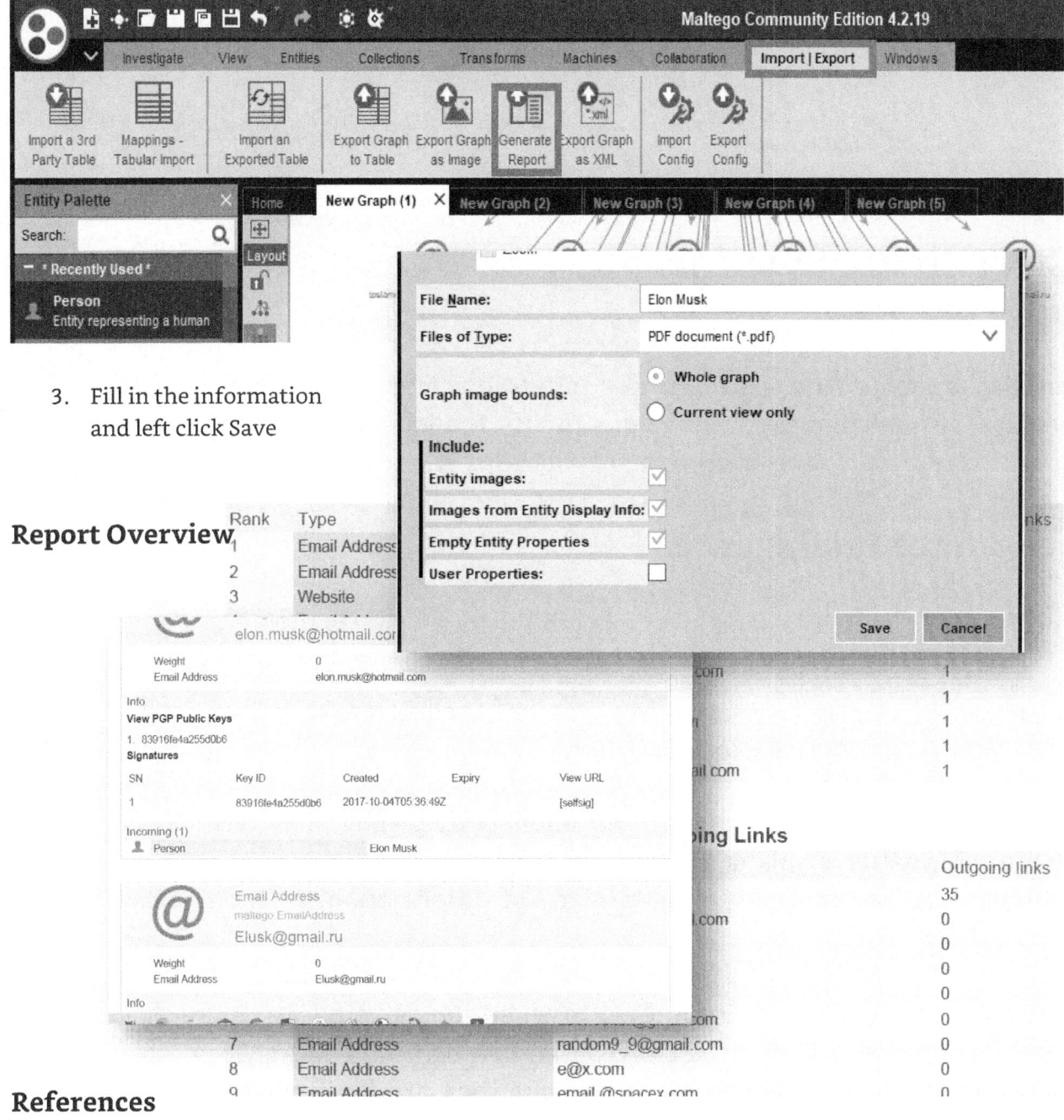

3. Fill in the information and left click Save

Report Overview

References

https://en.wikipedia.org/wiki/Maltego
https://www.maltego.com/

OSINT In ICS Systems

By: Frederico Ferreira

Industrial systems are getting more attention from an attacker's perspective; nowadays, search engines like Shodan simplify the job of finding vulnerable SCADA, ICS or IoT connected to the internet that is not correctly protected.

Open Source Intelligence

According to U.S. public law, open-source intelligence:

- Is produced from publicly available information
- Is collected, analyzed, and disseminated promptly to an appropriate audience
- Addresses a specific intelligence requirement

The critical phrase to focus on here is "publicly available." The term "open source" refers to information available for public consumption. If any specialist skills, tools, or techniques are required to access a piece of information, it can't reasonably be considered open source.

Open-source information is not limited to what you can find using the major search engines. Web pages and other resources that can be found using Google constitute a massive open-source information source, but they are far from the only sources.[1] Attackers and defenders collect OSINT from a variety of sources. This is not an exhaustive list but demonstrates the types of publicly available information that could facilitate attack planning:[2]

- Search engines
- Social media websites
- Job listings
- Websites
- Vendor websites and documentation, including installation docs containing default passwords
- Financial and legal resources such as 10-K filings or indictments
- Government and regulation authority body websites
- Reconnaissance tools such as Shodan or Censys
- Online scanning engines such as VirusTotal
- Business solicitation portals such as VendorLink
- Usernames and passwords in public repositories dumped by attackers or stored in GitHub
- Using tools like the OSINT Framework

Attackers may seek multiple types of information to conduct reconnaissance on a target and create a plan of attack. Identifying this information and educating company personnel on the potential risks of public exposure can enable defenders to proactively assess or remove likely information used in an attack. The following definitions can help identify relevant and potentially exploitable information:[2]

- **Personal/Personnel Information:** Allows for identification of critical personnel, general personnel, or outside source personnel (e.g., contractors, third-party operators):
    - LinkedIn profiles or construction contractors are building a new facility for the target.
- **Criticality Information:** Informs an adversary of the impact of an attack on a target's continued operations. A target's criticality is determined if its compromise or destruction has a highly significant impact on the overall organization and its ability to conduct business or operations:
    - "Crown Jewels" of operations, like safety controllers in oil and gas operations or data historians in manufacturing.
- **Accessibility Information:** Informs the adversary of the ability or method to remotely/physically access or egress from a target:
    - Remote Desktop Protocol (RDP) exposed to the internet.
- **Recoverability Information:** Gives an adversary insight into the ability for a target's process, system, or network infrastructure to recover from an attack or compromise:
    - Information about electric utility service restoration in the event of a disruptive event.
- **Vulnerability Information:** Informs an adversary of a vulnerability that exists in the target's infrastructure, processes, or response actions:
    - An unpatched vulnerability affects Virtual Private Network (VPN) appliances that enable initial access.
- **Effect Information:** Information about the amount of direct or indirect loss a target would have from an attack or compromise. Information on the effects that losses would have on the target, its organization, processes, or operations:
    - Physical effects of a disruptive cyber attack targeting a Safety Instrumented System (SIS); financial losses accrued from multiple days of downtime.
- **Recognizability Information:** Assists adversaries in the ease of identifying targets for operational gain and the level of obscurity that the target has from internal and external sources:
    - MAC address of target workstation within the ICS environment.

Targeting ICS and the Critical Infrastructure

OSINT and critical infrastructure sectors, we can combine those two things to gather intelligence on a country's critical assets. Collecting this information is essential to understand an adversary's cyber potential and weaknesses, and it's done as the first step in every cyber-attack.[3]

The first stage of an ICS Cyber-attack is best categorized as the type of activity traditionally classified as espionage or an intelligence operation. It is very similar to attacks covered in Lockheed Martin's Kill Chain. It often aims to gain access to information about the ICS, learn the system, and provide mechanisms to defeat internal perimeter protections or gain access to production environments. Image 1 below illustrates the first stage of the ICS Cyber Kill Chain.[4]

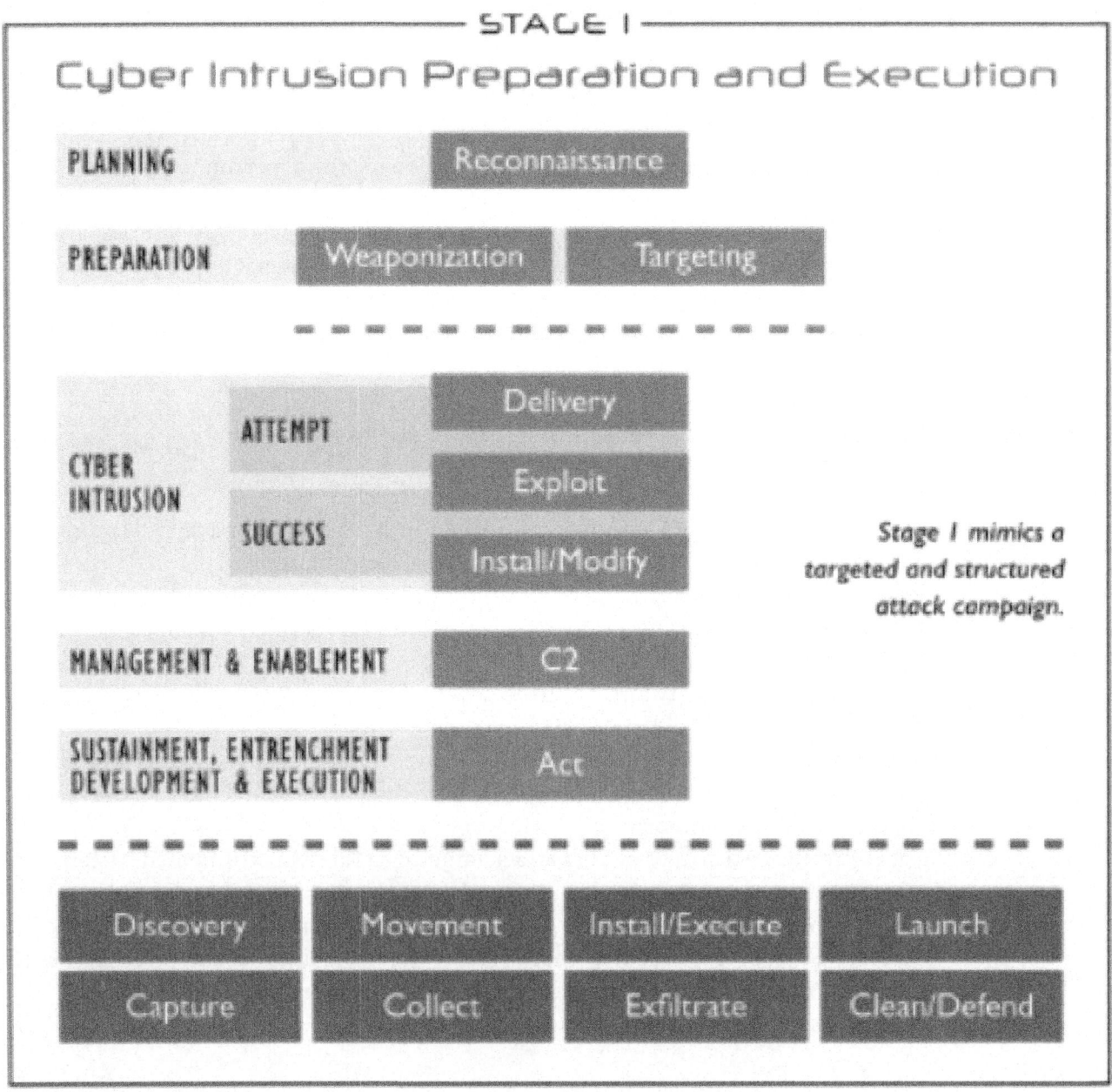

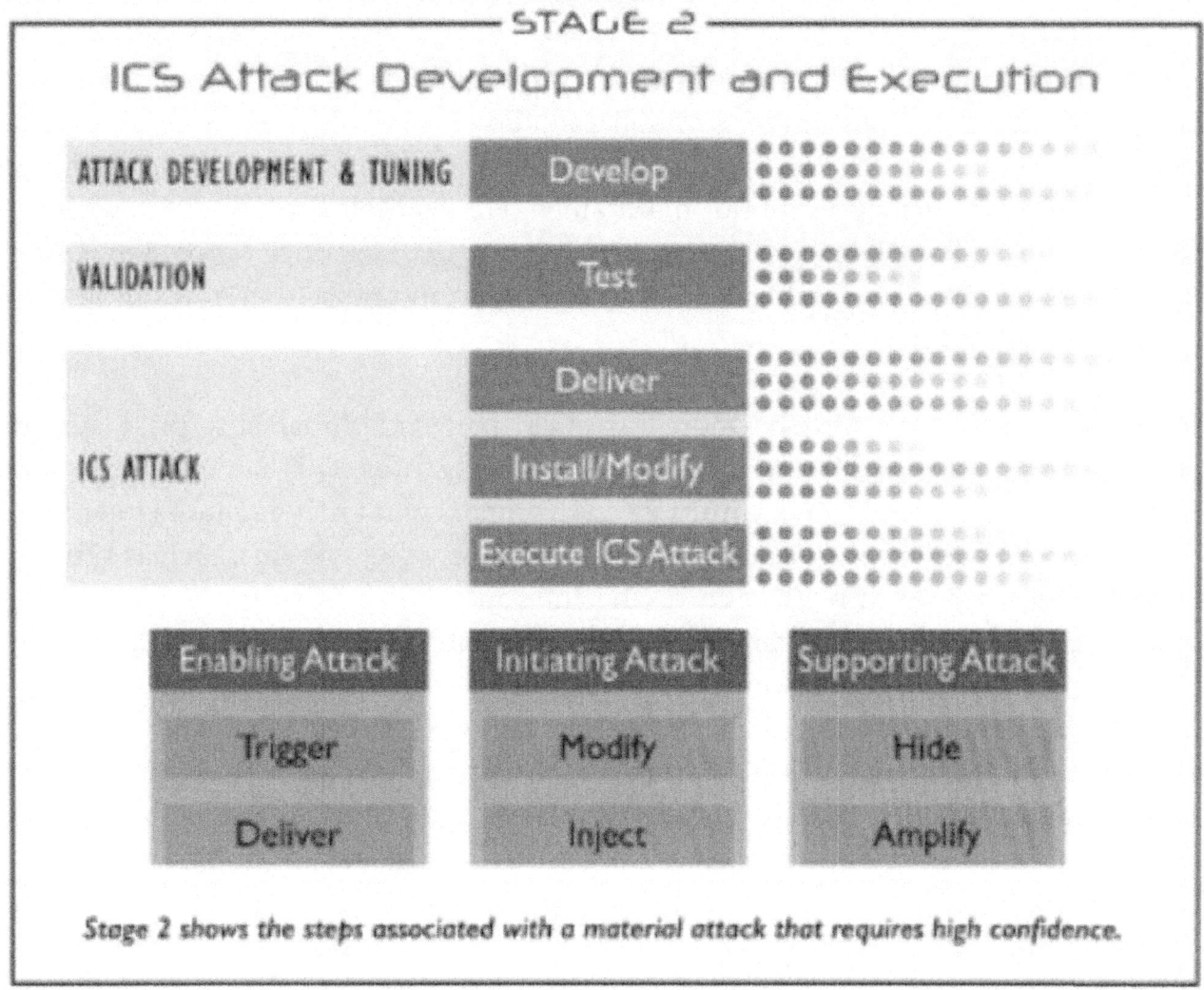

Image 2: ICS Cyber Kill Chain Stage 2 – SANS White Paper[4]

When mapped to the ICS Cyber Kill Chain, OSINT largely represents Stage 1 (Image 1) reconnaissance activity supporting Stage 2 (Image 2) objectives. It can be used to identify potential vulnerabilities, identify detections, implement persistence mechanisms, or reduce the time required to achieve objectives and avoid detection. Details on equipment, vendors, and processes can be used for later malware or malicious tool development.

Attackers target industrial entities for a variety of reasons. Attacks on ICS entities that serve critical functions within society can further political, economic, or national security goals. Depending on an attacker's objective, attacks can be used for messaging purposes or retaliation. The potential impact may extend to citizens of a target's community. Understanding critical infrastructure can put an attacker at a tactical advantage in times of conflict to establish a foothold as a contingency option when conflict occurs.

Targeting ICS can provide monetary value to an adversary. ICS entities increasingly experience ransomware attacks that, in many cases, disrupt operations. Disrupting operations can have significant daily financial impacts for some companies, costing thousands and sometimes millions of dollars in downtime. In these cases, an operator may be more willing to pay a ransom to unlock computers and limit downtime, especially if proper backups are not maintained. For example, in July 2020, wearables manufacturer and Global Positioning System (GPS) service provider Garmin experienced a ransomware attack. They opted to pay an undisclosed ransom to get its operations back online.

ICS environments may also be more insecure than traditional enterprise systems, especially for entities with immature cybersecurity postures. This can be due to various legacy operating systems across multiple environments and inadequate segmentation. It is not uncommon to observe outdated Windows operating systems, such as Windows XP or Windows 7, within ICS due to the interoperability of some ICS devices and limitations on patch management. ICS systems are fundamentally complex, and security mechanisms like patching are conducted based on weighing the risk of compromise against the outcome of a potential cyberattack. Practicing defense-in-depth, including conducting OSINT risk assessments to strengthen external security postures, and limiting the ability of adversaries to operationalize public information, can prevent initial access and movement within an operational environment.[2]

We can also map OSINT to the MITRE ATT&CK Matrix framework, specifically the PRE-ATT&CK. Whereas the ATT&CK framework concentrates on the steps taken once an attack is launched, the PRE-ATT&CK framework focuses on the preceding preparation phases. Bellow a table with the techniques to map OSINT to the PRE-ATT&CK.

Technique Name	Technique ID
Active Scanning	T1595
Gather Victim Host Information	T1592
Gather Victim Identity Information	T1589
Gather Victim Network Information	T1590
Gather Victim Org Information	T1591
Search Closed Sources	T1597
Search Open Technical Databases	T1596
Search Open Websites/Domains	T1593
Search Victim-Owned Websites	T1594

Table 1: OSINT mapped to PRE-ATT&CK framework

Shodan.io

It is not possible to be in Cyber Security and never come across the Shodan search engine. Today Shodan is essentially a vulnerability search engine. By providing it with a name, an IP address, a port, or even the name of some industrial protocols, it returns all the systems in its databases that match. This makes it one of the most effective intelligence sources when it comes to infrastructure and IoT. It's like Google for internet-connected devices. Shodan constantly scans the Internet and saves the results into a public database. While this database is searchable using the Shodan website (https://www.shodan.io).

Shodan is the most popular device engine and supports more ICS/SCADA Protocols.

Engine	BACnet	CodeSys	Crimson v3	DNP3	EtherNet/IP	GE-SRTP	HART-IP	IEC60870-5-104	IEC61850	MELSEC-Q	Modbus	Tridium	OMRON-FINS	PCWorx	ProConOS	Siemens S7
shodan.io	✓	✓	✓	✓	✓	✓	✓	✓	✓	✓	✓	✓	✓	✓	✓	✓
censys.io	✓			✓							✓					✓

Image 3: SCADA protocols supported by the most popular device search engines[5]

We can easily find ICS devices using Shodan; we will search for very well-known protocols: ModBus and DNP3

We can search for ModBus devices using the Modbus word or even by the Modbus TCP port by using port:502 on the search. Shodan will return results where the Modbus word is found or devices where the port 502 is open; not all are ICS Devices or even have the Modbus function on the port 502. Bellow, we can check the Shoran report for both searches.

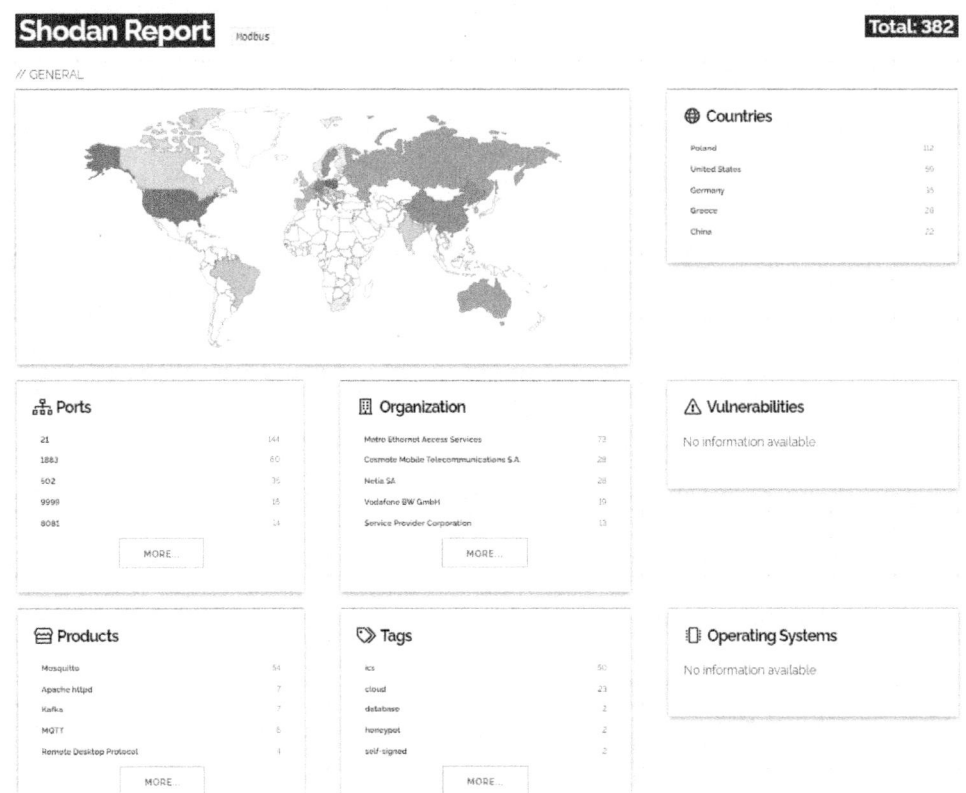

Image 4: Shodan Report for Modbus word search

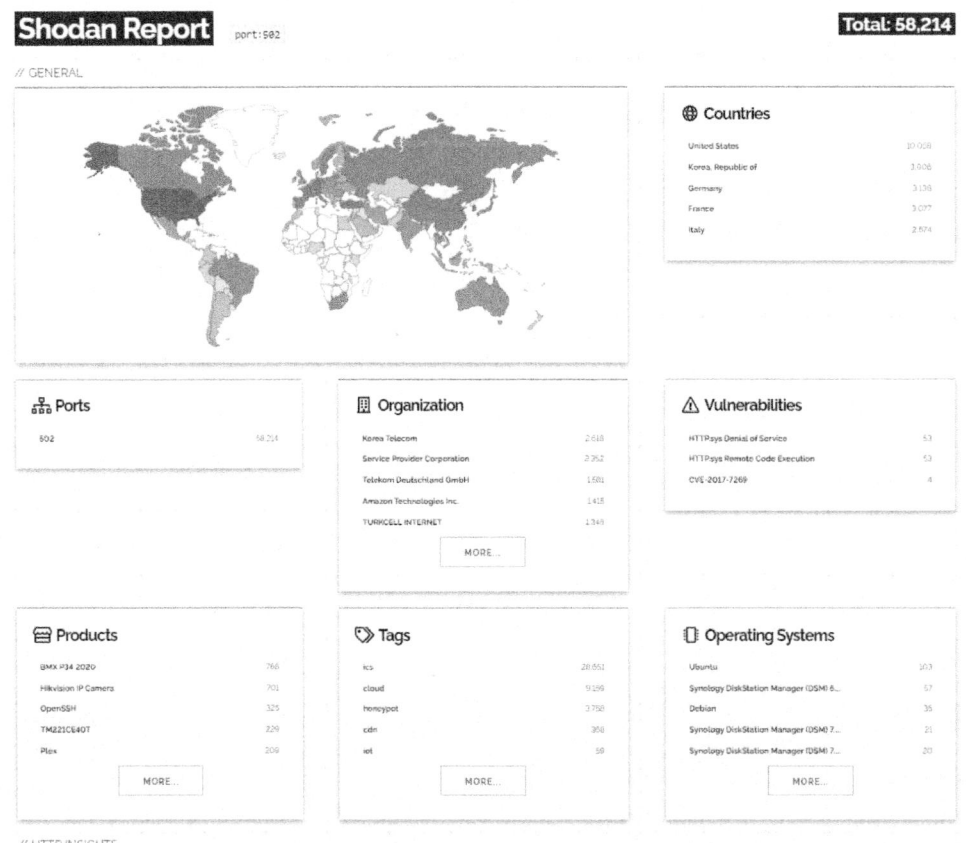

Image 5: Shodan Report for Modbus port 502 search

After checking a few of the IP addresses, we came across the one below (Image 6); it has port 502 open and a few more like port 80 for HTTP or port 22 for SSH, looking in more detail, we find that the equipment is running Linux. It might be equipment from 3S-Smart Software Solutions or equipment used in Chemical Processing. Shodan also informs of a possible vulnerability affecting the equipment.

Image 6: Shodan Image Details

Exploring the IP address in Internet Explorer, we can see an HMI with some information; after quick research, we conclude it has indications for some transactions running, program, and some pump information (Image 6). Exploring what we call the HMI Mail Menu a little more, we can access a login menu (Image 7).

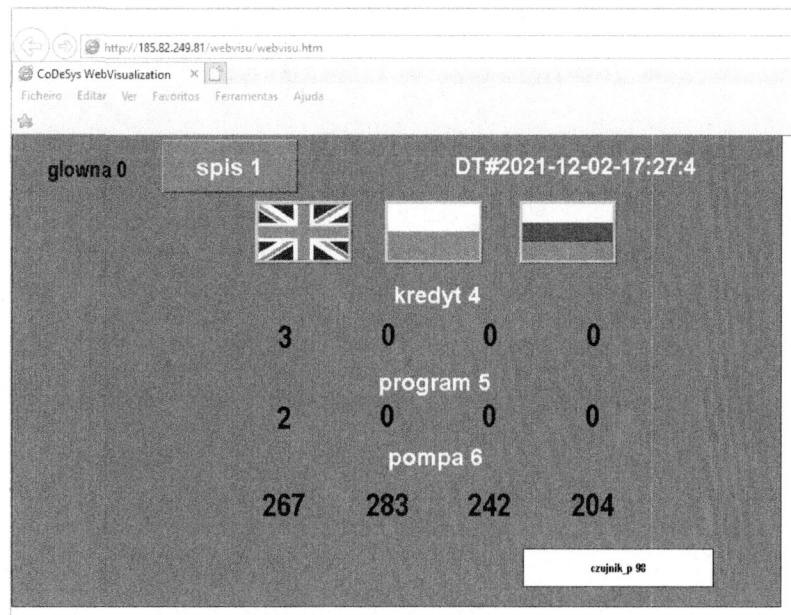

Image 6: HMI Main Menu

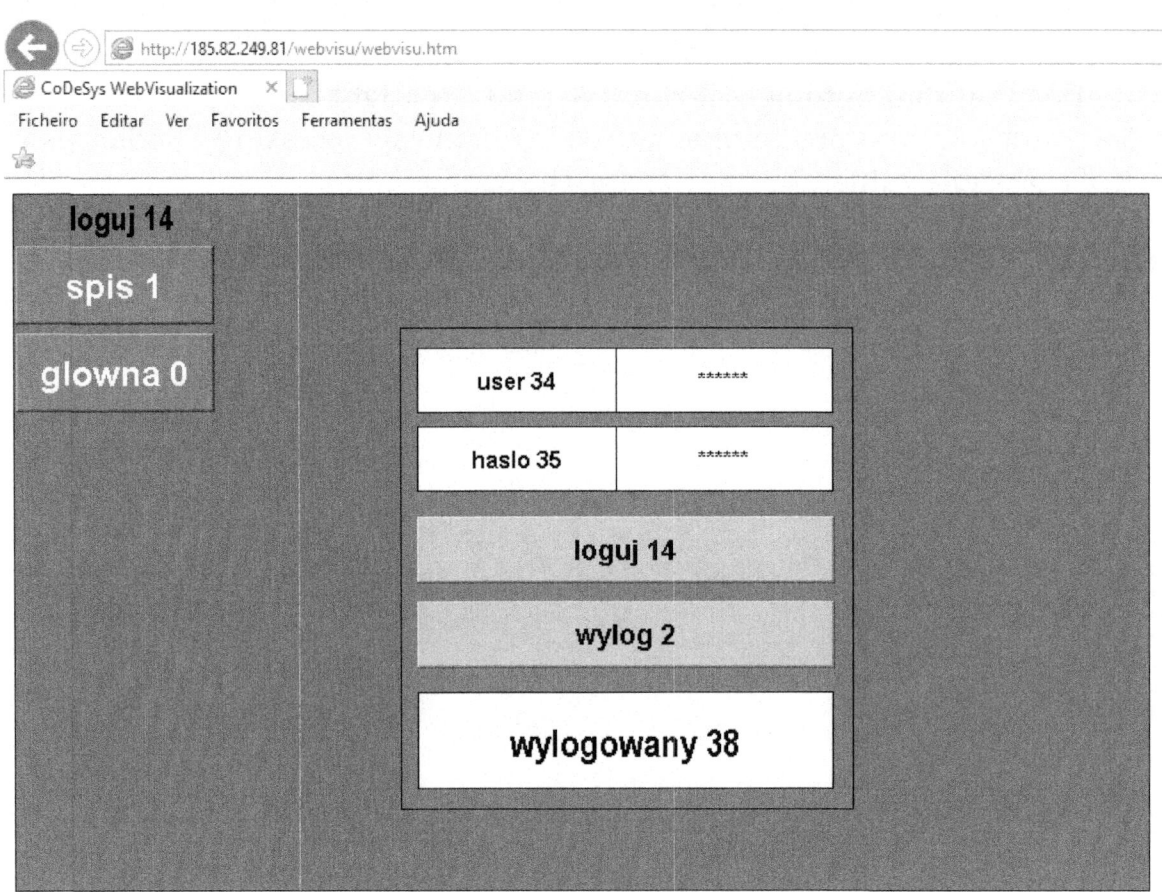

Image 7: HMI Login Menu

When performing the same search for the protocol DNP3 (port: 20000), we also found an IP address (Image 8) that takes us to an HMI from a Schneider PowerLogic Meter (Image 9), where we can check a lot of parameters from Operation, Consumption and even Power Quality. Also, the Setup menu is visible but disables Web Interface changes. A quick search on google with some information from the HMI and Google Maps reveals that this Meter is in the City of Guayaquil and might belong to Concrete Plant.

Image 8: DNP3 protocol

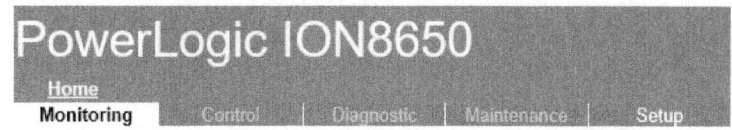

Operation
Consumption
Power Quality

Operation

Voltage		Current		Power	
Vln avg	39722.81 V	I avg	18.48 A	kW total	1983.61 kW
Vln a	39879.34 V	I a	18.22 A	kW a	634.93 kW
Vln b	39235.96 V	I b	17.57 A	kW b	634.94 kW
Vln c	40053.13 V	I c	19.65 A	kW c	713.74 kW
Vll avg	68802.71 V			kVA total	2198.77 kVA
Vll a-b	68364.68 V	I unbal	6.31 %	kVA a	726.72 kVA
Vll b-c	68584.19 V			kVA b	689.47 kVA
Vll c-a	69459.27 V	**Power Factor**		kVA c	786.91 kVA
V unbal	1.23 %	PF sign total	-90.21 %	kVAR total	948.64 kVAR
		PF sign a	-87.37 %	kVAR a	351.71 kVAR
Frequency		PF sign b	-92.09 %	kVAR b	267.38 kVAR
Freq	59.99 Hz	PF sign c	-90.70 %	kVAR c	329.55 kVAR

Owner	TESAL-GYE		Meter Type	8650
Tag 1	RESPALDO		Firmware Version	004.020.001
Tag 2	HSBARTOLO		Template	8650C_FAC_V4.2.0.0.2
Device Time	2021-12-02 11:22:29 GMT -05:00		Serial Number	MW-1603A920-02

Image 9: PowerLogin HMI

We also find interesting results if we search for VNC devices online. Default VNC ports are 5901, 5900, and 5800, so we need to search for additional parameters like country, region, or even with no authentication. We will search for the VNC service with "Authentication Disabled," this means that the VNC service is running on the specific port 5901 and will be available without any authentication, which means we can log in and watch the screen. There were 2195 results for VNC port: 5901 without authentication when writing this article.

Editor's Note

PowerLogic ION8650 series

https://download.schneider-electric.com/files?p_enDocType=User+guide&p_File_Name=7EN02-0306-06.pdf

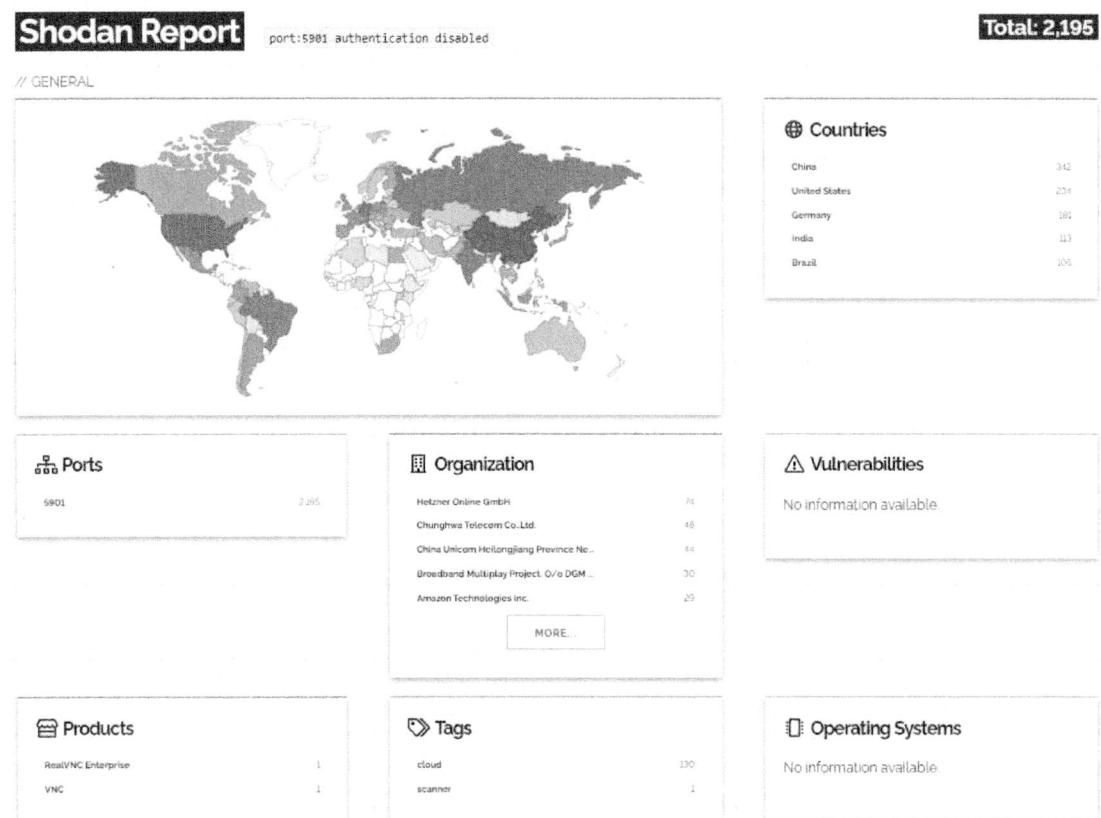

Image 10: Shodan Search result VNC

Image 11: VNC without authentication https://beta.shodan.io/host/150.164.46.16#5901

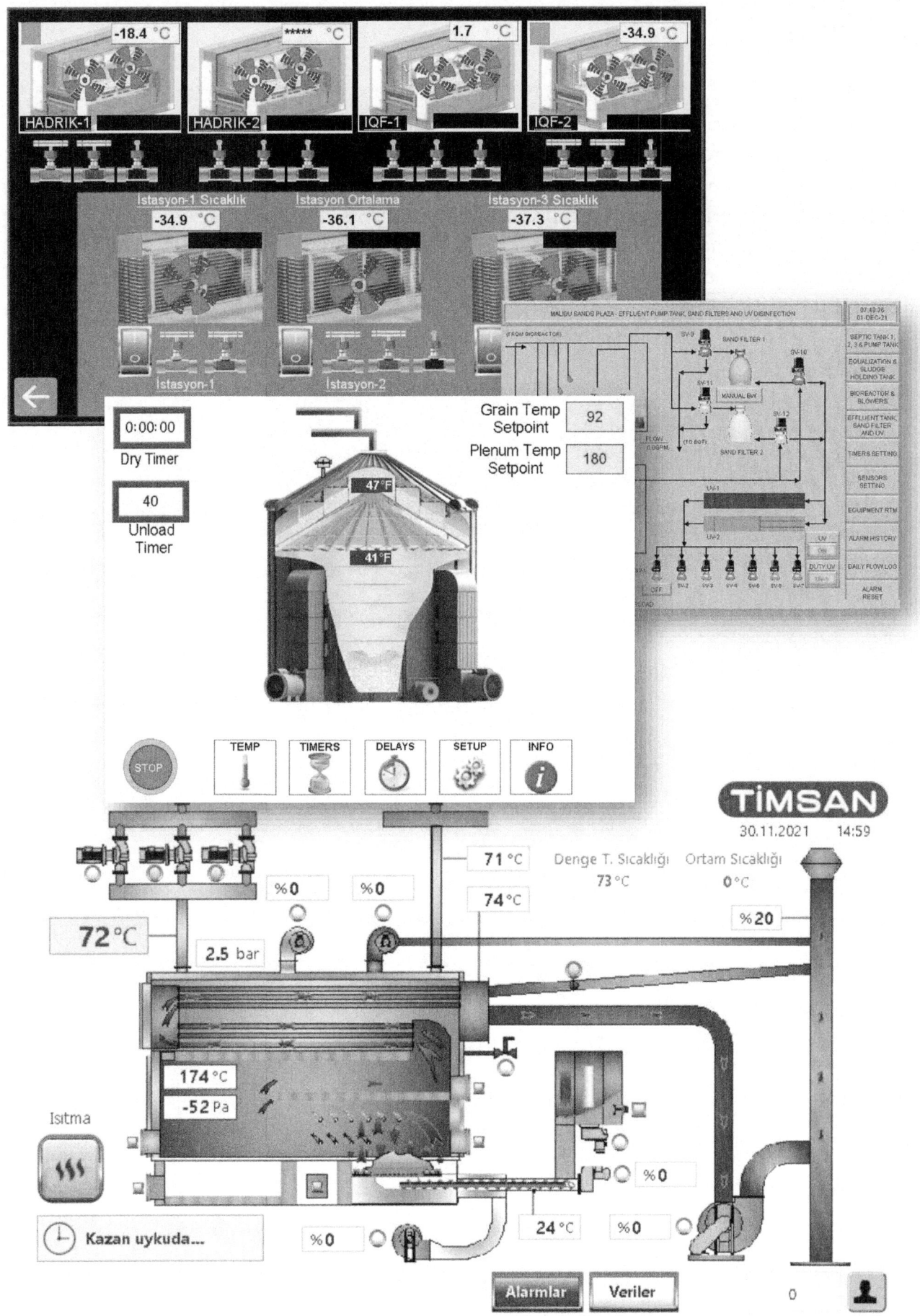

Final words

Since the inception of OSINT by the US military in the late 1980s, a lot has changed in the world, along with the advancement of technology and society. The revolution of Internet technology resulted in a paradigm shift. The widespread popularity of social media, search engines, mobile data, and the internet, in general, has enriched the accumulation of open-source content on the web. OSINT is now being used in many other fields such as marketing, cyber security, political strategy analysis, etc. The flood of data during this era was beneficial not only to law enforcement agencies and professional practitioners but also to threat actors.

References:

- [1] What Is Open Source Intelligence and How Is it Used?
  https://www.recordedfuture.com/open-source-intelligence-definition/
- [2] Dragos Whitepaper, Open Source Intelligence;
  https://f.hubspotusercontent10.net/hubfs/5943619/Whitepaper-Downloads/Dragos-OSINT-Framework.pdf?utm_referrer=https%3A%2F%2Fwww.dragos.com%2Fresource%2Fopen-source-intelligence%2F
- [3] Intelligence Gathering on U.S. Critical Infrastructure:
  https://www.icscybersecurityconference.com/intelligence-gathering-on-u-s-critical-infrastructure/
- [4] SANS White Paper, https://sansorg.egnyte.com/dl/HHa9fCekmc
- [5] https://ris.utwente.nl/ws/portalfiles/portal/124347608/wodc_report_scada_final.pdf

Cool Tool: Ӿamerka GUI

Ultimate Internet of Things/Industrial Control Systems reconnaissance tool. Powered by Shodan - Supported by Binary Edge & WhoisXMLAPI

https://github.com/woj-ciech/Kamerka-GUI

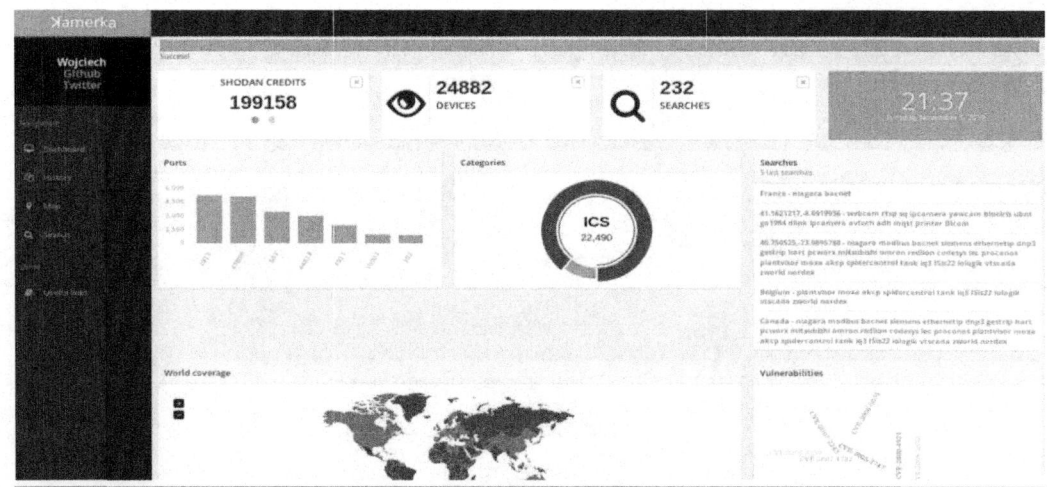

Who is watching you?

By Jeremy Martin

Do you have a security system or Internet (IP) camera installed in your home or business? If you do, was it easy to install? How easy? Probably too easy... Many people do not go through all the configurations to pick what will add more security to their environment and want to make the new equipment work. Sometimes the configurations can be complex and confusing, leading to many "default settings" is kept. If you pick the wrong settings, things can be even worse.

Are you at risk?

First, we must discuss what "risk" is.

> Risk = Threat * Vulnerability * Impact

To answer the question, are you at risk... What are your vulnerabilities? Seriously, do you know? Most people do not think about risk or look for their vulnerabilities. Most security solutions are there to keep the honest person honest. Threats are everywhere, especially on the Internet. The exciting thing about a threat is that it takes two items to become a threat. The threat agent (hacker, nosey neighbor, government, etc.) and the likelihood of occurrence (targeted attack versus a target of opportunity). Targeted attacks are made with focus while the later victim has terrible luck.

The impact needs to be realistic. For example:

With remote access to your home security system, a home invasion with a loss of life is possible. Criminals would know the who/what/when/and where of their target.
If someone has access to a Department of Transportation camera monitoring road conditions, they may take another route. Or they could use that to track a target driving from point A to point B.

So, are you at risk? Maybe...

Realized risk

A **Threat** just exploited your **Vulnerability** to produce an **Impact.**

For example, you want to monitor your baby's room remotely to make sure they are safe. So, you configure your IP camera to be accessible from the Internet by making a small change on your wireless broadband modem. This allows you to check in from time to time while you are in another room or working at the office. Unfortunately, this may let anyone on the Internet do the same.

> *"Hacker shouts at baby through the baby monitor*
>
> *An Ohio family is asleep when a man's voice reportedly is heard coming from the baby's room. It turns out to be someone who thought it funny to hack into the device."* - cnet.com
>
> *"Hacker yells expletives at toddler after hacking baby monitor*
>
> *An unknown hacker gained access to a 2-year-old girl's baby monitor, calling her by name and harassing her, and her parents, with insults and profanity."* - CNN
>
> *"I'm in your baby's room: A hacker took over a baby monitor and broadcast threats, parents say*
>
> *'A stranger's voice, spouting sexual expletives,' wafted through a baby monitor in the Rigneys.' ... 'I am going to kidnap your baby,' the voice said next, Ellen Rigney recalled to the news station. 'I am in your baby's room.'"* - Washington Post

These are three different headlines from three separate incidents. When you do not secure your environment from either physical or electronic attacks, you are allowing bad actors the opportunity to do bad things.

Why are default settings a vulnerability?

Anyone can look up default settings of devices using a google search or Reading the Fine Manual (RTFM). This means other people may know things that would help them access the devices without your knowledge or consent. Default usernames and passwords are one of those configs that will leave your security wide open.

If you plug-n-play your cameras without changing the passwords to get it to work, you are keeping the system open for anyone else that wants to plug-n-play right into the device. At a minimum, change the password.

A list of default credentials for common IP Cameras:

- 3xLogic: admin/12345
- ACTi: admin/123456 or Admin/123456
- Amcrest: admin/admin
- American Dynamics: admin/admin or admin/9999
- Arecont Vision: <blank>
- AvertX: admin/1234
- Avigilon: admin/admin or administrator/<blank>
- Axis: root/pass or root/<blank> - some require users to create password on first login
- Basler: admin/admin
- Bosch: <blank>/<blank>, service/service, or Dinion/<blank> - (6.0+) users create passwords on first login
- Brickcom: admin/admin
- Canon: root/camera or root/Model # of camera
- CBC Ganz: admin/admin
- Cisco: admin/<blank>
- CNB: root/admin
- Costar: root/root
- Dahua: admin/admin, 888888/888888, or 666666/666666 - some require users to create password on first login
- Digital Watchdog: admin/admin
- DRS: admin/1234
- DVTel: Admin/1234
- DynaColor: Admin/1234
- FLIR: admin/fliradmin
- FLIR (Dahua OEM): admin/admin
- FLIR (Quasar/Ariel): admin/admin
- Foscam: admin/<blank>
- GeoVision: admin/admin
- Grandstream: admin/admin
- GVI: Admin/1234
- Hikvision: admin/12345 - some require users to create password on first login
- Honeywell: admin/1234 or administrator/1234
- IndigoVision (Ultra): <blank>/<blank>
- IndigoVision (BX/GX): Admin/1234
- Intellio: admin/admin
- Interlogix admin/1234
- IQinVision: root/system
- IPX-DDK: root/admin or root/Admin
- JVC: admin/jvc
- IQInvision: root/system
- Longse: admin/12345
- Lorex: admin/admin
- LTS Security: admin/12345 or admin/123456 - some require users to create password on first login
- March Networks: admin/<blank>
- Merit Lilin Camera: admin/pass

- Marit Lilin Recorder: admin:1111
- Messoa: admin/Model # of camera
- Mobotix: admin/meinsm
- Northern: admin/12345 - some require users to create password on first login
- Oncam: admin/admin
- Panasonic: admin/12345 or admin1/password - some require users to create password on first login
- Pelco: admin/admin - some require users to create password on first login
- Pixord: admin/admin or root/pass
- Q-See: admin/admin or admin/123456
- QVIS: Admin/1234
- Reolink: admin/<blank>
- Samsung: root/root, admin/4321, root/admin, or root/4321 - some require users to create password on first login
- Samsung Techwin (old): admin/1111111
- Sanyo: admin/admin
- Scallop: admin/password
- Sentry360: admin/1234, <blank>/<blank>, Admin/1234, or admin/<blank>
- Sony: admin/admin
- Speco: admin/1234, root/root, or admin/admin
- Stardot: admin/admin
- Starvedia: admin/<blank>
- Sunell: admin/admin
- SV3C: admin/123456
- Swann: admin/12345
- Toshiba: root/ikwd
- Trendnet: admin/admin
- Ubiquiti: ubnt/ubnt
- Uniview: admin/123456
- Verint: admin/admin
- VideoIQ: supervisor/supervisor
- Vivotek: root/<blank>
- W-Box (Hikvision OEM, old): admin/wbox123
- W-Box (Sunell OEM, new): admin/admin
- Wodsee: admin/<blank>

If you haven't changed your default credentials on your camera or other network devices, now is time to do it! Knowing there are things you can do to protect yourself from prying eyes is half the battle. Going through the steps to protect yourself is the path to minimizing risk.

If WPS is enabled on the wireless device, turn it off if you need it. A PIN exchange mechanism is susceptible to brute-force attacks that could allow an attacker to gain access to an encrypted Wi-Fi network. The WPS PIN is only 8-digits.

Why Are Default Settings a Vulnerability?
Examples

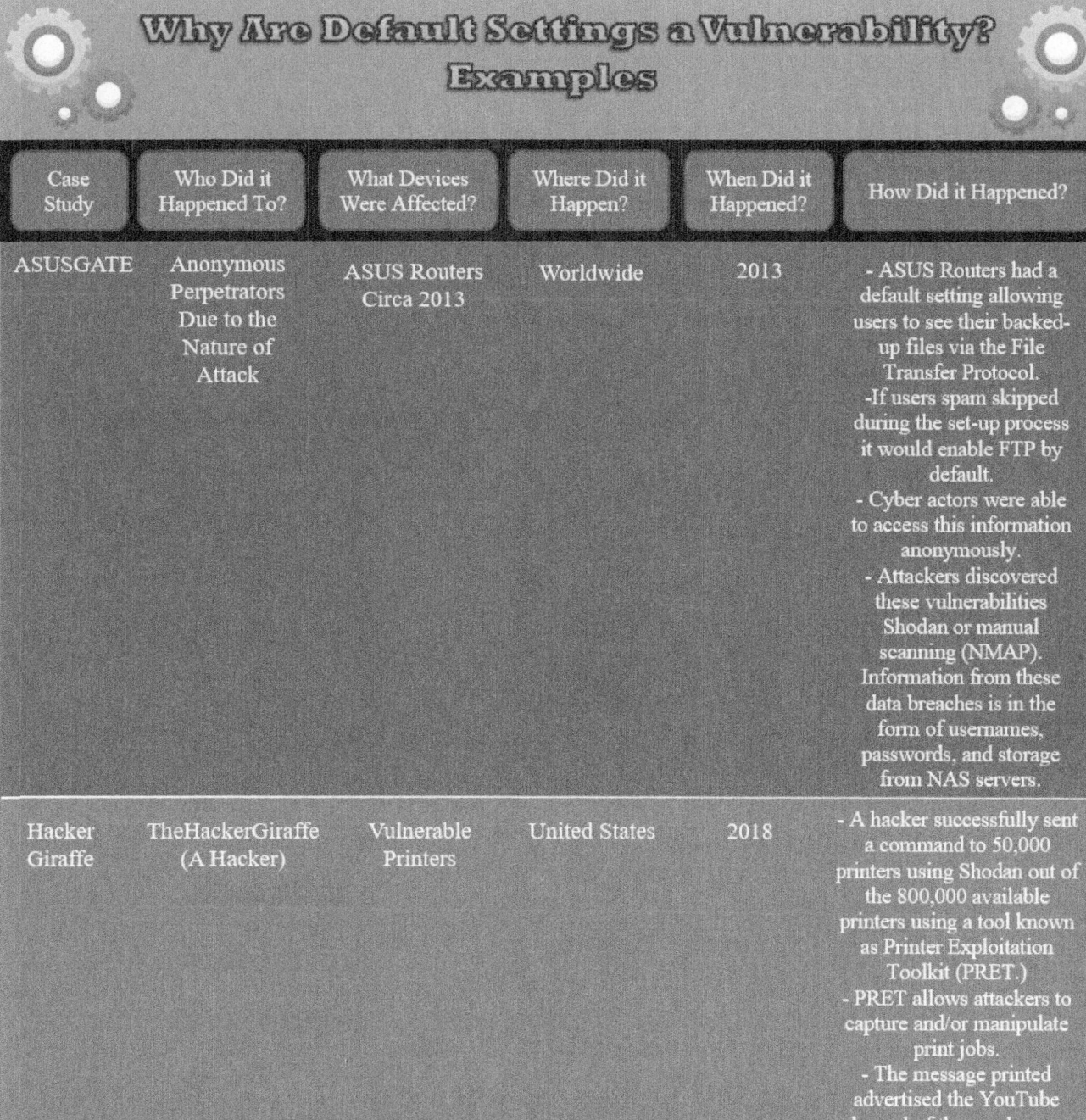

Case Study	Who Did it Happened To?	What Devices Were Affected?	Where Did it Happen?	When Did it Happened?	How Did it Happened?
ASUSGATE	Anonymous Perpetrators Due to the Nature of Attack	ASUS Routers Circa 2013	Worldwide	2013	- ASUS Routers had a default setting allowing users to see their backed-up files via the File Transfer Protocol. -If users spam skipped during the set-up process it would enable FTP by default. - Cyber actors were able to access this information anonymously. - Attackers discovered these vulnerabilities Shodan or manual scanning (NMAP). Information from these data breaches is in the form of usernames, passwords, and storage from NAS servers.
Hacker Giraffe	TheHackerGiraffe (A Hacker)	Vulnerable Printers	United States	2018	- A hacker successfully sent a command to 50,000 printers using Shodan out of the 800,000 available printers using a tool known as Printer Exploitation Toolkit (PRET.) - PRET allows attackers to capture and/or manipulate print jobs. - The message printed advertised the YouTube channel of the number one individual YouTube content creator PewDiePie.

Why is misconfiguration of a device a vulnerability?

Many things can go wrong when you misconfigure a device. One would be making the system inoperable or turning it into a "brick." Another would be allowing unauthorized people to access your system remotely through either exploitation or handing them the keys to the kingdom with default or no credentials. Sometimes what makes it easier for you is to make it easier for everyone else.

Vendors try to make it easier for users to implement their tools and, in doing so, have made a lot of their tools unsecured. They expect you to secure the devices once you have set them up. Unfortunately, many vendors do not explain this very well to the consumer. This puts the responsibility on the user or YOU to do the research and figure out what you are supposed to do.

Some websites are dedicated to searching out unsecured devices, and some focus on IP cameras. Two sites that focus on cameras while giving links to them are:

- insecam.org
- www.opentopia.com

These cameras range from public places to businesses to the privacy of people's homes.

Shodan is a site that focuses on all devices on the Internet they can find, or others find and submit to them. They even post vulnerabilities and misconfigurations that were identified:

shodan.io

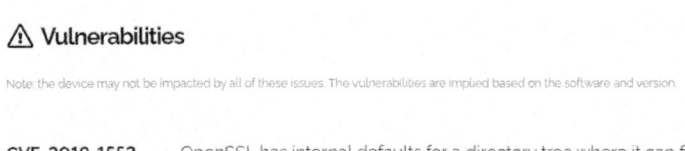

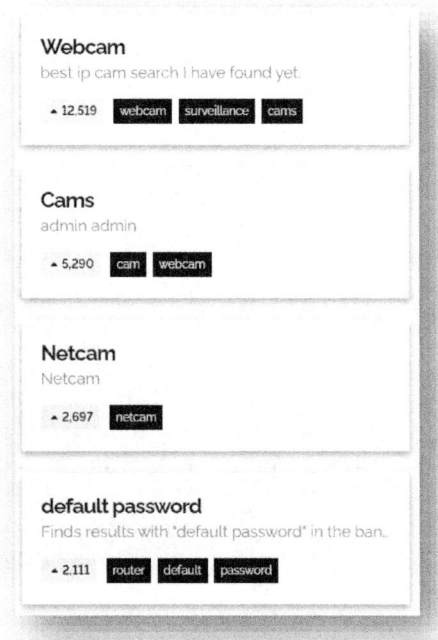

War spying

War spying (also known as war viewing) is the search for unencrypted wireless signals transmitted from video cameras to nearby receivers or recorders. If your wireless cameras broadcast unencrypted signals, you should be aware of this risk. This allows anyone with a Software Defined Radio (SDR) and know-how can capture the signal and watch it like they would with a TV. You have no reasonable expectation of privacy if you don't encrypt over public bandwidths.

This whitepaper walks you through the process of building your own war spying device focusing on the 2.4 GHz range:
qsl.net/kb9mwr/projects/uwave/2.4%20GHz%20Warspying%20Device.pdf

The likelihood of this attack is moderately low due to the knowledge, equipment, and physical access to the area in the range of the wireless signal. Suppose it is a targeted attack, the risk increases. Encrypting the signal will prevent war spies from eavesdropping.

Cameras turned into wiretaps

In 2019, it was found that devices that allow for voice commands like the Alexa, Echo, and some cameras are vulnerable to a laser attack. Yes, lasers...

"researchers who have discovered that when a laser is aimed at the devices' microphones, an electrical signal is created, just as it is when a voice command is made. Using an oscilloscope, the academics found they could make it, so the microphone created the same signal when receiving light as it did with sound. In doing so, they effectively mimicked a voice with a laser beam." - Forbes

Is the likelihood of this attack higher than someone stumbling across your IP camera online and guessing the default password? Absolutely not. This would most likely be a targeted attack due to the knowledge and equipment needed to exploit such a vulnerability. It is also straightforward to prevent. Move the device out of the line of sight from windows and other places where evildoers would be able to set up lasers.

Fortunately, there is a lot of information that can help you if you know where to look. This means you need to know you need to look in the first place. This does not mean that you shouldn't use IP cameras or other Internet of Things (IoT) devices to make your life easier or more secure. When you are adding things to your environment, you may be increasing the risk to your business, home, or family.

Here is a list of things you can do to minimize your risk:

1. Change the default passwords to your devices
2. Do not "port forward" traffic directly to your camera or device from your modem.
    a. This puts your device directly on the Internet for Shodan and the world to see
3. Use encryption when available
    a. Use the HTTPS interfaces when available or encrypted services for remote access
4. Keep your systems patched and up to date
    a. Some systems have internal mechanisms that will help automate the process. Sometimes you may need to update the systems manually.
5. Segment all your IoT devices from your regular network.
    a. You may need to purchase another WiFi access point for your IoT devices
6. Secure your WiFi
    a. Use a strong password on your WiFi.
        i.   This means your administrative access AND your connection
        ii. Do NOT use WPS. This can be brute forced in many cases, giving easy access to the devices on the network.
    b. Use encryption
        i.   Prevents attackers from "tuning in" to your wireless cameras.

You can find guidance for IoT vulnerabilities from OWASP:
www.owasp.org/images/1/1c/OWASP-IoT-Top-10-2018-final.pdf

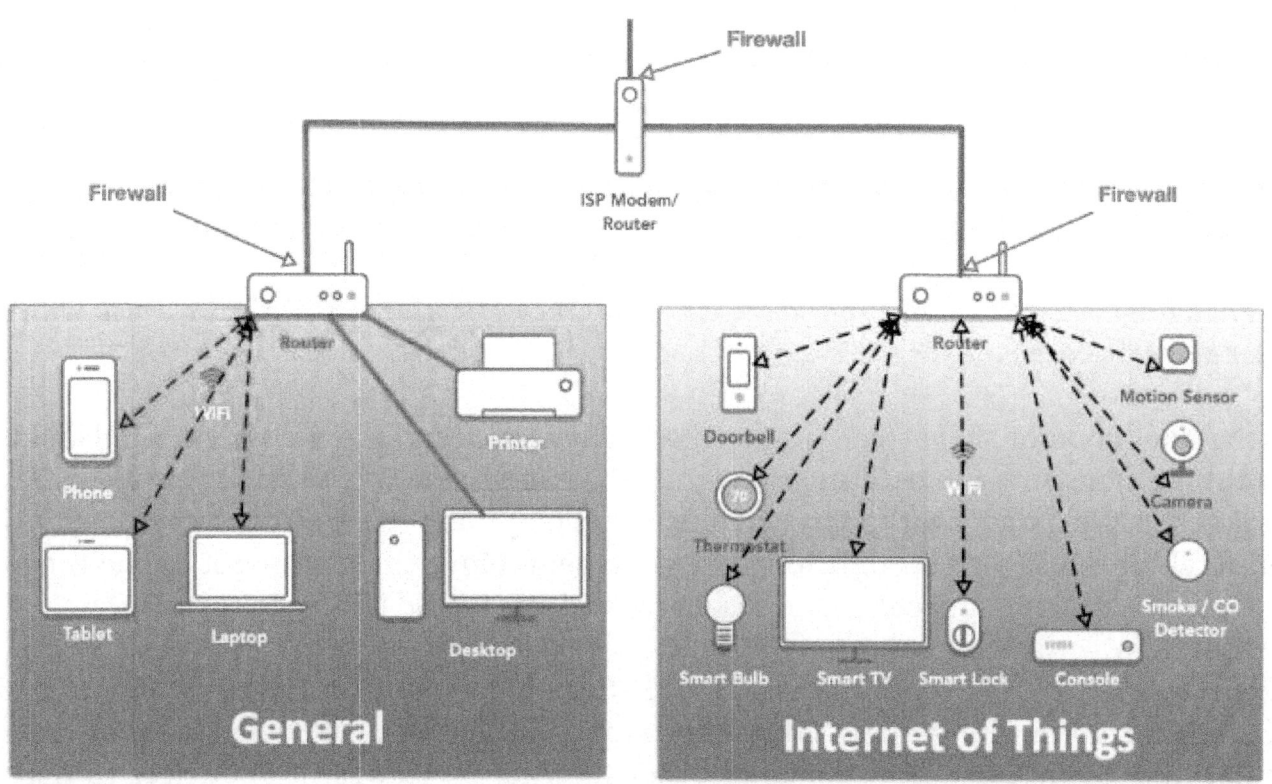

IP Cameras, IoT, and OSINT

Disclaimer: DO NOT BREAK THE LAW!!! Accessing a system without authorization or over authorization is a criminal offense as it may qualify for Title 18 U.S.C 1030's Computer Fraud and Abuse Act. This includes default passwords, password cracking, and exploits.

When a Person of Interest (POI) doesn't follow Operational Security (OPSEC) best practices, some of them mentioned above; may make identifying and tracking them more straightforward. If you are trying to use something like IP cameras in your investigation, a few pieces of information can help narrow down the hunt. Here are some of them:

- Geographic location
- IP Address or range
- Social Media accounts
- Etc...

Some of the "open camera" websites will let you search by map or city. If there are enough cameras in the area, you might get lucky and get a camera that can be useful.

If you know the geographic location and don't have a camera listed, that is useful; you can throw a Hail Mary, identify the Internet Service Providers in the area and get their IP address ranges. Use Shodan to search those ranges or use a tool like nmapify to scan for standard ports or services IP cameras use within those ranges. You may find several cameras in the area, and you may even get luckier and find a useful one.

If you know the POI's IP address or network range, you can scan it for open cameras or services. A Nmap scan can shed a lot of light on the services running. You will need to use "sudo" on Linux/Unix systems for the following command.

    nmap -A -p- -sTU -vv -oA casename IPADDRESS

If you don't have the IP address, you can set up a web server and send the URL link to the POI. If they click it, you will have their Internet-facing IP address. Hopefully, they are not using a proxy, VPN, or Tor. If you go one step further, you can add an API request in the HTML code to request their location. If the POI accepts the request, it will give up its geolocation. This way, you have the location and can verify where the device says they are and if they are where you are trying to find cameras.

CSI Linux has these capabilities already built in.

Capturing online or streaming video

By Jeremy Martin

When doing an OSINT investigation, sometimes you will need to capture video evidence for your case. I will cover several tools that can help you capture videos posted on websites, streaming video from IPTV, and IP camera sources. There are other times that you may need to screen capture what you are doing on your system.

Imagine that a Person of Interest recorded committing a crime and posted it on a social media site. Yes, this does happen. You need to pull the data to preserve it for an ongoing instigation. There are many options out there, and we will cover a few of them.

Let's first cover some of the primary video formats, encoding, and file types you might see that you may need to add as evidence.

Common video formats

- **MP4:** (MPEG-4 Part 14) is the most common type of video file format. It uses the MPEG-4 encoding algorithm to store video and audio files and text, but it offers a lower definition than some others. MP4 works well for videos posted on YouTube, Facebook, Twitter, and Instagram.
- **MOV:** (QuickTime Movie) stores high-quality video, audio, and effects, but these files tend to be quite large. Developed for QuickTime Player by Apple, MOV files use MPEG-4 encoding to play in QuickTime for Windows. MOV is supported by Facebook and YouTube and can support transparency when using 32-bit.
- **WMV:** (Windows Media Viewer) files offer good video quality and large file sizes like MOV. YouTube supports WMV.
- **AVI:** (Audio Video Interleave) works with nearly every web browser on Windows, Mac, and Linux machines. Developed by Microsoft, AVI offers the highest quality and large file sizes. YouTube supports it.
- **AVCHD:** Advanced Video Coding High Definition is specifically for high-definition video. Built for Panasonic and Sony digital camcorders, these files compress for easy storage without losing definition.
- **Flash video formats:** FLV, F4V, and SWF (Shockwave Flash) are designed for Flash Player, but they were used to stream video on YouTube.
- **MKV:** Developed in Russia, Matroska Multimedia Container format is free and open source. It supports nearly every codec, but many programs do not support it.
- **WEBM:** These formats are best for videos embedded on your personal or business website. They are small files, so they load quickly and stream easily.

Common streaming Protocols formats

- **HLS:** HTTP Live Streaming protocol, or HTTP Live Streaming, was developed by Apple. The HLS standard supports adaptive-bitrate streaming.
- **MPEG-DASH:** Dynamic Adaptive Streaming over HTTP is open source and like HLS and works by breaking the content into small segments. Each segment contains a short interval of playback time of content that is potentially many hours in duration, such as a movie or the live broadcast of a sporting event.
- **RTMP:** Real-Time Messaging Protocol was initially developed by Macromedia in the early days of streaming; it is rarely used as a viewer-facing video streaming protocol like it once was. As an adaptable feed, the viewers do not have to watch in one linear direction. With content hosted on an RTMP server, the feed allows them to skip and rewind parts of the meal or to join a live stream after it's begun.
- **RTSP:** Real-Time Streaming Protocol allows viewers to watch content before the download is complete and uses either TCP or UDP.
- **SRT:** Secure Reliable Transport is an open-source video transport protocol that utilizes the UDP transport protocol and supports AES encryption.

Common Streaming Video Codec

- **AVC/H.264:** Advanced Video Coding is a video compression standard based on block-oriented, motion-compensated integer-DCT coding. It is the most used format for recording, compression, and distributing video content, used by most video industry developers.
- **HEVC/H.265:** High Efficiency Video Coding is a video compression standard designed as part of the MPEG-H project as a successor to the widely used Advanced Video Coding (AVC, H.264, or MPEG-4 Part 10). It uses the hardware to support the compression/decompressing twice the video quality at the same file size as H.264.

Common Streaming File Formats

- **M3U8:** HLS file broadcasting server divides the stream into separate 10 seconds sections of mp4. This is great when the broadcaster requires to stream multiple streaming qualities so that the spectator could use the fitting bitrate of the video considering the network bandwidth. There may be a 10-30 second lag.
- **TS:** MPEGTS has two parts which are MPEG and TS. The TS stands for Transport Stream. This format can provide audio, video, and metadata like subtitle, EPG, or a different form of data to lock the stream. Mpeg has an error correction feature to keep the integrity of the video whenever the signal is low.

CSI Linux Case Management System

Within CSI Linux, a video capture utility ties the captures to the case you are working on using several different tools in the background to maximize your chances to capture the evidence. This automates the process and works for most scenarios.

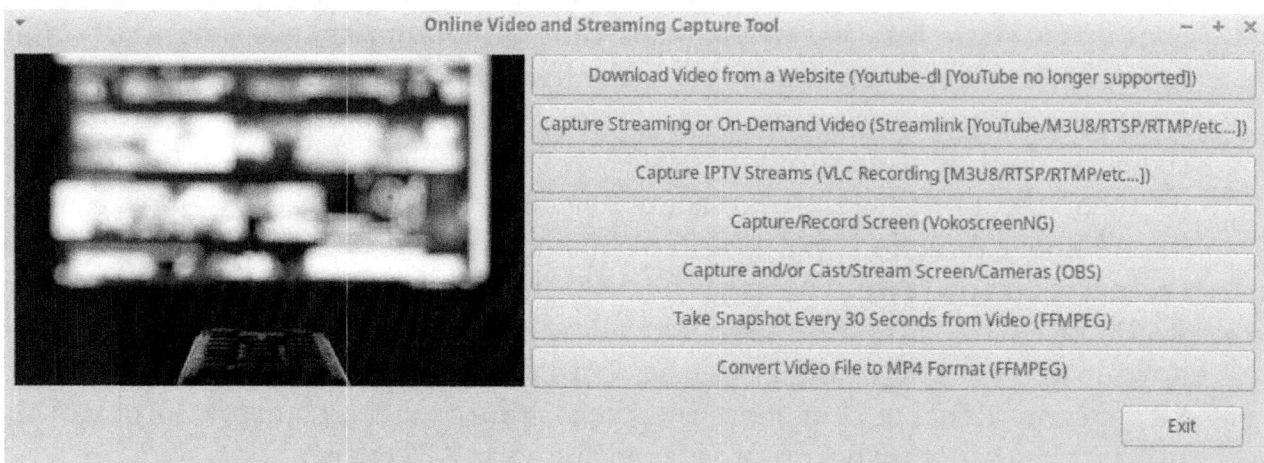

Most of the options use tools in the background to record, stream, or convert while saving the evidence to the ~/Cases/"Case Name"/Videos folder. These tools are listed below:

- **Youtube-dl** - Video-n-Demand downloader
- **Streamlink** - Video-n-Demand downloader & Streaming Video Capture
- **VLC** - Streaming Video Capture
- **FFMPEG** - Video/Audio conversion, Streaming Video, Snapshots Capture

Note: When done with the streaming video using Streamlink, close the VLC player, and the recorded file will finish posting to the case.

You will need to save the files to your case folder manually.

- **VokoscreenNG** - Screen Capture
- **OBS** - Screen Capture and Streaming

It is good to know how to do this manually. This helps with troubleshooting when things don't work the way you think they should and may be needed in certain situations.

Note: Video files can get large. Each time you close the Case Management application, it archives the evidence in zip files, and over time, this can take up space.

CSI Linux Video Capture Walkthrough – M3U8 Stream

In this example, we *will* capture a live stream from the Al Jazeera English live stream and save it as a file called AJ-001.mp4. Then we will use the screenshot tool *to* get an idea of what the video was about without having to watch the whole thing. This can be very useful when investigating a large video or *several* large videos. There are a few ways to open the video capture application, but we *will* use the icon located at the bottom of the screen.

1. Left click on the icon that is outlined in red.

2. Enter the name of the case you are working on and left-click on "OK."

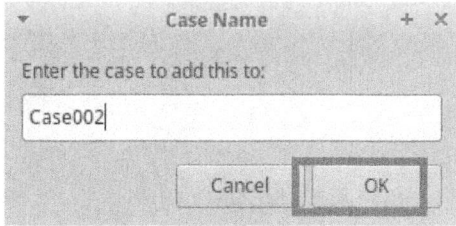

Note: We are going to use the Streamlink and the Snapshot options

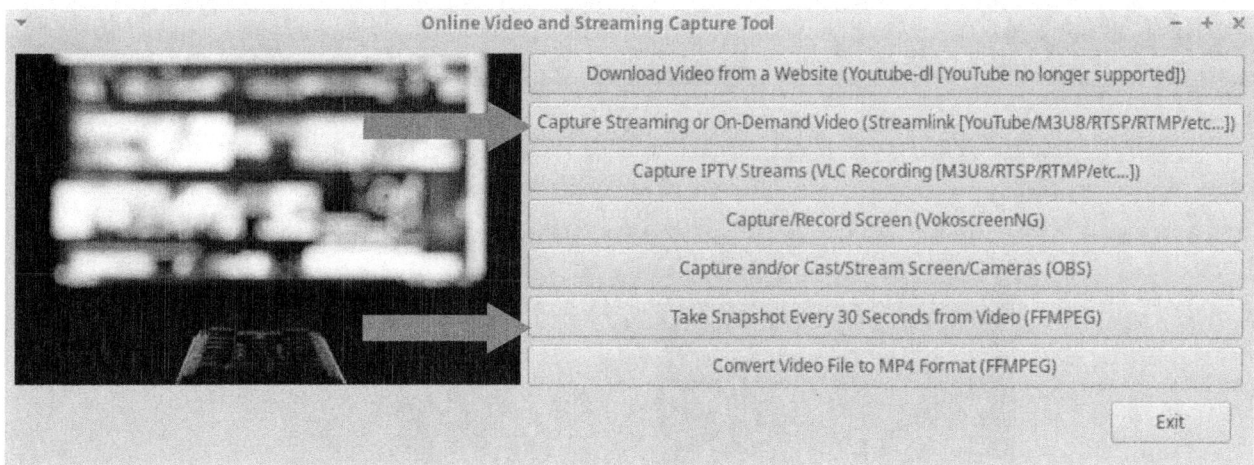

3. Left click on Capture Streaming … Streamlink
4. Enter the M3U8 file link **for Al** *Jazeera* **English** in the first field:
    a. " live-hls-web-aje.getaj.net/AJE/index.m3u8"
5. Enter the File name to create in the second field:
    b. "AJ-001"
6. Left click "OK."

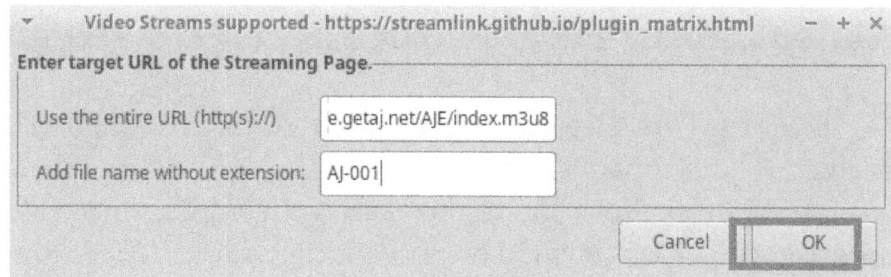

Note: You should see VLC Player pop up with the video feed running. If the link provided doesn't work, find one that does.

7. When you are done recording, close the VLC Player, and the file should now be saved into your ~/Cases/"Case Name"/Videos folder with the name "AJ-001.mp4."

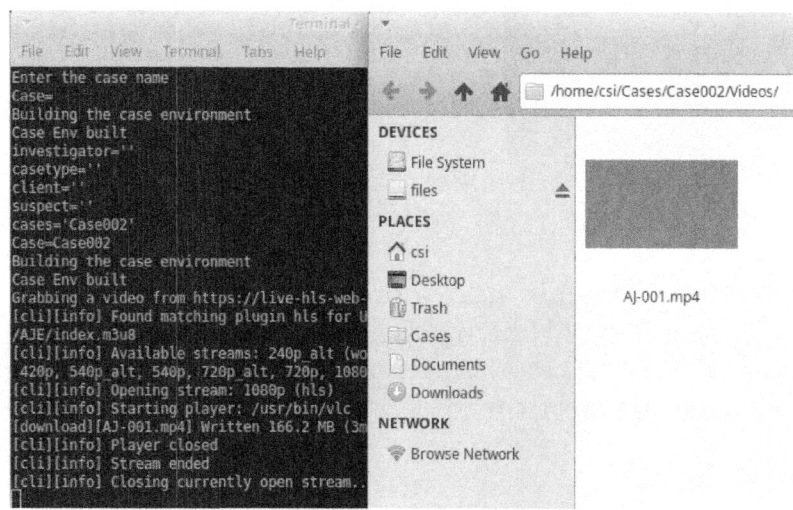

Note: You can double left click on the AJ-001.mp4 if you want to verify the capture.

8. Back in the video capture tool, left-click on the "Take Snapshot Every 30 Seconds from Video (FFMPEG)" button.

9. Find the "AJ-001.mp4" file and left-click on "OK."

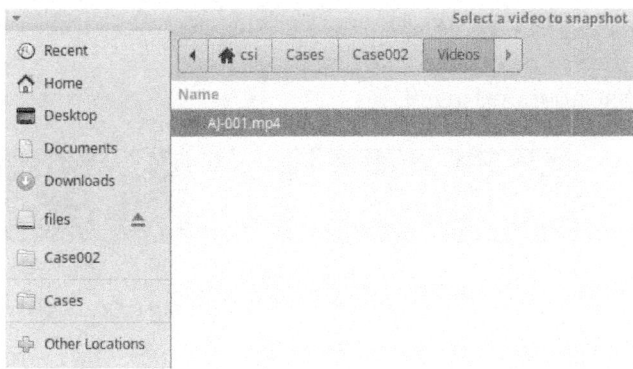

Note: the video will start being analyzed by FFMPEG and capture a screenshot every 30 seconds. Each image will be added to a folder with the name of the video. In this case, there will be a folder called "AJ-001". Each image will be named image#.jpg

10. Go into the ~/Cases/"Case Name"/Videos/AJ-001 folder to see the images

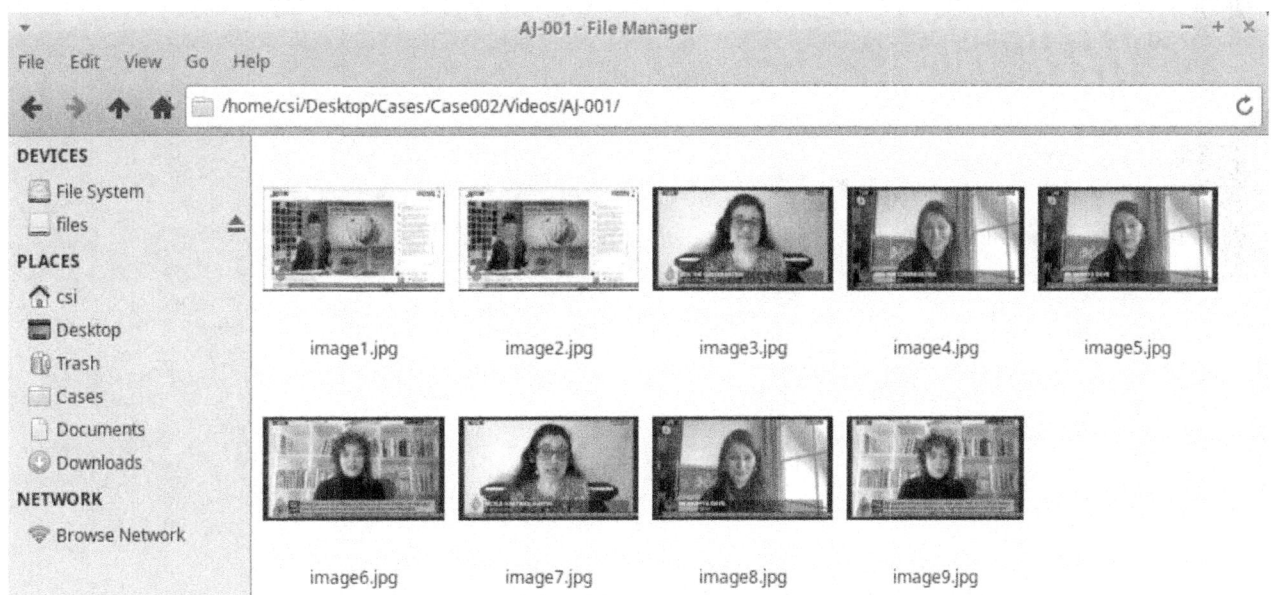

This process will give you a good idea of what the video contains without having to watch the entire video while separating everything into the folders associated with the specific video.

191

CSI Linux Video Capture Walkthrough – YouTube Capture

Now, you want to download a video that was posted on Vimeo.com that is related to an ongoing investigation. We are going to use the Youtube-dl option.

Note: If Youtube-dl doesn't work for a site, try the Streamlink option

1. Left click on the icon that is outlined in red.

2. Enter the name of the case you are working on and left-click on "OK."

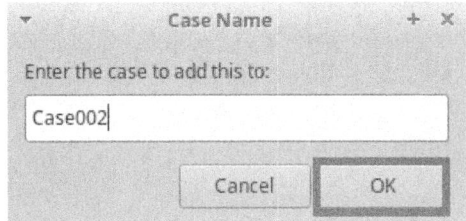

Note: We are going to use the Youtube-dl option

3. Left click on Download Video from a Website button

   We are going to download the "XnView Image Analysis – Cyber Secrets" video

   vimeo.com/479570297

4. Enter the video URL of the video into the text field and left-click "OK."

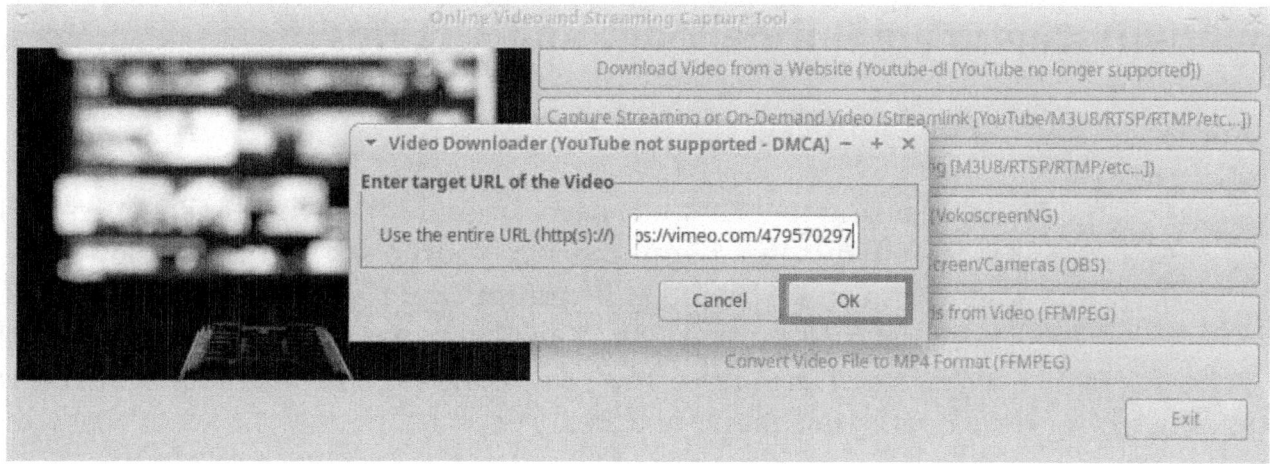

Wait until it is done, then the video should be saved into the ~/Cases/"Case Name"/Videos folder. Then double left click on the video to verify that it downloaded successfully.

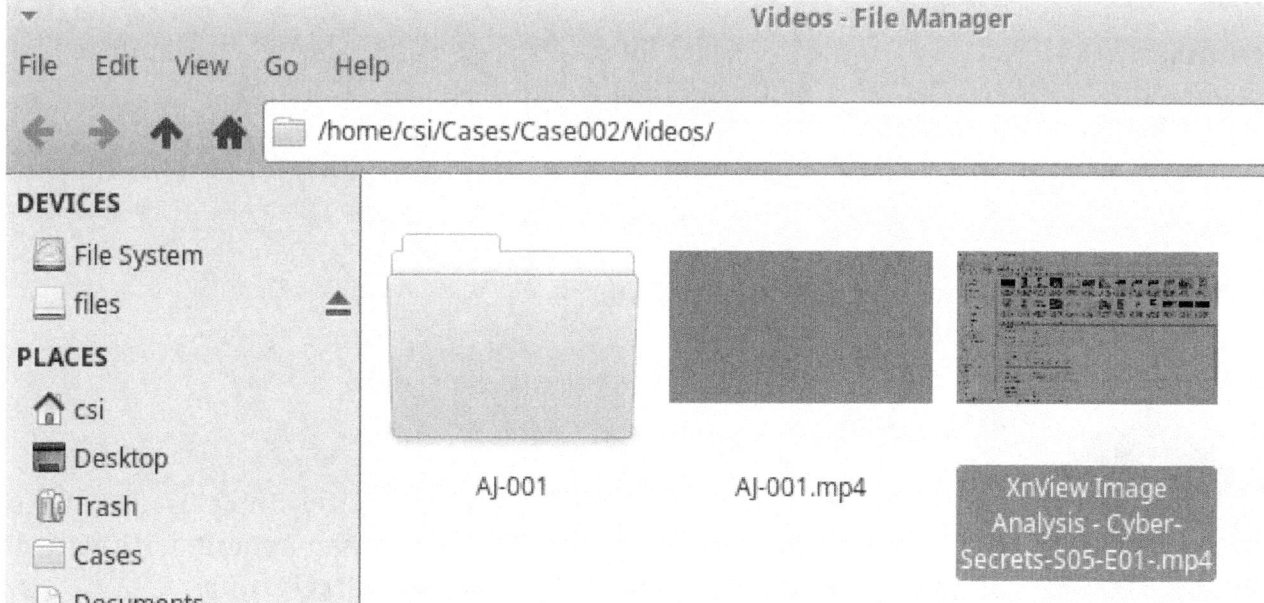

As you can see, Youtube-dl does a great job keeping the original name from the website associated with the file. You will need to name the file yourself for some of the other options. As a reminder, in the instance when Youtube-dl doesn't work, your options for troubleshooting are:

- Run a powerup to update CSI Linux and the dependencies
- Use Streamlink
- Look at the source code of the web page and identify the file
  - If the file is an actual stream (.ts, M3U8, etc.), copy that link
  - Use Streamlink again using that link

Manually Capturing Online Video and Streams

Youtube-DL

An amazing tool that has been around for a while and is a staple in video downloading applications. Youtube-dl was taken down for a short time for a Digital Millennium Copyright Act (DMCA) takedown notice served by YouTube. Luckily, it was brought back and is still available. Here is a link for content: Github.blog/2020-11-16-standing-up-for-developers-youtube-dl-is-back/

This tool supports over 1200 different sources, and their updated list can be found here:

ytdl-org.github.io/youtube-dl/supportedsites.html

Examples:

youtube-dl --list-extractors	(Supported)
youtube-dl "link" -o file.mp4	(Download)
youtube-dl "link" --write-thumbnail -o file.mp4	(Thumbnails)

Website: github.com/ytdl-org/youtube-dl
             youtube-dl.org

Streamlink

This tool has over 60 plugins for different sites and can also capture live streaming services using HLS. The other benefit is that it will also play the stream in the VLC player while recording.

Here is a list of supported plugins: streamlink.github.io/plugin_matrix.html

Examples:

streamlink "link" best	(VLC plays the "best" quality)
streamlink "link" best -r file.mp4	(Downloads the "file.mp4")

CLI help: streamlink.github.io/cli.html
Website: streamlink.github.io

VLC Player

This is a great tool that supports many video codec as a player. It can also record the feeds it plays. This means that you can convert to a different video format or record live streams (M3U8, RTSP, RTMP, etc.). If Streamlink doesn't capture live streams, this is a backup solution.

The only issue I have seen is the audio sometimes becomes out of sync.

Examples:

    vlc "link"
    --
    sout="#duplicate{dst=std{access=file,mux=mp4,dst='$file.mp4'},dst=display}" (Play stream and copies to a file)

Note: This syntax will split the file to VLC while saving it to a file named "filemp4".

    vlc -vvv "link"
    --sout '#standard{access=http,mux=ts,dst=0.0.0.0:1234}'
    (Open op a streaming server on port 1234)

    vlc ServerIP:1234   (Connect to the remote server no 1234)

URL syntax:

file:///path/file	Plain media file
host[:port]/file	HTTP URL
ftp://host[:port]/file	FTP URL
mms://host[:port]/file	MMS URL
screen://	Screen capture
dvd://[device]	DVD device
vcd://[device]	VCD device
cdda://[device]	Audio CD device
udp://[source address@bind address:bind port]	UDP stream
vlc://pause:<seconds>	Pause the playlist
vlc://quit	Special item to quit VLC

CLI help: wiki.videolan.org/VLC_command-line_help/
Website: videolan.org

Manually Capturing or Streaming your Desktop

VokoscreenNG

"vokoscreenNG is a powerful screencast creator in 38 languages to record the screen, an area, or a window (Linux only). Recording of audio from multiple sources is supported. With the built-in camera support, you can make your video more personal." - linuxecke.volkoh.de

Just make sure the "Videopath" is set to your ~/Cases/"Case Name"/Video folder.

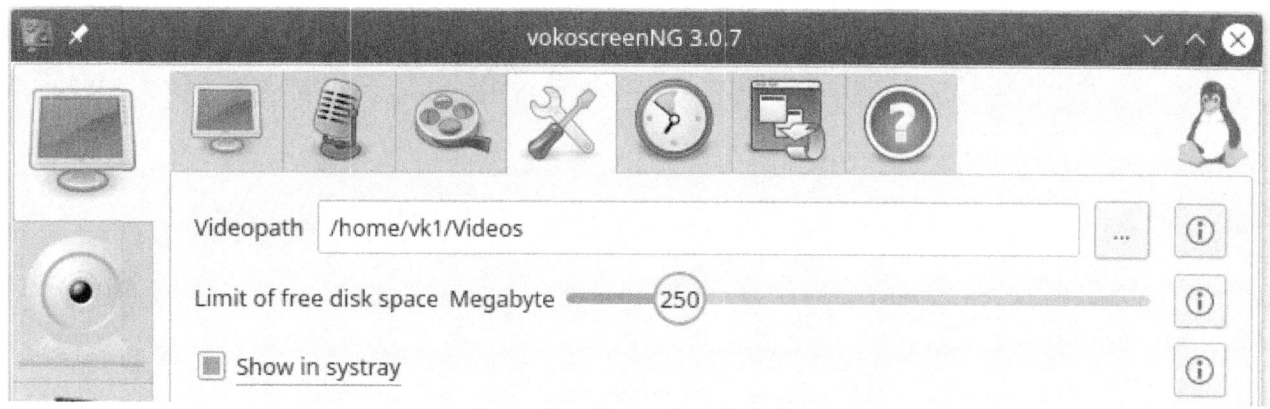

Image from linuxecke.volkoh.de

CLI Help: non at this time.
Website: github.com/vkohaupt/vokoscreenNG

OBS Studio

"OBS (Open Broadcaster Software) is free and open-source software for video recording and live streaming. Stream to Twitch, YouTube, and many other providers" obsproject.com

Examples:

```
obs --startstreaming --startrecording      (Stream/Record)
obs --studio-mode --startrecording          (Studio Mode/Record)
```

CLI Help: obsproject.com/wiki/Launch-Parameters
Website: obsproject.com

Manual Convert Videos and Capture Streaming

FFmpeg FFMPEG

"FFmpeg is a free and open-source software project consisting of a suite of libraries and programs for handling video, audio, and other multimedia files and streams. At its core is the command-line FFmpeg tool itself, designed for processing of video and audio files." - Wikipedia

This tool allows you to manually convert video file formats, separate audio from video, and record or "convert" live streams to a file. It is the base much video-focused software is based on or around.

Examples:

ffmpeg -i input.mp4 -hide_banner   (Get video info)

ffmpeg -i "link" -bsf:a aac_adtstoasc -vcodec copy -c copy -crf 50 file.mp4

-bsf:a aac_adtstoasc
bsf = (bit stream filter)
use aac_adtstoasc bsf for a audio streams, this is need if .m3u8 file consists with .ts files and output is .mp4
reference ffmpeg.org/ffmpeg-bitstream-filters.html#aac_005fadtstoasc

-c copy -vcodec copy
skip codec (encode and decode), just demux and mux
reference ffmpeg.org/ffmpeg.html#Stream-copy

-crf 50
0 is lossless, 23 is the default, and 51 bad
reference trac.ffmpeg.org/wiki/Encode/H.264#CRFExample

ffmpeg -i input.mp4 -vn output.mp3   (Pull audio)

ffmpeg -i input.mp4 -r 5 image%d.jpg   (Turn video into images)

-r   Set the frame rate per second. The default value is 25 per second.
1   = 1 shot per second
1/30   = 1 shot per 30 seconds

CLI Help: ffmpeg.org/ffmpeg.html
Website: ffmpeg.org

GEOINT: Geo-locating Images Using Landmarks

By: Umar Farooq

This article is going to be focused on geolocating images, specifically using Landmarks. Geolocation means finding the real world location of an object, such as the place where a photograph was taken. This process is rather straightforward but there are various methods - some more creative than others - of doing so. You don't always get enough clues from an image's metadata (data about data) and most images won't typically show a famous landmark in the background to help you locate the area, town or even country.

According to Geo-INT expert *Benjamin Strick*, there are 5 key elements one should consider when looking at an image:

- Context
- Foreground
- Background
- Map markings
- Trial and error

Methodology: Reduce Your Area of Interest

Usually, we have a context in which the image was produced or shared, called context clues. For example, things like type of architecture, important landmarks, and any other clues where this location could be in relation to land. Any piece of information, no matter how minor it may appear, could give an image more context. As an example, while searching for a missing person, an image of a banana leaf led investigators to research where banana production exists in the world.

One of the more obvious ways we can geolocate an image is to look at the image details:

- Who posted the image?
- Where was it posted?
- Does it contain metadata?
- Is there a location tagged on social media?
- Your investigation also serves as context

Image Analysis

Be creative and scan the image for visual clues. Look for Point-Of-Interests in the image like its landscape, terrain, road layouts, a river, bridge, statue, or a steep hill or for unique features like vegetation, specific trees, windows, street art, business names, architectural details like light-posts, balconies, or rooftops in the Background as well as Foreground.

Reverse image search

One of the methods for geolocating an image is to do an image reverse search. This means that if the image has been indexed by search engines, we may find the exact image, or we can do a visual or crop search to help us find similar images. Remember that changing the crop and the keywords for searching an image may yield completely different results. I like to use this browser addon to ease the workflow when I find images online that I want to do an image reverse on:

Addon description: "Perform a search by image. Choose between the image search engines Google, Bing, Yandex, TinEye and Baidu."

Chrome: https://chrome.google.com/webstore/search/RevEye%20Reverse%20Image%20Search?hl=no
Firefox: https://addons.mozilla.org/nb-NO/firefox/addon/reveye-ris/

Let's see an Example

Consider we are provided below image for analysis:

From the things we discussed above, we can see some odd buildings which really stand out and something like a playground in the background (marked in red).

If we play close attention, we notice something in the foreground (marked in cyan) also which, probably, is a railing. We can later use it for confirmation purposes like from where the photo was taken.

Keeping this point of interests in sight, a reverse image search tells us that the image was taken in London and the skyscrapers and railing help confirm it.

Map Markings

Orienting an image on a map provides valuable insights. If compared to Traditional mapping platforms, Local mapping platforms or data sets sometimes provide more valuable information. Sources like *Weather Underground* can be used to check historical weather data to corroborate image dates with weather at various locations, *WolframAlpha* to establish a time frame based on rainfall or *London Street Trees* to locate a particular type of tree across the city. *SunCalc* is another useful resource to identify a particular location using the sun's direction and shadow in an image.

A tool like *Wikimapia* allows users to annotate maps, include adding the names and locations of various structures. We can later add place marks on *Google Earth* or *Google Maps* as they have variety of different other options.

Keep an Eye for what is NOT in your image/video?

During a *Bellingcat* investigation to geolocate an image of mass executions in or near Benghazi, a Twitter user noticed the color of the sand was grey compared to other areas of Benghazi, where colors of the sand are more orange or yellow. This tip helped investigators identify the location to be in the southwest area of Benghazi. Furthermore, this was the first instance when (in August 2017) the International Criminal Court (ICC) issued its first ever arrest warrant solely based on evidence gathered via social media.

Trial and Error

Sometimes you need to revisit previous assumptions. When you feel like giving up, go back repeatedly and revisit your assumptions, check if any possible suspicion or guess may be correct or not. Try to look for what is not in an image. Even when an image shows no clear horizon, the lack of a horizon could become just as useful to reduce your area of interest.

Further Tips

While geolocating, it's important to know what is and isn't likely to be in a country. For example, it is unlikely for a regular Catholic church to appear in places where Buddhism / Islam is the most popular religion. The language used on the shops and vehicles matter too. We can use Google translate to predict what language it could be. Which side of the road the cars are on, the license plates, the markings on the road (different countries have different markings), the style of traffic lights, the clothing choices of those walking around.

To be good at geolocation, we've got to open our eyes to all that could be. In your country, for example, it may be common to wear coats during the winter periods. However, in other countries it may not be (think). Even the smallest of things that we wouldn't normally think twice about can reveal to us the possible location.

> Still wandering? Here's a nice (beginner) geolocation challenge write-up
> *https://www.secjuice.com/geolocation-osint-amateur-hour/*

For Improving Skills

> *@quiztime* on Twitter
> Play a lot of *Geoguesser!*

References:

- Benjamin Strick (on Twitter): *https://twitter.com/BenDoBrown*
- Weather Underground: https://www.wunderground.com/history
- WolframAlpha: https://www.wolframalpha.com/examples/science-and-technology/weather-and-meteorology/
- London Street Trees: https://apps.london.gov.uk/street-trees/
- SunCalc: https://www.suncalc.org/
- Wikimapia: https://wikimapia.org/
- Geoguesser: https://geoguessr.com/
- Identify a location from a photo or video: *https://youtu.be/RoqWbpZUOSo*
- Robin Taylor's session "More Than Meets the Eye: Geolocation for human rights investigations" at the Investigation is Collaboration conference: *https://cdn.ttc.io/s/exposingtheinvisible.org/iic-conf/slides/Geolocation_RTaylor.pdf*
- OSINT Geo Location: https://rallypoint.withyouwithme.com/cyber_challenges/osint-geo-location/
- Geolocation Techniques – Mapping Landmarks: *https://www.bellingcat.com/resources/how-tos/2014/07/15/geolocation-techniques-mapping-landmarks/*
- Google Earth: https://earth.google.com/
- Google Maps: https://www.google.com/maps
- Bellingcat: https://www.bellingcat.com/

Using Sublist3r

By: Kevin John O. Hermosa

Subdomain enumeration is an essential step in reconnaissance as it helps in discovering assets owned and connected to the primary party subject to ethical hacking.

It isn't essential at first, especially when dealing with small-time domains. But when you consider domains on the level of, say, googlevideo.com, one could see that it can be quite a daunting task to be managing hundreds or even thousands of these subdomains. You could even overlook the fact that some of them could already be pointing to malicious servers—which are just some of the things that one should be on the lookout for.

With all that said, the subject of this section is all about a subdomain enumeration tool named Sublist3r, which is designed to query a wide variety of search engines and DNS databases to gather subdomain information about the domain provided as input.

Installation

For this article, Python 3 will be installed to fulfill the dependencies needed for the successful execution of the Sublist3r tool. Still, the author claims that it should work for both 2 and 3, where he recommended versions 2.7.x and 3.4.x in Sublist3r's GitHub repository.

Installation involves installing python3 and python3-pip, which are Sublist3r's main dependencies as it is a python script. Using Kali Linux or a Debian-based distro is assumed but installing python on other distros is typically a trivial task.

    sudo apt install python3 python3-pip

The next step is grabbing Sublist3r itself, which is quickly done by git cloning the Sublist3r git repository.
Keep in mind that the folder will be created in the current working directory of your shell session. And you can quickly check that by plainly using the "pwd" command.

    git clone github.com/aboul3la/Sublist3r.git

What needs to be done after this is that you will have to install other Python packages that Sublist3r depends on. Oh, and don't forget to cd into what you just cloned.

```
cd Sublist3r
pip3 install --user -r requirements.txt
```

We're almost done! Since sublist3r.py uses python instead of python3, a symlink pointing to python3 will be created.

```
sudo ln -sfv /usr/bin/python3 /usr/bin/python
```

Then last, but not least is making it easy for you to invoke your new tool.

```
sudo ln -sfv ./sublist3r.py /usr/bin/sublist3r
```

Now go and rock hard with it!

```
sublist3r -d [targetdomain.com]
```

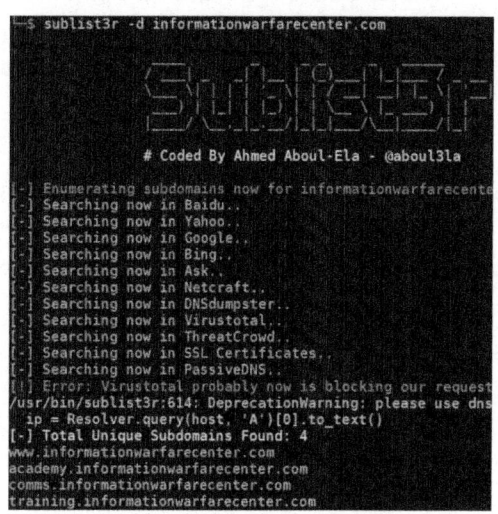

It's OK to ignore the deprecation warning as it is, and it should go away once Sublist3r's code gets changed to update the deprecated code.

Final words

With that, you should enumerate subdomains with confidence, thanks to people like Ahmed Aboul-Ela. They write valuable programs that dramatically ease cumbersome tasks like enumerating domains.

Execution of Sublist3r targeting informationwarfarecenter.com

Feel free to play with Sublist3r as it offers you the ability to specify many things about its operation, like the number of threads to allocate for the enumeration process, using only specific search engines, etc.

References

- Sublist3r's official git repository
    - Link: github.com/aboul3la/Sublist3r

DNSRecon

By: MUHAMMAD ABUBAKAR

"DNSRecon, as it is known today, is the Python equivalent of a Ruby script originally written by Carlos Perez toward the end of 2006. In his own words, this tool largely emerged from his personal need to reflect DNS-related data collection in an intuitive manner while the Python version allowed him to practice his newly acquired skills with the programming language." - securitytrails.com

This script provides the ability to perform:

> Check all NS Records for Zone Transfers.
> Enumerate General DNS Records for a given Domain (MX, SOA, NS, A, AAAA, SPF and TXT).
> Perform common SRV Record Enumeration.
> Top Level Domain (TLD) Expansion.
> Check for Wildcard Resolution.
> Brute Force sub-domain and host A and AAAA records given a domain and a word-list.
> Perform a PTR Record lookup for a given IP Range or CIDR.
> Check a DNS Server Cached records for A, AAAA and CNAME Records provided a list of host records in a text file to check.

This script has seen some development recently but its most of its code base is old.

Following are general enumeration results are from a search of "google.com" using dnsrecon with the "-d" option

$ dnsrecon -d google.com

```
[*] Performing General Enumeration of Domain: google.com
[-] DNSSEC is not configured for google.com
[*] NS ns1.google.com 216.239.32.10
[*] NS ns1.google.com 2001:4860:4802:32::a
[*] NS ns3.google.com 216.239.36.10
[*] NS ns3.google.com 2001:4860:4802:36::a
[*] NS ns4.google.com 216.239.38.10
[*] NS ns4.google.com 2001:4860:4802:38::a
[*] NS ns2.google.com 216.239.34.10
[*] NS ns2.google.com 2001:4860:4802:34::a
[*] MX alt1.aspmx.l.google.com 142.251.9.27
[*] MX alt3.aspmx.l.google.com 74.125.200.27
[*] MX aspmx.l.google.com 142.251.5.27
[*] MX alt2.aspmx.l.google.com 142.250.150.26
[*] MX alt4.aspmx.l.google.com 142.250.157.26
[*] MX alt1.aspmx.l.google.com 2a00:1450:4025:c03::1a
[*] MX alt3.aspmx.l.google.com 2404:6800:4003:c00::1b
[*] MX aspmx.l.google.com 2a00:1450:400c:c06::1b
[*] MX alt2.aspmx.l.google.com 2a00:1450:4010:c1c::1b
[*] MX alt4.aspmx.l.google.com 2404:6800:4008:c13::1b
```

[*] A google.com 172.217.19.174
[*] AAAA google.com 2a00:1450:4019:801::200e
[*] Enumerating SRV Records
[+] SRV _ldap._tcp.google.com ldap.google.com 216.239.32.58 389
[+] SRV _ldap._tcp.google.com ldap.google.com 2001:4860:4802:32::3a 389
[+] SRV _xmpp-client._tcp.google.com xmpp.l.google.com 66.102.1.125 5222
[+] SRV _xmpp-client._tcp.google.com alt2.xmpp.l.google.com 142.250.150.125 5222
[+]   SRV _xmpp-client._tcp.google.com alt2.xmpp.l.google.com 2a00:1450:4010:c1c::7d 5222
[+]   SRV _xmpp-client._tcp.google.com alt3.xmpp.l.google.com 74.125.200.125 5222
[+]   SRV _xmpp-client._tcp.google.com alt3.xmpp.l.google.com 2404:6800:4003:c00::7d 5222
[+] SRV _xmpp-client._tcp.google.com alt1.xmpp.l.google.com 142.251.9.125 5222
[+]   SRV _xmpp-client._tcp.google.com alt1.xmpp.l.google.com 2a00:1450:4025:c03::7d 5222
[+]   SRV _xmpp-client._tcp.google.com alt4.xmpp.l.google.com 142.250.157.125 5222
[+]   SRV _xmpp-client._tcp.google.com alt4.xmpp.l.google.com 2404:6800:4008:c13::7d 5222
[+]   SRV _xmpp-server._tcp.google.com alt2.xmpp-server.l.google.com 142.250.150.125 5269
[+]   SRV _xmpp-server._tcp.google.com alt3.xmpp-server.l.google.com 74.125.200.125
[+] SRV _xmpp-server._tcp.google.com xmpp-server.l.google.com 142.251.5.125 5269
[+] SRV _xmpp-server._tcp.google.com alt4.xmpp-server.l.google.com 142.250.157.125 5269
[+] SRV _xmpp-server._tcp.google.com alt1.xmpp-server.l.google.com 142.251.9.125
[+] SRV _jabber._tcp.google.com alt4.xmpp-server.l.google.com 142.250.157.125
[+] SRV _jabber._tcp.google.com alt1.xmpp-server.l.google.com 142.251.9.125 5269
[+] SRV _jabber._tcp.google.com alt3.xmpp-server.l.google.com 74.125.200.125 5269
[+] SRV _jabber._tcp.google.com xmpp-server.l.google.com 142.251.5.125 5269
[+] SRV _jabber._tcp.google.com alt2.xmpp-server.l.google.com 142.250.150.125
[+] SRV _caldavs._tcp.google.com calendar.google.com 172.217.21.46 443
[+] SRV _caldavs._tcp.google.com calendar.google.com 2a00:1450:4019:806::200e 443
[+] SRV _carddavs._tcp.google.com google.com 172.217.19.174 443
[+] SRV _carddavs._tcp.google.com google.com 2a00:1450:4019:801::200e 443
[+] SRV _caldav._tcp.google.com calendar.google.com 172.217.21.46 80
[+] SRV _caldav._tcp.google.com calendar.google.com 2a00:1450:4019:806::200e 80
[+] SRV _jabber-client._tcp.google.com alt1.xmpp.l.google.com 142.251.9.125 5222
[+] SRV _jabber-client._tcp.google.com alt1.xmpp.l.google.com 2a00:1450:4025:c03::7d 5222
[+] SRV _jabber-client._tcp.google.com alt2.xmpp.l.google.com 142.250.150.125
[+] SRV _jabber-client._tcp.google.com alt2.xmpp.l.google.com 2a00:1450:4010:c1c::7d 5222
[+] SRV _jabber-client._tcp.google.com alt3.xmpp.l.google.com 74.125.200.125 5222
[+] SRV _jabber-client._tcp.google.com alt3.xmpp.l.google.com 2404:6800:4003:c00::7d 5222
[+] SRV _jabber-client._tcp.google.com xmpp.l.google.com 66.102.1.125 5222
[+] SRV _jabber-client._tcp.google.com xmpp.l.google.com 2a00:1450:400c:c1b::7d 5
[+] SRV _jabber-client._tcp.google.com alt4.xmpp.l.google.com 142.250.157.125
[+] SRV _jabber-client._tcp.google.com alt4.xmpp.l.google.com 2404:6800:4008:c13::7d 5222
[+] 38 Records Found

Note: This is not the entire list of Internet facing systems, but now we have a good list of subdomains and IPV4/6 IP addresses to get started with. If you use other tools like Sublist3r, Fierce, Recon-NG, etc, you will probably find more to add to your evidence capture.

ReconDog

ReconDog v2.0
By: Maria Segarra

The use of Open-Source tools is becoming more and more popular these days; more businesses are opting for minimizing certain technology costs. Therefore, administrative decisions sometimes lead to taking advantage of exploring and experimenting with Open-Source tools that are available on the internet. Tools such as *ReconDog* can bring many great benefits and utilities that can facilitate some of the basic but valuable techniques for reconnaissance.

It is an Open-Source tool that is used for basic information reconnaissance. It exploits external databases and locally driven searches to collect information about its scan targets. *ReconDog* can scan websites and web applications to help find possible vulnerabilities. It uses API to gather and extract all the data from different resources. The tool can be downloaded from GitHub. Many utility modules are available in ReconDog, such as a Port scanner, Detect Content Management Systems (CMS), Honeypot detector, Whois Lookup, NS Lookup, and reverse Ip Lookup, among others. The software can be run on Windows, Linux, and Mac.

There are two requirements needed before installing *ReconDog* in your system. You will need to ensure that you have the Python interpreter 2.7 and/or 3.6 installed and Git installed.

Pre-Installation:

1. Open your preferred web browser and go to https://github.com/s0md3v/ReconDog (To check if needed files are still available in the repository)
2. Open your Linux System (virtual machine preferred)
3. Open a CLI/CMD prompt Terminal window

Ensure to check for any needed updates/upgrades available by entering the following command on the terminal.

    sudo apt update && apt upgrade

Ensure that Git is already installed or installed by entering the following command on the terminal.

sudo apt install git

Ensure that Python is already installed or installed by entering the following command on the terminal.

sudo apt install python

After confirming that the installation packages mentioned above are set in place, install *ReconDog* by entering the following commands in the terminal.

git clone https://github.com/UltimateHackers/ReconDog
cd ReconDog
ls
sudo chmod +x dog
./dog

The first command below refers to where the *ReconDog* files will be downloaded and installed.

git clone https://github.com/UltimateHackers/ReconDog

The second command below will open the *ReconDog* Directory for its navigation.

cd ReconDog

The third command below will enlist any existing files located inside the ReconDog Directory that can be accessed.

ls

The fourth command below will give the execute permission to the file/tool.

sudo chmod +x dog

Permission was successfully applied, and now the fifth command below will run its instructions and execute the tool.

$ ./dog

Congratulations! You have successfully installed ReconDog.

Terminal Command Line Argument (CLA) Interface Usage:

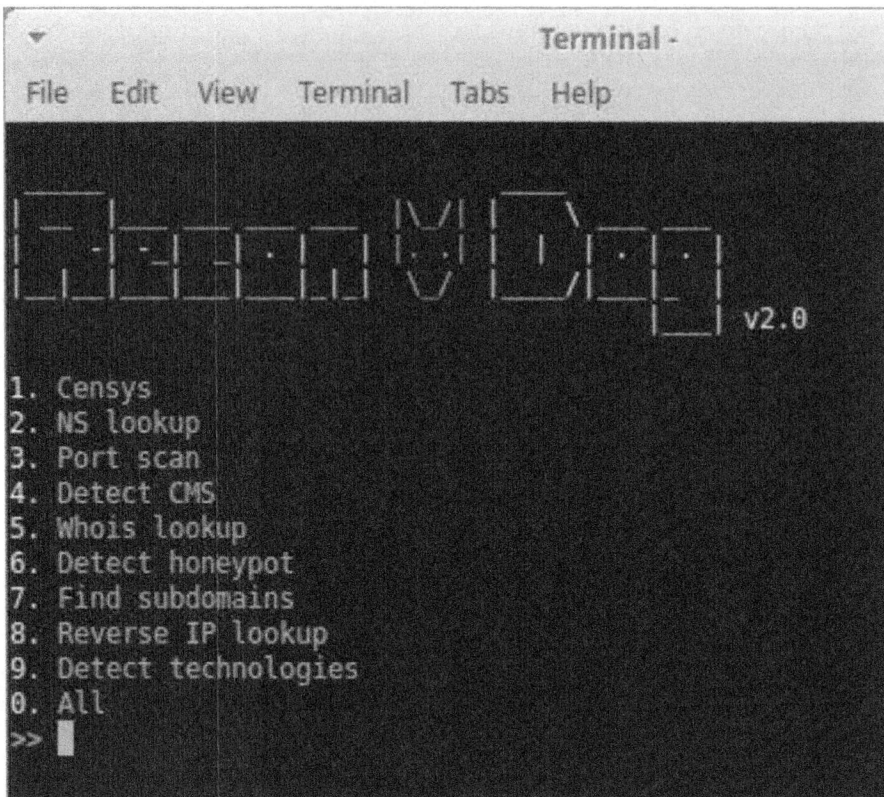

Figure 1-13 CSI Linux

Terminal CLA Interface

The CLA Interface encompasses the capability of pipelining, i.e., passing the output of some operation as input to a subsequent one. This will aid in searching subdomains-sample screenshots and command output below.

dog -c 3 -t <domain>

Figure 3-13 Nicholas Kolokotronis, Stavros Shiaeles (Ref below)

In the area below, you will find a sample of some of the tool modules with a brief description of what it does and some screenshots of the command outputs for better understanding and visibility.

210

Utility Modules:

ReconDog has around ten different utility modules, and each performs various searches and provides excellent information about targeted resources. A sample of the modules and their outputs are provided below for your appreciation.

Websites Consulted for ReconDog Functionality Realization

Website	ReconDog Feature(s) Supported
hackertarget.com	NS lookup, Port Scan, Whois lookup, Reverse IP lookup
censys.io	Censys (device discovery and analysis)
whatcms.org	Detect CMS
shodan.io	Detect honeypot
findsubdomains.com	Find subdomains
wappalyzer.com	Detect technologies

Figure 2-13 Nicholas Kolokotronis, Stavros Shiaeles (Ref below)

Censys

This module can be used along with the *ReconDog* tool to scan the target's IP address to gather country and city location information. Sample screenshot of the command output below.

1. Input/type the number 1
2. provide the target <IP address>

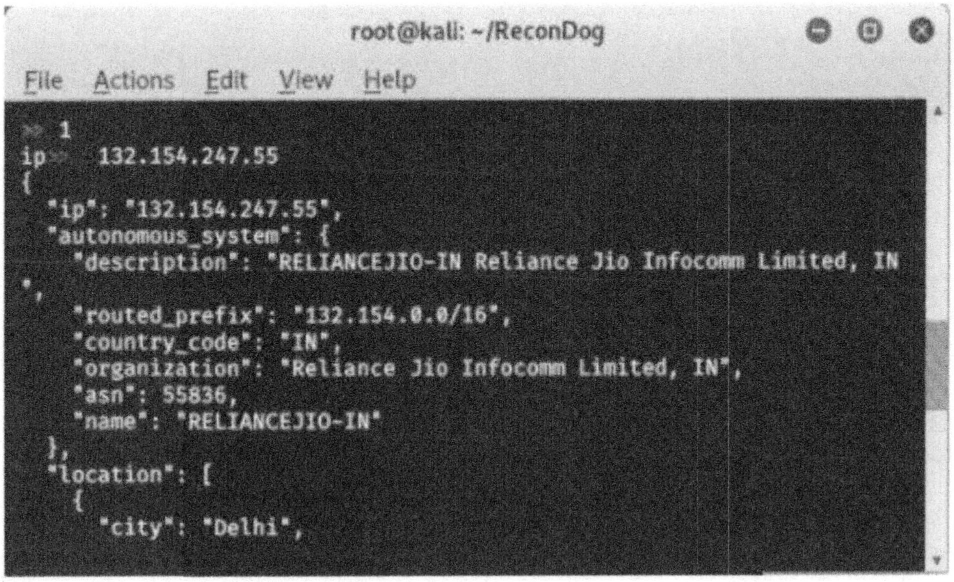

```
root@kali: ~/ReconDog

File  Actions  Edit  View  Help

>> 1
ip    132.154.247.55
{
  "ip": "132.154.247.55",
  "autonomous_system": {
    "description": "RELIANCEJIO-IN Reliance Jio Infocomm Limited, IN
",
    "routed_prefix": "132.154.0.0/16",
    "country_code": "IN",
    "organization": "Reliance Jio Infocomm Limited, IN",
    "asn": 55836,
    "name": "RELIANCEJIO-IN"
  },
  "location": [
    {
      "city": "Delhi",
```

Figure 4-13 geeksforgeeks.org

NS Lookup

This module can gather some information about the targeted domain and network. NS Lookup takes as input a domain name and queries the DNS servers to obtain the records of this domain. The records provided can be A (Address) records, NS (Name Server) records, MX (Mail eXchanger) records, SOA (Start of Authority) records, among other NS records are of interest to attackers because they can be exploited in the context of DNS poisoning attacks. Sample screenshot of the command output below.

1. Input/type the number 2
2. provide the target <domain>

7 This is a domain we set up solely for the demonstration purposes of this chapter, since the information that can be uncovered by this process is sensitive. All addresses used in the domain correspond to private IPs. Since the external APIs used by ReconDog do not work with private IPs, local installations of APIs delivering the required functionalities were set up and used in place of the APIs/websites utilized by the ReconDog distribution.

```
root@kali:~/ReconDog# python dog
```

```
1. Censys
2. NS lookup
3. Port scan
4. Detect CMS
5. Whois lookup
6. Detect honeypot
7. Find subdomains
8. Reverse IP lookup
9. Detect technologies
0. All
>> 2
domain>> scantest.uop.gr

scantest.uop.gr.        17304    IN    MX     10 bigserver.scantest.uop.gr.
scantest.uop.gr.        17304    IN    MX     20 backupserver.scantest.uop.gr.
scantest.uop.gr.        17304    IN    SOA    ns.scantest.uop.gr. noc.uop.gr.
2020011501 3600 7200 1209600 86400
scantest.uop.gr.        17303    IN    NS     ns.scantest.uop.gr.
```

Figure 5-13 Nicholas Kolokotronis, Stavros Shiaeles (Ref below)

Port Scan

This module can be used anonymously to run a port scan and gather information on the most used TCP ports and their port state and service. The module functionality consults *hackertaget.com* for its scans. Sample screenshot of the command output below.

1. Input/type the number 3
2. provide the target <domain> or <IP Address>

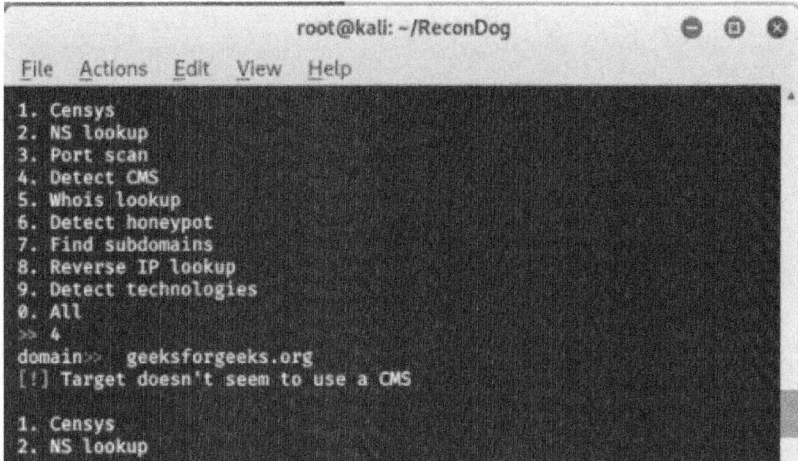

Figure 6-13 vodoo666.wordpress.com

Detect CMS

This module can be used to check if a domain is using Content Management System (CMS) or not. A Content Management System is software that aids users in creating, modifying, and managing website content without having a very vast technical knowledge, making It easy for anyone to use. This tool can detect more than 400+ CMS. The module uses *whatems.org* for its CMS detection. Sample screenshot of the command output below.

1. Input/type the number 4
2. provide the target <domain>

Figure 7-13 geeksforgeeks.org

213

Whois Lookup

This module can be used to run a WHOIS lookup. It provides information about the Registry Domain ID, Registrar Whois Server, Registrar URL, owner, domain provider, creation date, and the organization that registered the domain with its geographical location. Whois is a Plain Text Protocol that queries a database with internet resources. Whois Service can also gather information regarding allocated pools of IP addresses. This was initially designed for UNIX, but now it is available for Windows and other platforms. Sample screenshot of the command and its output below.

1. Input/type the number 5
2. provide the target <domain> or <IP Address>

8 Again, we used a locally installed Whois service provider, which we populated with test data, since the domain *scantest.uop.gr* is not officially registered.

```
domain or ip>> scantest.uop.gr
    Domain Name: SCANTEST.UOP.GR
    Registry Domain ID: 12345678-PrivateWhoIsReg
    Registrar WHOIS Server: privatereg.uop.gr
    Registrar URL: http://privatereg.uop.gr
    Updated Date: 2020-01-18T19:38:04Z
    Creation Date: 2020-01-16T15:12:53Z
    Registry Expiry Date: 2030-01-18T20:00:00Z
    Registrar: ScanTest temporary registrar
    Registrar Abuse Contact Email: abuse@privatereg.uop.gr
    Registrar Abuse Contact Phone: +30.2710999999
    Domain Status: clientDeleteProhibited https://icann.org/epp#clientDeleteProhibit
    Domain Status: clientTransferProhibited https://icann.org/epp#clientTransferProh
    Domain Status: clientUpdateProhibited https://icann.org/epp#clientUpdateProhibit
    Registrant Organization: UoP Cyber-Trust Experiments
    ''-trant Country: GR
    Name Server: NS.SCANTEST.UOP.GR
    DNSSEC: unsigned
>>> Last update of whois database: 2020-01-18T19:38:04Z <<<

For more information on Whois status codes, please visit https://icann.org/epp
```

Whois for domain *scantest.uop.gr*

Figure 8-13 Nicholas Kolokotronis, Stavros Shiaeles (Ref below)

```
domain or ip>> 192.168.38.77
% Information related to '192.168.38.0 - 192.168.38.255'

% No abuse contact registered for 192.168.38.0 - 192.168.38.255

inetnum:        192.168.38.0 - 192.168.38.255
netname:        NON-RIPE-NCC-MANAGED-ADDRESS-BLOCK
descr:          IPv4 address block not managed by the RIPE NCC
country:        GR
admin-c:        PRIVATE-DOMAIN
tech-c:         PRIVATE-DOMAIN
status:         ALLOCATED UNSPECIFIED
mnt-by:         PRIVATE-SCANTEST
created:        2020-01-16T10:44:59Z
last-modified:  2020-01-16T10:44:59Z
source:         PRIVATE-DOMAIN
```

Whois for IP lookup

Figure 9-13 Nicholas Kolokotronis, Stavros Shiaeles (Ref below)

Detect Honeypot

This utility module can be used to check if a target could be a honeypot. It uses *Shodan.io* for honeypot detection and enlists the output as a probability percentage. Sample screenshot of the command and its output below.

1. Input/type the number 6
2. provide the target <IP Address>

Figure 10-13 geeksforgeeks.org

Find Subdomains

This utility module can be used to enumerate subdomains. This tool uses *findsubdomains.com* to do its search. It will provide information about the different available subdomains and their IP Address. A sample screenshot of the command and the output is below.

1. Input/type the number 7
2. provide the target <domain>

```
>> 7
domain>> scantest.uop.gr
Subdomains of scantest.uop.gr
  scantest.uop.gr
  backupserver.scantest.uop.gr
  bigserver.scantest.uop.gr
  ns.scantest.uop.gr
  pc-1.scantest.uop.gr
  pc-10.scantest.uop.gr
  pc-11.scantest.uop.gr
  pc-12.scantest.uop.gr
  pc-13-4.scantest.uop.gr
  pc-14.scantest.uop.gr
  pc-15.scantest.uop.gr
  pc-2.scantest.uop.gr
  pc-3.scantest.uop.gr
  pc-4.scantest.uop.gr
  pc-5.scantest.uop.gr
  pc-6.scantest.uop.gr
  pc-7.scantest.uop.gr
  pc-8.scantest.uop.gr
  pc-9.scantest.uop.gr
  pc-19-1.scantest.uop.gr
  sub.scantest.uop.gr
  www.scantest.uop.gr
```

Figure 11-13 Nicholas Kolokotronis, Stavros Shiaeles (Ref below)

Reverse IP Lookup

This utility module can be used to run a Reverse IP Lookup. It will run a search for all DNS names registered in the DNS to find what domain name/sites are associated with a given IP Address on the same local server. Sample screenshot of the command and its output below.

1. Input/type the number 8
2. provide the target <IP Address>

```
>> 8
ip>>  192.168.20.21
appserver.intranet
www.scantest.uop.gr
```

Figure 12-13 Nicholas Kolokotronis, Stavros Shiaeles (Ref below)

Detect Technologies

This utility module can be used to detect what technologies are used. It utilizes *wappalyzer.com,* and it can see more than 1000+ technologies available. It can identify technologies used on websites, eCommerce platforms, web frameworks, server software, and analytics tools, among others-sample screenshot of the command and its output below.

1. Input/type the number 9
2. provide the target <web site>

9 wappalyzer.com; this utility is also available as a Docker container at https://hub.docker.com/u/ wappalyzer

```
>> 9
url>>  www.scantest.uop.gr
Apache Bootstrap Debian Google Font API Joomla jQuery jQuery Migrate PHP
```

Detect technologies

Figure 13-13 Nicholas Kolokotronis, Stavros Shiaeles (Ref below)

All (Utilities)

This module can run all the modules together on the target. All the utilities mentioned before will be executed in the same target. Sample command below.

1. Input/type the number 0
2. provide the target <web site>

Why use ReconDog?

Well, why not? First, take advantage of this tool because it is Open-Source. It is currently free, fully available, and can continue to expand into a more sophisticated tool as it matures. Second, because it can perform a lot of different discoveries that can produce excellent output to aid in the analysis of a project and case reconnaissance, last, because this tool is simple, user-friendly, and valuable, technology and tools were made to be used when needed and make our lives somewhat more accessible.

References:

[1] open-Source Photo by www.freeimages.com
[2] ReconDog Photo by https://github.com/s0md3v/ReconDog
[3] Terminal CLI screenshots & descriptions by Cyber-Security Threats, Actors, and Dynamic Mitigation edited by Nicholas Kolokotronis, Stavros Shiaeles (scantest.uop.gr)
[4] Terminal CLI screenshots by vodoo666.wordpress.com
[5] Terminal CLI screenshots by geeksforgeeks.org/
Link: https://github.com/s0md3v/ReconDog
Link: https://www.kitploit.com/

Other references:

Link: https://censys.io/
Link: https://hackertarget.com/dns-lookup/
Link: https://hackertarget.com/tcp-port-scan/
Link: https://hackertarget.com/whois-lookup/
Link: https://honeyscore.shodan.io/
Link: https://spyse.com/tools/subdomain-finder
Link: https://hackertarget.com/reverse-ip-lookup/
Link: https://www.wappalyzer.com/

Cool Tool: ThreatResponder Forensics

Investigate Windows endpoints that are infected/compromised and offline, on-line, dead, in on-premises, remote, or the cloud, with speed and accuracy.

This is an agentless stand-alone software (which requires no installation) that allows ANYONE to investigate ANY Windows endpoint ANYWHERE the endpoint may be--whether on-premises, in the cloud, offline, "dead" hard drives, with or without an Internet connection

https://www.netsecurity.com/threatresponder-forensics/

Reports and Document Templates in CSI Linux

By: Jeremy Martin

The report template is very basic currently. The goal of it is to take the setting from both the current case and the organization/agency and propagate that data into one of the three report templates located in the **"~/Documents/Templates/"** folder. The new file will then be saved into the **"~/Cases/<case name>/Report/Report for <case>.odt"** file.

There will save some time while adding consistency to your reporting. As the project grows, we will add contents that were found during you investigation. This section will walk you through modifying the template to meet your needs.

The Template files are located here:

> path: /home/csi/Documents/Templates/

The easiest way to get there is to

1. Double left click on the **Home** icon on the desktop
2. Double left click on **Documents**
3. Double left click on **Templates**
4. Double left click on the template you want to use.
   a. Shadowdragon-Dossier-Template.odt
   b. Forensic-investigation-report-template.odt
   c. Custom-Template.odt

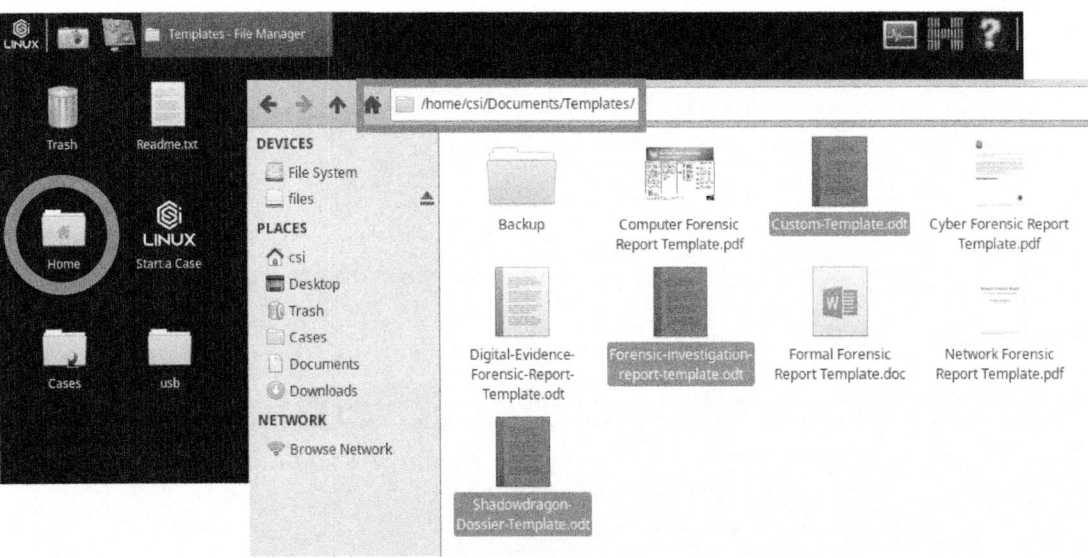

When you open the csi-template.odt, you should see some of the variable names within "<" ">" symbols.

The variables are pulled from two different files:

1. Global: /opt/csitools/startcsiconfig
2. Local: ~/Cases/Case Name/caseinfo.txt

The local file is in your case folder. The global file and Local file can be easily accessed from the CSI Case Management Menu.

○ Edit Document Generator Variables
◉ Document Templates for the Case

Investigation Reports

Here are the report variables you can modify.

	Variable	Value	Template Field Variable
Global	AgencyName	"Name of the Agency"	\<Agency Name\>
Global	AgencyAddress1	"Agency Mailing Address"	\<Agency Address\>
Global	AgencyCountry	"Country the Agency is in"	\<Agency Country\>
Global	AgencyState	"State the Agency is in"	\<Agency State\>
Global	AgencyCity	"City the Agency is in"	\<Agency City\>
Global	AgencyZip	"The zip code for the Agency"	\<Agency Zip\>
Global	AgencyPhone	"The Agency phone number"	\<Agency Phone\>
Global	AgencyWebsite	"URL of the agency"	\<Agency Website\>
Global	AgencyEmail	"Email address of the Agency"	\<Agency Email\>
Global	AgencyMessage	"Powered by CSI Linux"	\<Agency Tagline\>
Global	AgencyClassification	"FOUO"	\<Agency Classification\>
Case	Investigator	"Your Name"	\<Investigator\>
Case	cases	"Case Number/Name"	\<case\>
Case	casetype	"OSINT"	\<Case Type\>
Case	client	"Your Client's Name"	\<Client\>
Case	clientaddy	"Client Address"	\<Client Address\>
Case	clientcity	"Client City"	\<Client City\>
Case	clientstate	"Client State"	\<Client State\>
Case	clientzip	"Client Zip Code"	\<Client Zip\>
Case	clientphone	"Client Phone #"	\<Client Phone\>
Case	suspect	"Suspect Name"	\<Suspect\>

There can't be any formatting within the variable names, or the replacement will not work. Once the variables are added, you should be able to modify the entire variable. For example:

Change \<Client\> to *\<Client\>*

This will result in the \<Recipient of Report\> being replaced with a larger red font. If this does not work, you may have to delete the "\<client\>" and type it in again. This is an Open office issue if formatting is switched within a word and not around a word.

Now, you can change the report from the one that is included with the CSI Linux distribution to your own. You just need to save the file as a .ODT file and make sure to use the same file name: /home/csi/Documents/Templates/Custom-Template.odt.

If you would like to modify any of the templates, you can add the fields mentioned above to any place within the 3 documents.

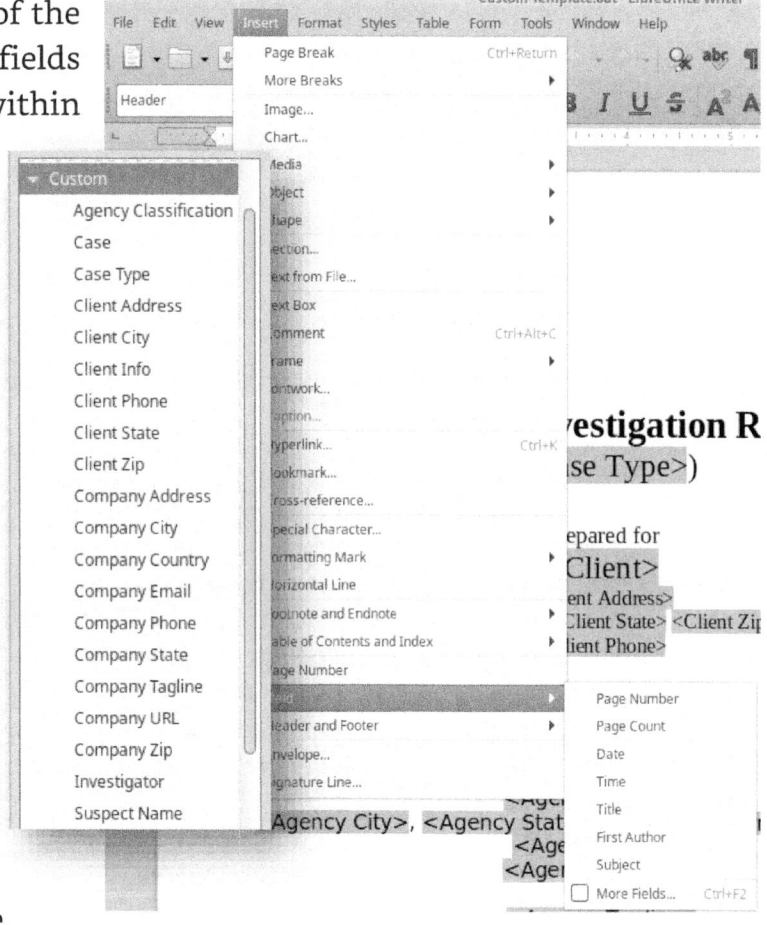

1. Open the template
2. Left click Insert
3. Left click Field
4. Left click More Fields
5. Left click on Custom
6. Pick the field to insert

This allows you to insert any one of these fields anywhere in the document you want. When the report is generated, it will be replaced with both the Local and the Global case variable values.

If you already have a report template built in Microsoft Word and saved as a .DOCX file, simply open it in word as save it as an OpenDocument Text (*.odt) file with a name that is **NOT** "Custom-Template.odt", and then copy the file into CSI Linux. Make sure to move it into the /home/csi/Documents/Templates/ folder.

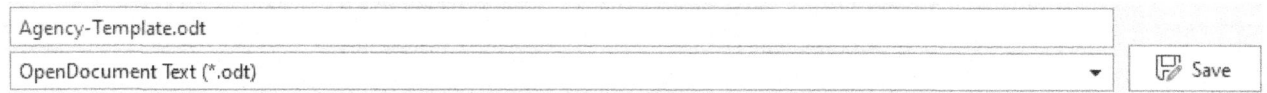

Then just copy the contents of your template into the Custom-Template.odt through Libre Office. This will be easier than adding each individual custom field into your pre-built template. Save the new Custom-Template.odt and add your fields accordingly.

Make sure your Global and Local variables are set. When you start a new case, the variables are stored when you fill out the case information, but it is always good to double check.

Open up the Case Management application and start a new case. The wizard allows you to add information that will be used within the Template Management system.

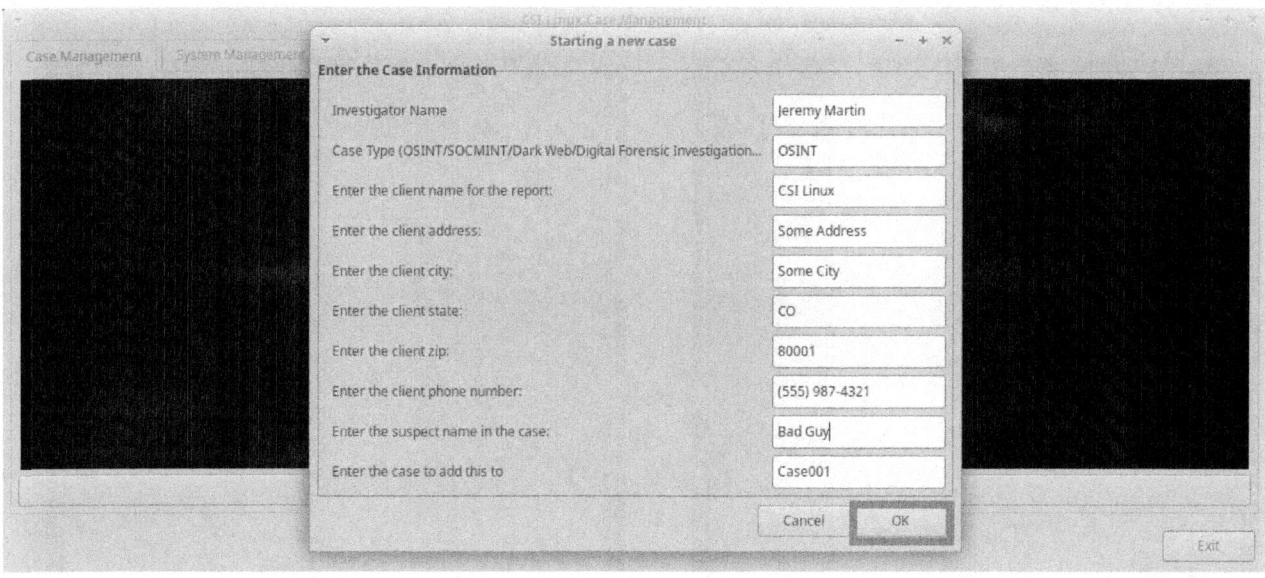

Once the case information is filled out, left click on OK. Now it is time to generate the report template.

P ick the Report section

Pick your report. In this instance we will pick the Suspect Dossier.

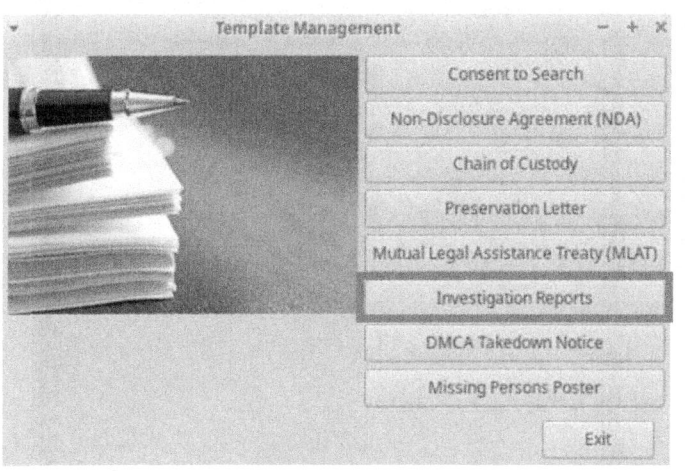

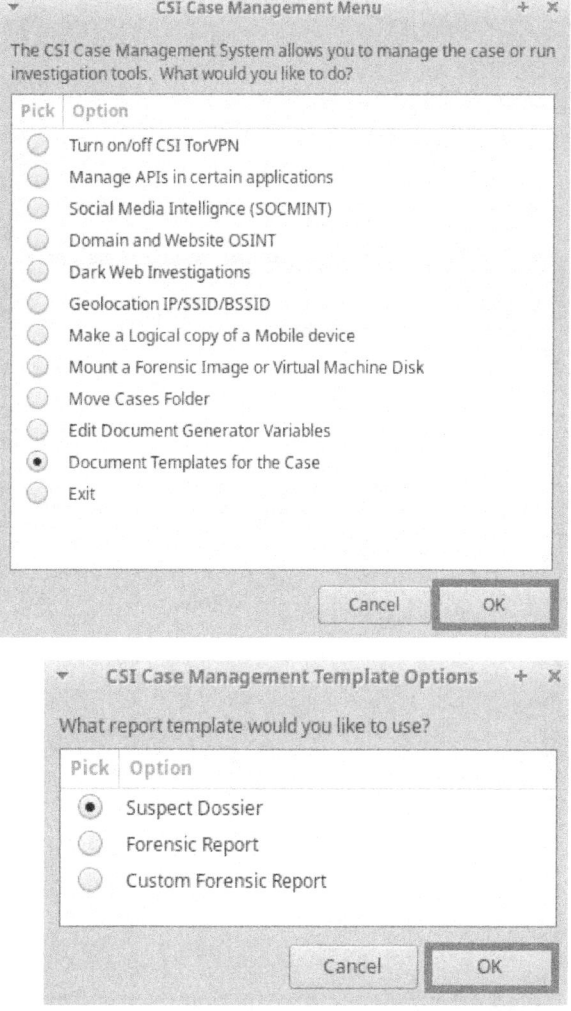

This should change the reports template like these:

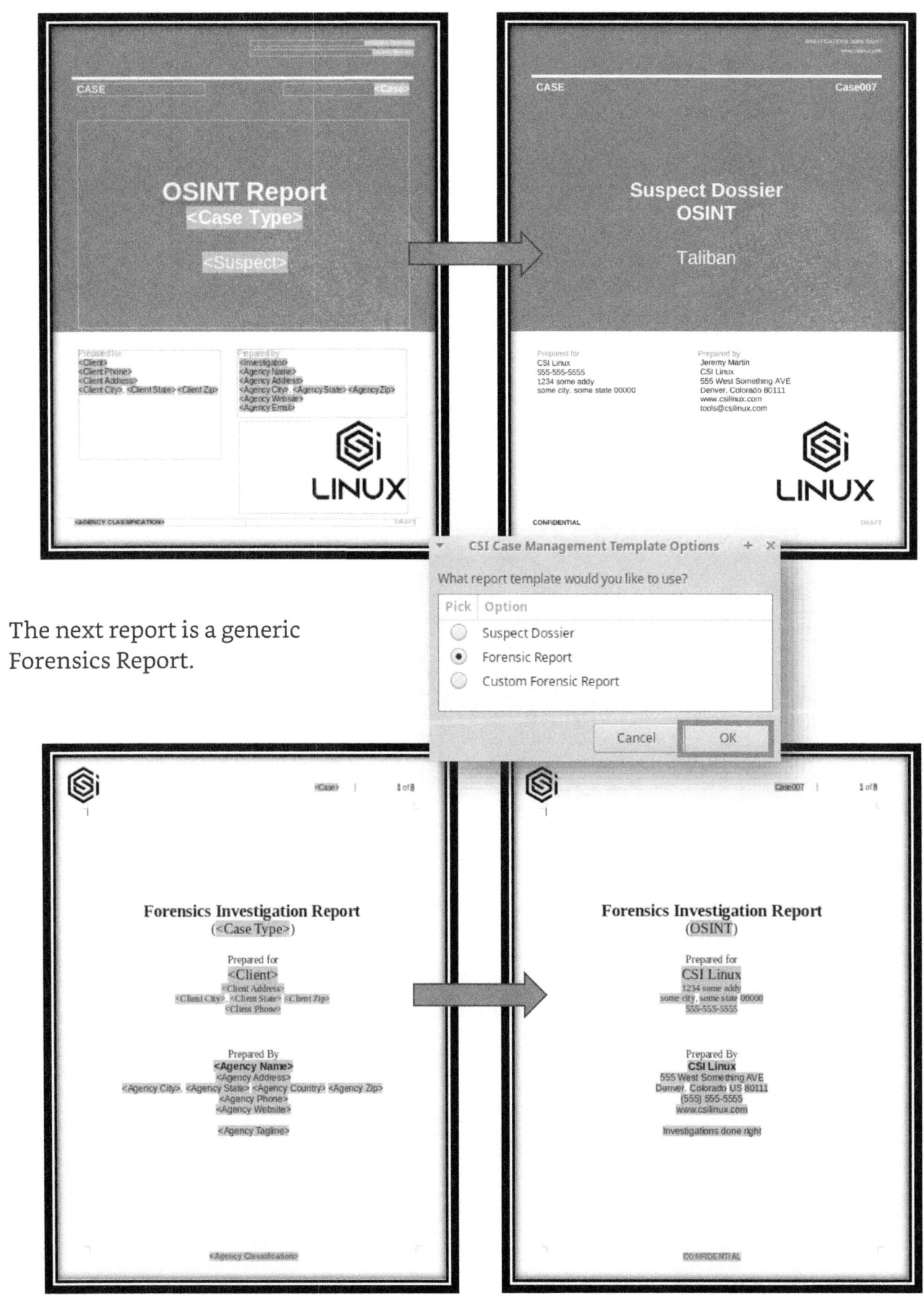

The next report is a generic Forensics Report.

More Templates

We have added a few more templates that are commonly used in digital investigations. It is always a good idea to have your Attorney look over the templates to make sure they work well for your organization. These template files are also located in the same /home/csi/Documents/Templates/ folder. If you make changes, make sure to back up the files before and after you make modifications.

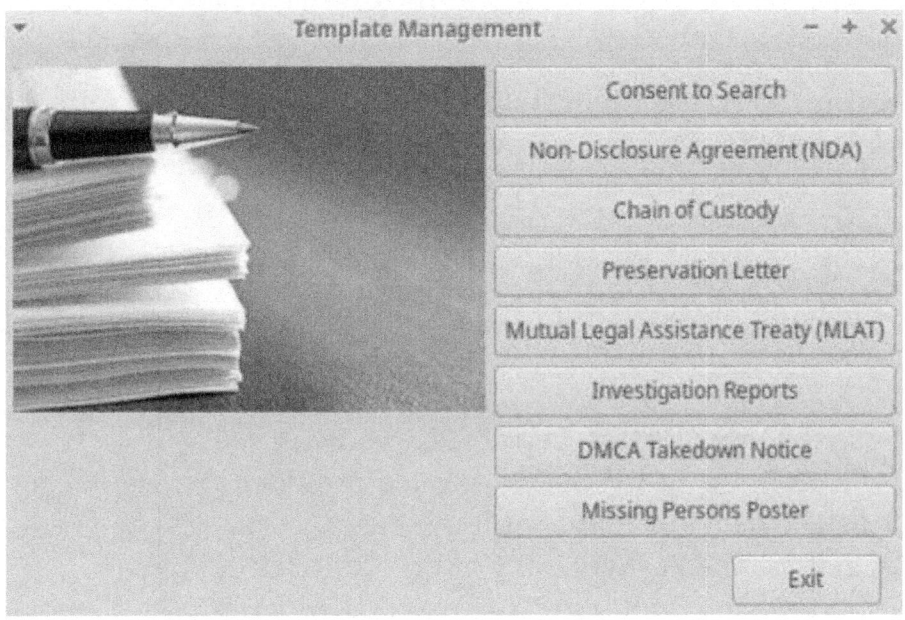

Note: The powerup update will overwrite the template files. Make sure to copy your modified files into the Backup folder and to an external drive. Backup and backup often.

Some of the documents do have some extra variables that can be modified and there will be a popup with asking for the extra information. For example, the Preservation Letter contains the following information for the "Service Provider":

- Provider Name
- Provider PoC
- Provider Address
- Provider City
- Provider State
- Provider Zip
- Provider Number

The Template Management will continue to evolve and will keep the main goal of trying to automate as much of the mundane work so you can focus on the real work, the investigations.

Preservation Letter

"A preservation letter is a request for a service provider to retain logs or "Due to the dynamic and temporary nature of digital records, and because of the variability in the duration of time that records are retained by service providers, law enforcement agencies may issue a preservation letter under 18 U.S.C. §2703(f). Generally, no regulations pertain to the retention of records held by service providers. These records may be retained briefly or not at all. The use of a preservation letter or order will prevent these records from being destroyed."
- itlaw.wikia.org

There is a time limit for these requests. If the provider complies with the request, you must get a court order to retrieve the evidence within the time limit of the request. If you do not, the evidence may be destroyed.

There is a generic preservation letter template that has been added to the template repository that you can edit for your organization or agency's needs

When you choose the Preservation Letter (PL), you will see a popup that will ask you to fill in the service provider's information. This allows you to have multiple PLs in a case. The naming format for the PLs will be "Preservation Letter for <PL Name> - <Case001>.odt". In this instance, our file name is: *"Preservation Letter for Provider Name - Case00.odt"*.

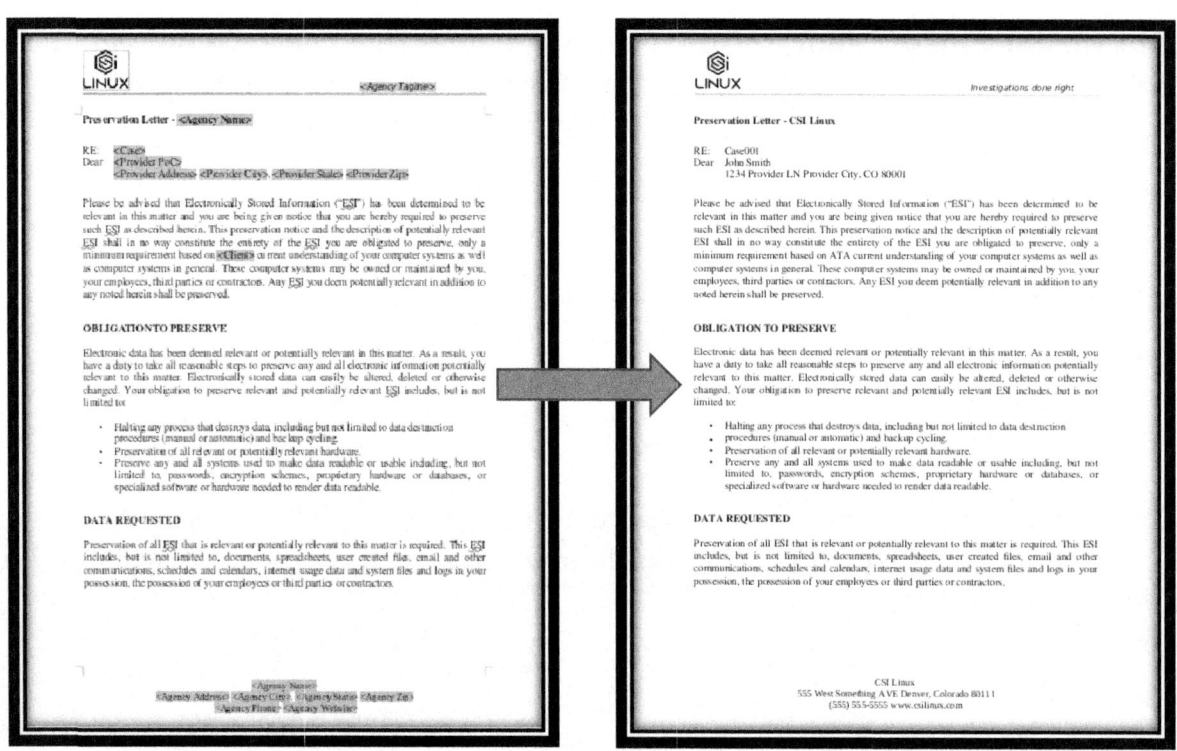

The Missing Persons Template

The missing persons set is growing, and we are constantly looking for improvement. If you have any suggestions, please let us know. The goal is to help speed up the process for the investigation and make it more standardized to minimize any issues so the information can be more easily distributed to those that need it and help save the victims.

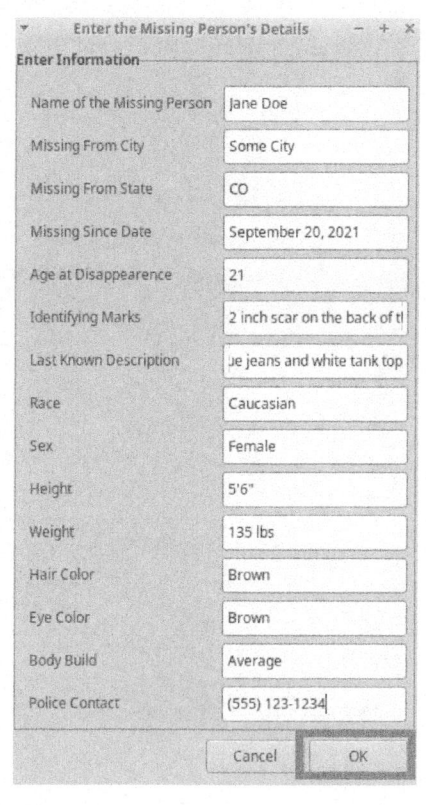

This template does require information specific to the missing person. This data will be added to the template when it is built and will be saved with the following format: "Missing Persons Poster for <Name> - <Case>". You can have multiple posters per case.

In this case, it will be:
"Missing Persons Poster for Jane Doe - Case001.odt"

Fill in the rest of the information within the document including the picture. When you are finished, safe the file and export it to a .PDF file. Once
you save the file as a PDF, you will no longer see the grey fields.

I wanted to take a moment to discuss some of the projects we are working on. They are a combination of commercial, community driven, & Open-Source projects.

Cyber WAR (Weekly Awareness Report)

Everyone needs a good source for Threat Intelligence and the Cyber WAR is one resource that brings together over a dozen other data feeds into one place. It contains the latest news, tools, malware, and other security related information.

InformationWarfareCenter.com/CIR

CSI Linux (Community Linux Distro)

CSI Linux is a freely downloadable Linux distribution that focuses on Open-Source Intelligence (OSINT) and SOCMINT investigation, traditional Digital Forensics, and Incident Response (DFIR), and Cover Communications with suspects and informants. This distribution was designed to help Law Enforcement with Online Investigations but has evolved and has been released to help anyone investigate both online and on the dark webs with relative security and peace of mind.

If you are interested in contributing to the CSI Linux project, please send an email to: conctribute@CSILinux.com

CSILinux.com

Cyber "Live Fire" Range (Linux Distro)

This is a commercial environment designed for both Cyber Incident Response Teams (CIRT) and Penetration Testers alike. This product is a standalone bootable external drive that allows you to practice both DFIR and Pentesting on an isolated network, so you do not have to worry about organizational antivirus, IDP/IPS, and SIEMs lighting up like a Christmas tree, causing unneeded paperwork and investigations. This environment incorporates Kali and a list of vulnerable virtual machines to practice with. This is a great system for offline exercises to help prepare for Certifications like the Pentest+, Licensed Penetration Tester (LPT), and the OSCP.

CyberSec.TV

We are building a site that pulls together Cyber Security videos from various sources to make great content easier to `find.

Cyber Secrets

Cyber Secrets originally aired in 2013 and covers issues ranging from Anonymity on the Internet to Mobile Device forensics using Open-Source tools, to hacking. Most of the episodes are technical in nature. Technology is constantly changing, so some subjects may be revisited with new ways to do what needs to be done.

- CyberSec.TV
- Amazon FireTV: amzn.to/3mpL1yU

Active Facebook Community: Facebook.com/groups/cybersecrets

Information Warfare Center Publications

Cyber Secrets publications is a cybersecurity series that focuses on all levels and sides while having content for all skill levels of technology and security practitioners. There are articles focusing on SCADA/ICS, Dark Web, Advanced Persistent Threats (APT)s, OSINT, Reconnaissance, computer forensics, threat intelligence, hacking, exploit development, reverse engineering, and much more.

Other publications

A network defender's guide to threat detection: Using Zeek, Elasticsearch, Logstash, Kibana, Tor, and more. This book covers the entire installation and setup of your own SOC in a Box with ZEEK IDS, Elasticstack, with visualizations in Kibana. amzn.to/2AZqBJW

IWC Labs: Encryption 101 – Cryptography Basics and Practical Usage is a great guide doe those just starting in the field or those that have been in for a while and want some extra ideas on tools to use. This book is also useful for those studying for cybersecurity certifications. amzn.to/3OaseOr

---

Are you getting into hacking or computer forensics and want some more hands-on practice with more tools and environments? Well, we have something that might just save you some time and money. amzn.to/306bTu0

This IWC Lab covers privilege escalation after exploitation. There are many ways to escalate privileges on both windows and Linux and we cover many of them including docker exploitation. amzn.to/3jCmGab

---

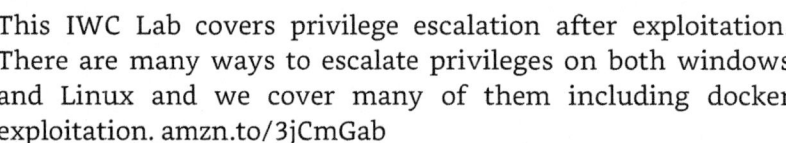

Containerization is increasing widely with the adoption of Docker for container workloads. It is always easy to spin a container and start working on it. But wait! Have you ever thought of the security of your container workloads? Did your Docker Container ecosystems can defend themselves against latest sophisticated attacks? Or you might be relying on legacy security systems to make them do the security work for you. You need to get this book... amzn.to/34KFDPq

Printed in Great Britain
by Amazon